CYBERMARKETING
Your Interactive Marketing Consultant

REGINA BRADY • EDWARD FORREST • RICHARD MIZERSKI

CYBERMARKETING
Your Interactive Marketing Consultant

REGINA BRADY • EDWARD FORREST • RICHARD MIZERSKI

Printed on recyclable paper

NTC Business Books
a division of *NTC Publishing Group* • Lincolnwood, Illinois USA

Cover illustration copyright © Ed Honowitz/Tony Stone Images.

Library of Congress Cataloging-in-Publication Data
Cybermarketing : your interactive marketing consultant/editors.
   Regina Brady, Edward Forrest, Richard Mizerski.
      p. cm.
     At head of title: American Marketing Association.
     Includes index.
     ISBN 0-8442-3442-7 (alk. paper)
      1. Interactive marketing. 2. Internet marketing. I. Brady,
Regina. II. Forrest, Edward. III. Mizerski, Richard. IV. American
Marketing Association.
HF5415.1264.C95 1997
658.8'00285'4678—dc21   96-47562
                                 CIP

Published in conjunction with the American Marketing Association,
250 South Wacker Drive, Chicago, Illinois 60606.

Published by NTC Business Books, a division of NTC Publishing Group
4255 West Touhy Avenue
Lincolnwood (Chicago), Illinois 60606–1975, U.S.A.

7 8 9 ML 0 9 8 7 6 5 4 3 2 1

CONTENTS

INTRODUCTION

The development of electronic interactive media is on the fast track in the United States, and the stage is being set for explosive global growth as well. Announcements about new technologies appear almost daily. Commercial online services such as American Online, CompuServe, and Prodigy; the World Wide Web; CD-ROM; electronic mail; interactive TV; interactive kiosks; screen telephones; interactive voice response; and fax-on-demand—these are just a few of the options open to consumers and marketers.

More sophisticated consumers are already using the leading electronic systems and services. And the number of marketers in this new electronic marketplace continues to expand, as telephone companies, newspapers, and other consumer communications "operatives" set strategies for exploration and growth. Virtually all of the participants in this new electronic marketplace share a common characteristic: frustration with the confusion and complexity of doing business.

The Marketing Challenge:
Coping with the Pace of Change

We have heard so much about the accelerating pace of change in our lives that we almost tend to ignore it. Yet it is unquestionably true, and nowhere is it more true than in the electronic marketplace. How quickly have things changed? Here are a few examples:

- In 1964 the yearbook for the electronics industry listed only 3 main consumer products: radios, phonographs, and television. The number of color TV sets sold was so small that it was not thought worthwhile to even record.

- Today this same yearbook lists dozens of different product categories. A typical superstore selling consumer electronics, major appliances, and home office equipment carries approximately 4,000 different pieces of merchandise.

- The products that existed in 1964 were much simpler than their counterparts today. A consumer who wished to purchase a television then could choose from about a dozen different models in a typical store. Selection was based on a few basic features, such as the type of tuner and picture tube, a simple mechanical channel switcher accessing VHF channels, and a choice of various furniture styles. Today's televisions include more than a hundred different features, and the typical dealer now offers more than 150 different models. If hobbyists have trouble keeping track of what's going on, how is the average consumer expected to cope?

As consumers we are faced daily with choices our parents only dreamed of. We must choose among hundreds of goods, services, pursuits, and lifestyles, many of which demand large amounts of time and energy to understand. Friends and family can no longer provide useful advice. And the salesperson from whom we purchase is likely to be an unknown—and probably untrusted—face. This trend will undoubtedly continue: products will keep proliferating, changing faster and faster, and our choices will become increasingly complex. In turn, we will have to depend more on the service of others for information about the items we buy. Can service keep up with product proliferation? Information, in and of itself, is currency.

All of which points to the basic problem with the new marketplace: choice versus clarity. The most basic rule of selling and marketing any product or service is "Make it easy for the buyer to understand what is being sold (the offer) and make it easy for the buyer to buy it." That rule is violated regularly in our society in general as the number of products continues to proliferate, but nowhere has this basic tenet of selling been violated more completely and consistently than in the new electronic media. Greater choice is generally considered a consumer benefit, but it must be accompanied by a product that is easy to understand and purchase terms that make sense.

Information Hungry and Time Starved

The time a consumer can devote to making a buying decision has changed. Most Americans are suffering under a time crunch. Since the end of the 1960s, the average working American has added about 160 hours of work to his or her annual schedule.[1] If an average work week were defined as 40 hours, that is almost an extra month of work time! Couple that with the fact that in the United States today more than 50 percent of families are two income families. What used to be a time crunch has become a time famine.

Even with a time-starved lifestyle the consumer of today still needs to shop and the way people shop has also changed with the times. In the late 1960s most companies distributed to the consumer through a limited number of channels: retailers, sales agents, and direct by mail. Those were the good old days! Now there are multiple distribution channels. The challenge for marketers is to determine how to exploit each channel to its fullest. With multiple ways to market goods and services marketers must consider interactive media as a new set of marketing channels to reach the consumer. These marketers must also keep in mind that the consumer has a vast array of products to choose from, multiple ways to purchase, and little time to make buying decisions.

Consumer Empowerment

Rather than throwing more facts at consumers, marketers need to use new technologies to help sift out better information and then synthesize and customize recommendations. Given the right information infrastructure, companies will emerge spontaneously, and they will grow and thrive as never before. New information technologies such as 900 telephone service, online computer networks, the Internet, and microcomputers with high-capacity storage (for example, CD-ROMs) have already led to the growth of a whole new range of marketing applications for both the consumer and the business-to-business market.

To be successful in cybermarketing requires a fundamental change in view. Traditional media appeals to the masses. New media attempts to appeal to the individual. Relationship marketing becomes vitally important, speaking to the consumer with their wants and needs in mind. The more the marketer can move down the continuum to working with the consumer on a one-to-one level, the more successful marketing efforts will be.

---

[1]Schor, Juliet B. (October 1, 1994). "Decline of leisure time in America: Cooperative movements are fundamental for making social change." Vital Speeches, v. 60, n 24, p 748.

Hype or Reality?

The media has been captivated by the possibilities that new technology brings. Turn on your television, open the morning paper, or read your favorite magazines and you'll inevitably find features and stories on the new media. Today, the cyber-landscape is getting a tremendous amount of hype. Business cards now carry e-mail addresses. Advertisements on television, in magazines, and even on billboards carry URLs or the World Wide Web address of the advertiser.

Does the general public understand these cryptic electronic signatures? While the omnipresent "www.company.com" appearing at the bottom of TV screens and magazine and newspaper ads may be interesting information, it is relevant to only one in five adults, says J. Walker Smith, managing partner of Yankelovich Partners in the second annual Yankelovich report on the behavior of cyberspace users. "Only 21.5 percent of all adults have any potential interest in a Web address in cyberspace," Smith said. Those who are so inclined tend to be mostly male, upscale baby boomers, although more women are plugging in, Smith said. Of those currently using the Internet, 35 percent are under age 30, 49 percent are age 30 to 39, and only 16 percent are age 50 and older, the report found.

We are receiving mixed signals about the current size and scope of opportunity. The Technology Adoption Life Cycle is a model for understanding the acceptance of new products and certainly applies to interactive media. Today the innovators and early adopters have embraced the new technology. We are beginning to move into the "early majority," which is the clear beginning of achieving mass market. Growth from year to year for new media has far outstripped normal growth patterns. In 1996 the number of women and seniors using the Internet has close to doubled. That shows a strong adoption pattern and supports the fact that we are on a slow march to mass market penetration.

The players in the electronic marketplace are also changing. Entrepreneurial firms have embraced technology and begun to make a name for themselves. Major corporations, including telephone companies, newspapers, and other consumer communications channel "players," are all setting strategies for exploration and growth. The strategic implications for marketers are tremendous.

It is almost impossible to ignore the constant stream of attention given to the new media. But the attention is not unwarranted. The possibilities that the new media bring have captured the imaginations of forward-looking thinkers in businesses, small entrepreneurial firms, academicians, and the government. Al Gore's vision of a networked society was criticized by some as pie-in-the-sky when he first espoused this view. Now grassroots efforts are in place that begin to reach out not only to the "haves" and but also to the "have nots." Visit your local library and you are likely to see an institution that has undergone wholesale change. Young and old alike are using multimedia encyclopedias, browsing the World Wide Web or conducting research on CD-ROM.

We have reached the point where technologies are beginning to converge and become more ubiquitous in the marketplace. But beyond technology there are other societal trends that have laid the foundation for the explosive growth that is on the horizon.

Why Is Now the Time to Get Involved?

Anyone who is serious about profiting in this new world needs to have the answers to a fundamental question: Why now? What makes this the right time to think about marketing in Cyberspace? Four key factors will contribute to continued growth.

THE GROWING AWARENESS AND USE OF NEW MEDIA

This is growing rapidly because of broader press coverage, the mass marketing efforts of the various online services, increased participation and related promotion on the part of software publishers and information providers (from Microsoft to Disney and from Standard & Poors to *Sports Illustrated*), and a greater use of electronic mail, groupware, and other connectivity applications in the business market.

In the business world the advent of laptop and portable PCs plus WANs (Wide Area Networks) and LANs (Local Area Networks) mean that more and more PCs have the ability to link electronically with others. Which is good for the future of online communication and information transfer.

In the consumer arena the proliferation of CD-ROMs, interactive kiosks in public spaces, and expanded audio and video PC capabilities have moved us quickly from an ASCII (or pure text) presentation to a richer and more vibrant environment. The term *user friendly* may be hackneyed, but simple point and click access to information that can be presented within a multimedia context is a far cry from the early DOS environment with arcane commands.

Both businesses and consumer markets are the beneficiaries of the increasing pace of advances in computer hardware, software, and communication technology. Rapid technological changes result in dynamic customer demands and frequent new product and service introductions. For example, the browser war between Netscape and Microsoft has paid off with enhancements and capabilities that rapidly increase functionality and presentation. Real audio, CU-See Me, streaming video, virtual phones—these are just some of the building blocks for innovative interactive marketers.

It is important to emphasize again that when the major consumer and business companies begin to get involved in new media there is a new degree of legitimacy. This is no longer the playground of technologically based companies. Media giants, major US corporations, and trade publications from every industry are involved. Some are involved in a major way and others are just getting their feet wet. New business ventures are being formed and announced from AT&T WorldNet, to Time-Warner's interactive television experiment in Florida to *The Wall Street Journal*'s interactive edition.

THE GROWTH OF THE HOME COMPUTER MARKET

This is being driven by lower hardware prices, expansion to mass-market retail distribution channels, and standardization of user-friendly graphical interfaces. More than 30 million American households (36 percent) today have a computer, and another 25 to 30 percent intend to purchase a computer, stated Graham Taylor, executive vice president of INTECO Corporation of Norwalk, Connecticut. "One of the biggest factors fueling this growth is the large number of families in America with school-age children. Another is the sheer volume of entertaining and educational multimedia products now available."

THE EXPANSION OF MODEM PENETRATION

Internet and online services access requires the use of a modem. A major factor inhibiting the trial of online services by consumers has been the infrequent installation of this device with PCs in the home. Modems are now being pre-installed in virtually all new computers introduced on the market today (and they are also multimedia equipped). When the consumer or business person powers up their new PC, they are also likely to see several of the online services and Internet Service Providers (ISPs) prominently displayed on their desktop. Being installed on the hard drive is the new battleground for visibility. Modem prices have declined substantially, making them more accessible to both new and existing computer users.

People want quick and efficient access to information. Beyond modem penetration increased modem speeds have made Internet and online services more usable. Local phone companies are offering ISDN lines which bring faster and faster connectivity. And with telephone companies planning to wire neighborhoods with fiber-optic or other superior communication lines at breathtaking cost for a digital future, the possibilities will be opened for even greater networking. The line between the personal computer and the television will begin to blur.

THE GROWTH OF MOBILE COMPUTING AND COMMUNICATION

There is an increasing range of mobile PCs, including laptops, notebooks, and pocket computers. Increasingly, these devices are incorporating telecommunications capabilities that enable them to access online services at work, at home, or while traveling. Pagers are now information delivery mechanisms that can keep individuals in touch with the latest communication, information, and entertainment. Users are now enabled to receive pages on everything from the latest score for their favorite sports team to current performance on that stock that they have been waiting for just the right time to buy.

The Personal Digital Assistant (PDA) is the new kid on the block. What, exactly, is a PDA? Basically, it's a handheld computer that acts as a pocket organizer and notepad. It might use a small keyboard, or it might use a special pen that enables the user to enter information by writing directly on the screen. Built-in software turns your handwriting into typed text. PDAs appeal to salespeople, freelancers, and others with busy lives often spent on the road. Users can attach their PDAs to a modem for communications links. Some PDAs offer a cellular phone option. Not only can you make and receive phone calls on the road, you can send and receive faxes and e-mail from the screen wirelessly.

Who Is the Interactive Consumer Today?

The factors discussed above have set the stage for burgeoning electronic and interactive commerce. It is also important to understand who is equipped to interact in cyberspace and what the prognosis is for the expansion.

There have been many studies with conflicting information about who is connected in cyberspace. As this is being written, the online services count 14 million global members, and of these it is estimated that approximately 9 million are in the United States. The majority of these members are now equipped to connect out to the Internet. That is a relevant piece of data; but a key question is how many people are connected to the Internet and what segments do they represent? FIND/ SVP Emerging Technologies Research Group reports lower numbers than their competitors, but their market definitions yield believable results. Their definition of Internet use calls for at least one Internet application besides e-mail.

They project the total number of adult U.S. Internet users to reach some 13.5 million by the start of 1997. And they have identified four segments of users:

1. **Recreational consumers** represent 27 percent of the total Internet user population. They pay personally for Internet access, primarily access from home, and use the Internet primarily for personal applications such as e-mail, news retrieval, or investment information.

2. **Occupational consumers** represent 12 percent of the total Internet user population. This segment pays personally for access, accesses primarily from home, and uses the Internet mainly for business-related activities such as conducting work at home or running a small business.

3. **Corporate users** represent 46 percent of the total Internet user population. Their Internet access is subsidized, they use the Internet primarily for work applications, and usually access from workplace locations.

4. **Academic users** represent 15 percent of the total Internet user population. Their usage is subsidized, they access from academic locations, and primarily uses the Internet for research and educational applications.

This is the base that will grow and change over time. Businesses will continue to embrace the efficiencies and capabilities available through interactivity and penetration in this arena will show a sharp and steep climb, particularly in the white collar professions. Looking at the consumer market a short way into the future, FIND/SVP forecasts that total Internet growth will reach 25 million adults by the year 2000. "At that time, we project that about 44 percent of all U.S. households will be equipped with desktop or notebook PCs, numbering more than 42 million homes," says Peter Clemente, an SVP Emerging Technologies Research Group analyst and author of the study. "Furthermore, we see 42 percent of PC households using the Internet by year-end 2000, for a total estimate of 17.8 million homes or 25.4 million users."

A Reality Check—Who Is Making Money Today?

There are several ways that marketers can make money today. They can:

- sell their content through subscriptions or special one-time charges;
- license their content to an online service or bulletin board operator;
- generate advertising revenues; and
- sell goods and services.

We are beginning to see the first forays into offering subscriptions on the Internet. Newspapers and magazines are moving gingerly into this arena. Several have tried and many have failed up to this point in time. This is because they are fighting the culture of the Internet where the perception is that everything is free. In actuality, this is not true, since in all cases someone is paying for Internet access, whether it is the taxpayer, a university, a corporation, or the individual.

It is likely that the typical content site is not yet making money on the Internet although a significant number are making money on the online services. The reason for this disparity is that today's online services have defined cohesive member segments to which they present an organized view of content. The online services will either license that content for the specific use of their members or they will often share in the revenues they derive.

Another way to make money in cyberspace is to sell advertising and therefore capitalize on the audience you are attracting to your site. Consensus estimates are that in 1996 total advertising revenues reached between $200 and $300 million but that this number should double in

1997. By the year 2000 interactive advertising is expected to reach $2 billion.

And online shopping is another application that has not yet reached its potential. Industry analysts projected revenues at somewhere between $400 million and $800 million by the end of 1996 and that this number will more than double in 1997.

In a very different arena screen phones may be making a comeback. There has been low market acceptance of screen phone-based home banking services partially fueled by the fascination with the Internet. Penetration is planned to reach 1.25 million by 1997. Driving the growth is the telephone companies' marketing of Call Waiting Deluxe, a new telephony service that allows residential customers to use Caller ID and Call Waiting simultaneously over a screen phone. There is also expanded distribution through retail, broader applications development, and new manufacturers helping to expand the market.

While the actual numbers and revenues in these various arenas do represent a reality check in light of all the current optimism and hype, it is important to note that the seeds are being sowed today for tremendous future growth. It is imperative that marketers begin now to explore the application of new media technology for their future economic potential.

Technology adoption curves have a classic pattern of introduction of trial and acceptance. Many point to the introduction of television as a good example. When it was introduced in the late 1940s, there was little market share, crude picture quality, and limited content. There was also not a lot of money to be made initially. After those first few years the adoption curve steepened and by the early 1960s television had become pervasive in society and gained wide acceptance. Ultimately, it was more than a vehicle to provide entertainment and information; it also evolved into a new marketing medium.

With the explosion of technology the adoption curves are becoming shorter and shorter. Look at the microwave oven, cellular phones, and the CD player. The fax machine seemed to grow almost overnight.

Why Is Interactive Marketing Different?

PERSONALIZATION AND RELEVANCY

Interactivity is one of the secret keys to successful marketing. It moves you from mass marketing and advertising on one end of the continuum to one-to-one marketing at the other extreme. In the middle there is target marketing, which also meets the needs of the individual by grouping people into appropriate segments for marketing purposes. Interactive marketing plays upon the demographic and psychographic characteristics of the consumer and overlays the immediacy of the contact. You can encourage direct communication with your customers and foster loyalty. The new media are perfect for relationship marketing.

People today want to make informed decisions. They want more information about the products they buy and support after the sale. Smart marketers can use interactivity to get customers involved. Smart marketers can find ways to customize the experience to the needs and wants of each individual. Instead of wading through a swamp of irrelevant information, consumers can be matched up with exactly the information they want and need. Marketers have the ability to tailor messages to different prospects. With database marketing and design you can store massive amounts of data but only give the customer the information he needs.

You can use interactive marketing for prospecting, for customer service, to create a dialog with your customer, to explore resell and cross-sell opportunities, and for ongoing promotion. This is also an enabling form of marketing because you can allow the customer to take control of the purchasing process. You can encourage customers to become engaged in your marketing efforts.

TIMELINESS AND UBIQUITY

Interactive marketing is generally not point-in-time marketing. Instead it is available to the customer when he or she wants it. Companies are provided with a marketing and sales presence in areas where they currently don't have stores, salespeople, or distributors. In this borderless world the company that can compete or fulfill on a global basis has the potential to open up new revenue streams.

COST STRUCTURES CHANGE

The economic investment in interactive marketing may be very different. Traditional marketing involves significant variable costs in production and printing of marketing and advertising materials. Support personnel must be kept on hand to answer inquiries from customers.

With new media the economics are different, and there may be insignificant variable costs.

Instead, what you must think about are "back-end" capabilities such as database marketing, customer segmentation, and customer service.

DELIVERY STRUCTURES CHANGE

Electronic versions of marketing materials don't have to be printed, packaged, stored, or shipped. They can also be updated almost at will. You get the opportunity to provide more marketing information to more prospects, and you also have the ability to customize that information.

SHIFTS IN NAME RECOGNITION

The playing field becomes level in the interactive game. Entrepreneurial companies that take the risk and keep up with the latest trends can establish strong franchises that can outshine the more traditional players who are slower to embrace new technology. Brand is still important because it enhances the marketer's ability to attract consumers to their new media "stores," but new brands such as C/Net, Amazon Books, and PC Flowers are capturing interest and attention.

When we look at the interactive superhighway today from a global perspective, there are many opportunities. It's still early. The traffic is light. Like fresh pavement stretching out before you, the interactive superhighway leads directly into the homes of millions of people. But it won't stay fresh for long. Those armed with an understanding of where we are today and what the immediate potential is can develop plans that will allow them to prosper and grow.

The Convergence of Technologies for Interactive Marketing

We are beginning to see the convergence of technologies that will be a boon for interactive marketers. The Internet is driving computing power in diverse forms; in the next year, expect to see Net-enabled phones, TV sets, and cars. Here are just a few examples of how this is occurring.

Now ET *can* phone home via the Internet. Several companies have already introduced products. The technology is new and there are some obstacles. Testers have reported that the actual transmission was impressive, but users must have specific sound cards that will enable them to both speak at the same time. Also, keep in mind that the individual you are calling has to be connected to the Internet. Nevertheless, the potential is vast. You will be able to talk to anyone, anywhere in the world assuming you each have the appropriate setup and an Internet connection.

There is technology in development that allows Internet phone users to call real telephone numbers from the Internet. The plan is to bypass, for the most part, the public telephone networks. Keep your eye on this one. It could significantly change how people and companies view Internet telephony.

WebTV Networks Inc., a privately held start-up founded in June 1995 by three former Apple Computer employees, recently announced that Sony and Philips had licensed their set-top box, which hooks up to the television and displays Web pages on the set. The boxes will be equipped with a 33.6 Kbps modem, software that eliminates flicker on the TV screen, and digital-quality audio and video output; plus, the design calls for an ISO Smart Card reader that will read credit and ATM cards. Cable modem functionality is planned for the future. Users of WebTV will be able to browse the net with WebTV's remote control, receive "smart advertising" and purchase in a secure manner.

High-speed telecommunications networks are in the planning stages. The telephone system today transfers information over its network using wavelike analog signals. By the early 21st century, sending digital, rather than sending analog information over current copper phone networks, will allow us to transmit data into the home more than 50 times faster than the rate that is commonly used today and allow us to transmit simultaneously voice, text, high quality graphics, and at least primitive video images.

We are switching from analog to digital technologies. This combined with the replacement of copper-wire networks with optical-fiber networks will not only make possible video-on-demand, but video-on-demand with images far better than anything we currently have on our TV or movie screens—images, for example, as good as those we are accustomed to seeing on a magazine page.

In the U.S., growth in this area has been slow, but it looks like things are speeding up. Optical fiber is not only becoming relatively affordable, decreasing in cost at a rate of roughly 30 percent per year. But both local phone companies and long distance carriers have already laid more than a million route miles of fiber in the past decade. Most intercity and regional telephone wiring is already fiber, many international calls also have shifted to fiber, and company spokespersons themselves are talking about how this new technology will allow them to bring consumers "video phones, push-button home shopping, news reports tailored to your interest, movies whenever you want to see them and even high-definition television" as conveniently as the telephone companies now bring phone service.

Once optical fibers reach the home, moreover, they could be connected to a wireless local-area-network within a single dwelling. This would provide consumers with even more convenient access to the world's information resources. Many business offices already use such high-speed wireless networks to access information, and it's only a matter of time before such networks become affordable to consumers.

Remember that the future begins today. The savvy marketer of today will begin to experiment with new media to learn the ins and outs so that as the adoption rate broadens they will be poised to exploit its true potential. Traditional marketers may not yet understand the importance of new electronic media. They may be intimidated by the technology. But interactive marketing is different, and the companies that understand how and why it is different will be the winners in the future.

About This Book

Interactive Marketing is a relevant topic for a broad spectrum of business people. Marketing, sales, and advertising professionals; entrepreneurs; corporate managers and executives; home office and small business owners and managers—these are all individuals who should benefit from this book. Whether you are an executive in a billion dollar enterprise or an entrepreneur just contemplating how to begin in cyberspace, this book should be for you.

There have been many books published about the subject. So, a key question you might be asking yourself is: What makes this book different from all the other sources available? The plain and simple answer is that you will have a true consultant at your fingertips. Not just one consultant . . . but more than 20 expert consultants. Each is an expert in his or her field.

Most books out in the marketplace today represent the viewpoint of one or two individuals. This book represents the viewpoints of experts in the many specific disciplines that make up interactive marketing. With a single author you receive one person's expertise and insights. With this book you have the benefits of the perspectives of experts in each field. This means that you will receive the more timely and relevant coverage of topics because the experts—those closest to what is happening in their area of expertise—are sharing their viewpoints. Subjects will be covered in depth and from the inside out.

This book also provides practical information coupled with overall perspective on the media. You want an overview of the interactive landscape from a high level, but you also demand applicability to your specific wants and needs. Both consumer and business-to-business marketers should be able to profit from the insights provided.

Cybermarketing: Your Interactive Marketing Consultant is divided into three sections. First, we cover the interactive marketing scene from a strategic standpoint. This will provide the "lay of the land" overview that is necessary to truly understand before you begin to choose and implement courses of action. Next, we begin to "roll up our sleeves" and examine tactics and techniques that will help to ensure success. Finally, we take a look at how to better understand that success. This last section deals with the metrics, the analysis, the customer, and ultimately the profitability of your efforts.

It is exciting to be thinking about cybermarketing today. A good deal of the groundwork has been done to help us point to a profitable future. There are charts that have been plotted. There have been successes and failures, and we can learn from each of these examples. We hope that this book will be a road map to success for you.

SECTION I

Marketing Strategies in the Interactive Age

This first section provides the framework for understanding the broad spectrum of interactive media today. It will provide a structure for creating a marketing strategy to reach the interactive consumer. This requires a change in mindset both about how to effectively exploit the opportunities new media brings and how to approach the consumer who uses the new media. Traditional marketing approaches do have a place in the interactive age, but there is no direct translation. Interactive communication technologies are having a major impact on the way we do business. The world of marketing and marketing communications must change in order to reap success.

The exploration of how to begin to deal with this change starts with a revolutionary strategy. It will challenge cherished beliefs and make a case for a total shift in how companies market. It is the perfect opening chapter for this book. Interactive marketing *is* different. Interactive marketing *requires* a different mindset. This chapter lays out a road map for competing in the future and how communication with the customer must quickly evolve.

Most businesses follow the time-honored mass marketing rules of selling to the greatest number of people. That has been the basis of all traditional advertising to date. But there are rumblings in the air . . . a sense that change is in the wind. One case in point is a challenge made recently to the advertising community by a representative of the pinnacle of traditional consumer brand marketing. Ed Artzt, who was Chairman of Procter & Gamble, recognized that "our most important ad medium, television is about to change big-time . . . " and he asked that the advertising community get together to "understand how consumer viewing habits will change as a result of these new technologies."

The information age has created a consumer who is overloaded with media options but who is also information-aware—almost an information junkie. They have their own specific wants, needs, and desires. A new approach must be put in place to effectively reach this individual. To win, marketers are challenged to change their mindset and embrace the concept of marketing to one customer at a time. Don Peppers and Martha Rogers call this "One-to-One Marketing" or in their special shorthand "1:1 Marketing." In "One-to-One Media in the Interactive Future: Building Dialogues and Learning Relationships with Individual Customers" marketers will hear the wake-up call.

Peppers and Rogers believe that "mass media are as bland as hospital food, or anything else that has to be served the same way to everybody." But when marketers use the new media of the 1:1 future, they will be able to communicate directly with customers, individually, rather than shouting at them in groups. Marketers will form unique relationships with individual customers. A 1:1 marketer will not try to sell a single product to as many customers as possible. Instead, the task will be to sell a single customer as many products as possible—over a long period of time and across different product lines.

Peppers and Rogers declare: "the instant a marketer begins thinking in terms of share of customer, rather than overall market share, new vistas of competitive opportunities will open up." This is good news for anyone involved with interactive media because the foundation of interactive media is customer focus. Interactive media are addressable media in that they can deliver a single message to a particular individual.

This focus on the individual provides a perfect lead-in to Michael Spalter's point of view. He reminds us that we must recognize the importance of a new strategic approach in "Maintaining a Customer Focus in an Interactive Age: The Seven I's to Success." Interactive media provide customers with the revolutionary ability to communicate from *anywhere* in the globe at *anytime*. Marketers need to act differently when the constraints of time and space are removed. They must recognize these differences, capitalize on them, and integrate them even further into future efforts. The process of marketing takes on a new dynamic with the consumer taking a much more active role. In fact, the consumer takes over the control over the marketing process as he or she chooses whether or not to interact with a marketer. Spalter stresses the value of *dialogue* over *monologue*. New media encourage dialogue, and this paradigm shift is redefining marketing practices and the businesses that depend on them.

"Now marketer and consumer not only transact but must interact." His Seven I's provide a solid framework for success— Interconnection, Interface, Interactivity, Involvement, Information, Individualism, and Integrity. Marketers may need to give more emphasis to one of the I's over the others; but to completely ignore any of them is risky.

With the groundwork laid for the need to redefine relationships with customers, Richard Cross and Janet Smith of Cross World Network present five specific examples of how the creative application of technology can provide added value and stimulate a dialog with the customer. "Customer-Focused Strategies and Tactics: Interactive Marketing Weighs in for Customers" explores actual programs that demonstrate how in new media the buyer-seller relationship changes for both consumer and business-to-business marketing.

The cases Cross and Smith present span media and markets and illuminate how different facilitating technologies can be used to create new benefits for marketers and consumers. A databased loyalty program, interactive voice response, a private on-line community, fax-on-demand, and the Internet—each example is developed with an eye toward building lasting customer relationships. The buyer-seller relationship is changing, with the consumer taking more control in the marketing process; but marketers who understand this can tip the balance in their favor by using every tool available to give their customers the reason to be *their* relationship choice.

As the consumer takes an active role in the marketing process, the role of the advertising agency and the advertising message will need to change out of necessity. "The Impact of Interactive Communication on Advertising and Marketing: And Now a Word from Our Consumer" discusses how agencies will reengineer their products. Ads today are generally contained in a space (a page in a publication) or a time (a television or radio commercial). In cybermedia the message must move from an entertaining delivery of small bits of information to advertising that invites consumers to choose the information they want to access. Advertising must move from a passive one-way delivery of information to a two-way medium in which consumers can choose the information they want to access. Edward Forrest, Lance Kinney, and Michael Chamberlain discuss how commercial messages will become multidimensional and transactional. They will be "more embedded with information being part and parcel of the program with which the individual is interacting."

In "Media and Marketing Strategies for the Internet: A Step-by-Step Guide" Tracy Emerick predicts that the Internet will "revolutionize marketing as it is known today" and will "bring about the end of distribution as it is structured today." He provides a recipe for companies to develop an Internet Marketing Strategy including how to develop a presence, how to promote product or service offerings, and how to develop interactions with potential customers. He includes tips on how to ask for and capture customer information and even provides comments on staffing considerations.

To be successful on the Internet marketers must also employ an integrated marketing strategy. The Internet is a communications medium. Like all media it should be used in combination with other media. Emerick presents several options to consider when developing a multi-media program.

Carol Nelson and Rocky James claim the Internet is "the wildest, most exciting, and most challenging advertising medium we've ever had the good/bad fortune to encounter." In "Creative Strategy for Interactive Marketing: 10 Rules for Adapting and Winning in the New Marketplace," they give practical rules to follow on how to integrate interactive advertising into existing ad campaigns while also taking advantage of the new marketing toolbox that new media present to marketers. At the top of the list of rules is "Passive messages are out. Absolutely. No exceptions." Nearly every one of the other rules stem from this first rule. The Internet has ushered in a new way to communicate, and if you play by these rules your result may not be "a brilliant campaign, but it should result in a completely professional campaign."

Richard Hodgson tempers the enthusiasm and optimism that surround interactive media in "Considerations for 21st-Century Direct Marketers: Focusing on the Basics in New Environments." He questions whether new media have reached the critical mass needed to ensure profitability. Plus, the proliferation of services, channels, offerings, and Web sites means that any individual advertising message may not attract a large enough number of people within a particular time frame. He cautions direct marketers to watch the numbers and trends with a wary eye.

In this high-tech world there is also a consumer need for ease of use and simplicity. The new media need to keep this in mind as they continue to evolve. Hodgson points to TV home shopping on QVC as one of direct marketing's greatest success stories. QVC examined the technology, but they realized that consumers gravitate to what is simple, common, and understandable; and this has shaped all of their activities. So, while there is a brave new world spread out before us with wonderful vistas near the horizon, marketers are advised to look before they leap and to spend time analyzing the market and the media.

CHAPTER 1

One-to-One Media in the Interactive Future

Building Dialogues and Learning Relationships with Individual Customers

Don Peppers
Martha Rogers

Don Peppers is founder and President of Marketing 1:1, Inc., a marketing consultancy specializing in relationship management business development, and marketing technology issues.

Martha Rogers is Professor of Telecommunications at Bowling Green State University and a founding partner of Marketing 1:1, Inc.

Peppers and Rogers are co-authors of *The One-to-One Future: Building Relationships One Customer at a Time*, called by *Inc.* Magazine "one of the two or three most important business books ever written."

In late 1991 the telegraph industry's life was taken, suddenly and bru-
tally, by the facsimile machine. For more than 150 years, the telegram stood for immediacy and importance. It was an icon for urgency.
But now, Western Union has closed down its telegraph service around
the world. The fax was a new technology the telegram could not
survive.[1]

The shift from teletype and telegram to facsimile transmission
represents one aspect of what some business consultants term a paradigm shift—a "discontinuity" in the otherwise steady march of business
progress.

The automobile was another discontinuity, one that radically transformed both the economy and society. When the automobile first
appeared, it seemed to be merely a horseless version of the well-known
carriage. Predicting the consequences of the automobile's introduction would have been nearly impossible. Who could have imagined that
a noisy, smelly, unreliable machine would eventually be responsible for
the creation of suburbs; the fractionalization of families; and the growth
of supermarkets, malls, and the Interstate Highway System?

It is as difficult to see beyond such a discontinuity as it would be for
a nine-year-old boy to imagine being fifteen. He can easily visualize
being ten, and he may dream about twelve, but it is virtually impossible
for him to plan on what his life will be like when his hormones kick in.
Hormones are a discontinuity.

Today we are passing through a technological discontinuity of epic
proportions, and most are not even remotely prepared. The old paradigm, a system of mass production, mass media, and mass marketing, is
being replaced by a totally new paradigm, a one-to-one (1:1) economic
system.

The 1:1 future will be characterized by customized production,
individually addressable media, and 1:1 marketing, totally changing the
rules of business competition and growth. Instead of share of *market*,
the goal of most business competition will be share of *customer*—one
customer at a time.

Economies of scale will never again be as important as they are
today. Having the size necessary to produce, advertise, and distribute
vast quantities of standardized products won't be a precondition for
success. Instead, products will be increasingly tailored to individual
tastes, electronic media will be inexpensively addressed to individual
consumers, and many products ordered over the phone will be delivered to the home in eight hours or less.

In the 1:1 future businesses will focus less on short-term profits derived from quarterly or annual transaction volumes and more on the kinds of profits that can be realized from long-term customer retention and lifetime values.

The discontinuity we are now living through will be every bit as disruptive to our lives, and as beneficial, as the Industrial Revolution was to the lives of our great-grandparents. The way we compete will change dramatically enough over just the next few years to alter the very structure of our society, empowering some and disenfranchising others.

The 1:1 future holds immense implications for individual privacy, social cohesiveness, and the alienation and fractionalization that could come from the breakdown of mass media. It will change forever how we seek our information, education, and entertainment, and how we pursue our happiness. In addition to the "haves" and "have nots," new class distinctions will be created between the "theres" and "there nots." Some people will have jobs that require them to be there—somewhere—while others will be able to work mostly from their homes, without having to be anywhere.

At the early Daimler-Benz Company, the Mercedes planning department was asked to forecast the ultimate size of the automobile market. Unable to visualize the profound changes the automobile would provoke, they planned forward from their own present, in which only the wealthy owned cars, and predicted an eventual total of one million automobiles worldwide. Today, of course, there are more than 500 million cars on the world's roads. Mercedes underestimated the car's potential because the planners correctly guessed the population could never support more than about one million *chauffeurs*. They didn't plan backward from a future in which people would drive their own automobiles and mass production would make millions of cars affordable to the middle class.[2]

In the same way that Mercedes' planners had difficulty seeing beyond the technological discontinuity represented by assembly line automobile production, it is difficult for most of us now to imagine life after mass marketing.

It will disrupt everything, but ultimately 1:1 technology will create an entrepreneurial froth of opportunities. When the dust has settled, a plethora of new businesses—millions of them—most not even conceived today, will have sprung up across the economic landscape as naturally and randomly as wild flowers after a severe winter.

In a world in which communication and information are practically free, ideas will be the new medium of exchange.

New Media for a New Future

Mass media are as bland as hospital food, or anything else that has to be served the same way to everybody.

The only reason "awareness" advertising plays much of a part at all in marketing today is that the mass media available for promoting a product electronically and inexpensively are not very good at doing anything else. Mass media carry a rising cacophony of competing messages, each one being shouted by a marketer intent on being heard above the surrounding noise of his competitors.

But just having one's shout heard above the clamor is clearly inferior to the ultimate goal as a business—the final purpose of all marketing activity—which is to generate sales and loyal customers.

Using the new media of the 1:1 future, a marketer will be able to communicate directly with customers, individually, rather than shouting at them in groups. Current and future 1:1 media are different from today's mass media in three important ways:

1. *1:1 media are individually addressable.* An addressable medium can deliver a single, separate message to a particular individual. Until very recently, virtually the only addressable medium of any significance was a slow, cumbersome, expensive postal system. Not any more. New 1:1 media allows a marketer to send information to individual consumers without using the mail at all.

2. *1:1 media are two-way, not one-way.* Today's mass media only convey one-way messages from the marketer to the customer. But new media are already available that allow customers to talk back to a business, and more are being invented literally every month. What will they say?

3. *1:1 media are inexpensive.* Imagine a business as small as a house painter, or an accountant, or a babysitter, reaching customers and prospective customers individually, in quantities small enough to be affordable. Businesses that today have little alternative but to send out printed flyers in the mail, or post 3 x 5

cards on supermarket bulletin boards, will be able to use individually addressable electronic media to reach new customers and to keep the ones they have.[3]

Many new media with 1:1 capabilities are already in place, and more are being proposed, invented, and deployed every year. We are already halfway through the discontinuity. But it is still difficult for most of us to see beyond it.

Paying Customers for Dialogue Opportunities

Marketers will be able to create dialogue opportunities with customers by providing them first with valuable information (such as investment counseling) or mass-customized news for free, and then paying for these services out of the revenue benefits of increased loyalty and product sales made possible by the dialogue. This "explicit" bargain, struck with individual consumers, resembles the "implicit" bargain that has driven mass media economics for decades. If commercial messages make up the difference between the $1.25 a reader pays for a Sunday *New York Times* and the $12.00 it actually costs to produce, why couldn't commercial messages pay for more individualized information?

And why not make the bargain even more explicit? Why not simply *pay* customers (or prospective customers) to generate dialogue opportunities?[4]

Creating Markets: Bringing Buyers and Sellers Together

Because a fax bulletin board resides on a computer and can be instantly updated or altered by computer input, it can be as flexible as necessary to convey very tailored information. A number of companies have recently gone into the business of creating markets for various products and commodities, using computers to convey information by interactive fax. If a jeweler in Topeka is looking for prices on a two-carat ice blue, she could call RapNet, a diamond exchange, and use her phone's touch tones to get the computer to fax back to her a list of prices from as far away as Antwerp.

If someone is looking for art, one new clearinghouse has a computer hooked up to answer inquiries by fax-response. Just step through Art Co-op's touch-tone menu, dial in a code number for the artist being looked for, and the computer will download to his fax machine a complete list of recent prices for the artist's work. Some of these information-dispensing firms charge subscription fees, while others give out information for one-time charges collected over 900 numbers.[5]

Fax-response can also be used to feed immense computerized data-bases directly to fax machines on request. One Rockford, Illinois company, Government Access & Information Network, Inc. (GAIN), offers a fax-response service that allows anyone with a fax machine to be able to tap into one of several extensive government databases. For $3.50 per document, anyone can call GAIN, use the touch tones on their fax machine to navigate around the system and retrieve, with relative ease, a document on, say, federal grants or assistance available under programs such as Women's Business Ownership Assistance, or Veterans Entrepreneurial Training and Counseling.[6]

When the video dial tone finally arrives, anyone with a phone and a camera will be able to go into the television "broadcasting" business. The video dial tone will spur the growth of an assortment of video service bureaus—companies that collect all sorts of video programming from all over the world, store it digitally in their own computers, and load it selectively into the video mailboxes of various consumer subscribers, according to the individual subscriber's preferences and needs.

Because anyone will be able to send a video signal to anyone else, the video service bureau business is likely to be highly competitive. Most such bureaus will offer not only a variety of video-on-demand but also access to sophisticated computing, gaming, and other interactive information and entertainment products.

And how will customers pay for this kind of video storing, sorting, and forwarding service custom-tailored to their own tastes?

They *could* simply pay for the service. They could elect to watch every program, news show, sporting event, beauty contest or movie on a pay-per-view basis. Since 25 cents worth of advertising enters each home every time someone watches a half-hour prime-time television show today, that's what a programming provider would have to collect to make it an economic proposition. Or maybe consumers may choose to pay a flat fee for a wide variety of choices, similar to the way cable services are sold today.

The alternative to paying for these services is to make deals with advertisers, through service bureaus, who will be only too happy to pay for it for a customer, provided that customer will agree to see their ads in the process. What does a customer have that's valuable enough to marketers to pay for services customers want? Information about themselves. Is a customer a cheap date if he or she trades information to a marketer in exchange for free media use? Everybody buys *something*. The information-for-media deal is, after all, foreplay to a transaction and, if all goes well, the precursor to a long-term relationship.

In the past, mass marketers have bought huge segments of audience—male 25–44, income $30,000 up, homeowners, white-collar, employed. In the 1:1 future, marketers have the wherewithal to use information about individuals—and to make deals with individuals to get that information. In the 1:1 future, running "commercials" will be practically free. What will be costly will be the time, attention, and information of individual customers.

Customers with Long Nails and Hair on Their Hands

When a marketer begins to engage in a dialogue with each customer individually, through whatever means, the customer he talks with is very unlikely to be totally satisfied, and will let him know. If every complaint is an opportunity to collaborate, once a marketer begins to facilitate genuine dialogue, he will be faced with many such opportunities.

Prodigy, a joint venture by Sears and IBM, has served as a good model of an interactive, dialogue-intensive marketing environment. The company provides a wide variety of interactive services to anyone with a personal computer and modem, but unlike most on-line computer operations, Prodigy's services are aimed primarily at home consumers, and many of the services are subsidized by commercial sponsors.

Prodigy has about 200 different advertisers operating on its network, and a good proportion of them sell their products on-line. Advertisers and merchants are free to engage any of the one million or so individual Prodigy subscribers in an e-mail dialogue designed to increase interest in their product and, eventually, to make a sale. Or a subscriber can interact with a Prodigy advertisement, within a limited framework.

For instance, an advertiser might have a questionnaire available and, if the consumer answers it, he or she will be sent a premium or discount of some kind.

Chevrolet offered a $500 rebate to Prodigy users who requested it, applicable to the purchase of a GEO. The subscribers who called up the Chevy ad offering the rebate, after being alerted by an "awareness" ad at the bottom of their screen, were mailed the rebate. Then, a few weeks later they were mailed a postcard from the local GEO dealer encouraging them to come in and test-drive the car.

Prodigy has a lot of problems. For one thing, subscribers find it to be friendly but extremely slow—so slow that relatively more computer-literate people turn their noses up at it. But the biggest problem with Prodigy, as an interactive medium, is not the engineering of its response time, but the engineering of its marketing structure. Believe it or not, even though Prodigy allows consumers to respond directly to messages from marketers, on the front end the system operates as if it were a totally non-addressable mass medium. The same "awareness" ads go to *every* subscriber, and because of the enormous time and expense required to program, produce, and manage the advertising, the company prefers to work mostly with national advertisers. Prodigy wants national advertisers despite the fact that for any service to be genuinely interactive it should be a low-barrier tool for local marketers. Nevertheless, the Prodigy system can still serve as a model for some kinds of consumer-to-marketer-to-consumer dialogue. This is the kind of interactive dialogue that will develop as genuinely 1:1 electronic media begin to proliferate. And it's not always a pretty picture.

Advertisers using the system and interacting with customers on an individual basis have found themselves forced to be extremely straightforward and, above all, responsive. Advertising rhetoric, and PR language, are not going to be sufficient to carry on a conversation.

PC Flowers is a company launched on Prodigy. William Tobin, its president, says that when consumers go on-line with a marketer their expectations of service increase exponentially. They

> grow long nails and hair on their hands . . .
> They tell you when you really didn't do a good job, and they want your firstborn back for it.[7]

One of the most important features of a 1:1 medium is that it will facilitate customer-initiated dialogue, and customer-initiated dialogue is going to be heavily weighted toward complaints—about product quality, about service, about pricing, about attitude. The perceived quality of a company's product or service will be the ruthless, brutal, and absolutely final arbiter of that firm's success. Today quality may be king, but tomorrow it will be somewhere between ayatollah and demi-god.

What is important to recognize, of course, is that all these individual customer complaints existed in the past. They were always there, but they weren't voiced directly to the marketer. The more dialogue a marketer can encourage from customers, the more complaints he has a right to expect. With any genuine mechanism in place for engaging in dialogues with customers, the marketer will have more opportunities than ever before to solve individual consumer problems. The marketer will have more opportunities to resolve difficulties, to create *customerized* products to address individual needs, to collaborate *individually* with each customer—and to gain a much greater share of each one's business.

Before a marketer begins to get all worried about the amount of time being consumed by having dialogues with customers, keep in mind that most of this dialogue is totally automated. Most customer "conversations" will consist of touch-tone interactions. Most actual text-based (keyboard) or audio (voice) communication from a customer will be "mailboxed" to the marketer, if his system has been organized the right way.

The key here is to ensure that the marketer uses automated, computer-intensive systems to absorb the vast, "middle" bulk of his dialogue cost burden. This will allow him to pay closer, more labor-intensive attention to conducting more specialized dialogues on either end of this middle. The marketer will need to allocate most of the firm's customer service labor costs to high-value customers on one end of the spectrum, and to complainers on the other—complainers who can be converted to ultra-loyal collaborators, but only through careful, personal attention.

The Future of Dialogue: Direct Response in Reverse

Soon electronic bulletin boards and mailboxes of various kinds will be common, on computer e-mail systems, "host" messaging systems like HomeFax, voice-mail audiotex, and, in a few years, video mail systems.

The real future of 1:1 media may be a form of direct-response marketing in reverse. Consumers will direct messages and offers to audiences of marketers, who will respond. Remember that most bulletin boards are based on low-cost, low-barrier technologies. So consumers will soon have their own bulletin boards that are scanned by marketers looking to sell them things.

Suppose a consumer could "post" a message for all interested retail electronics stores in his area saying that he was looking for a new 27-inch or bigger television with some digital capability. No reason to limit the offer to retailers. He could send his offer to the major electronics-by-mail companies too. Anyone interested in having his business? Absolute reliability in warranty service is a must, and any store wanting to sell him television should be prepared to give him two satisfied customer references.

This kind of shopping is done personally by many people now, but it is done in a series of phone calls or visits to different establishments. The criteria for a purchase could vary considerably, of course, from the hypothetical example above, depending on who the customer is and what her preferences are. She might just be looking for the lowest price on a particular model of new car. Or she might want a very low price, but not necessarily rock bottom, from a dealer with a good reputation in the service department. Or maybe she needs a bank to handle her IRA account. Or a grocery store willing to provide special help for the physically disabled.

What we're talking about is the fact that, eventually, an individual consumer will be able to send his or her own message to a collective group of marketers—sort of an upside-down "target audience" application.

Because there are few organized media for bulletin boards and mailboxing at present, this kind of message is rarely sent today, although it could blossom next year—or next week. The most direct way for it to occur would be for a host system to go into business, making money by imposing a charge, either explicitly or implicitly, to the consumer (an implicit charge might be in the form of a commission or transaction fee from marketers selling goods through this service).

The host company would have to provide several services to assure an orderly information market. First, it would need to provide the hardware and software to run the system. The system could be voice-mail audiotex, or fax-response, or computer e-mail. Audiotex, although awkward in some respects, would be the most easily accessible to the largest number of consumers today. Second, the host would have to guarantee the integrity of the system. For the consumer, this would mean not divulging the name and address to marketers. The host would know the consumer's identity, but a marketer would only be able to find it out when the consumer responded positively to one of his offers.

To attract marketers, the host would have to ensure that the users of the system were legitimate consumers, shopping for goods and services for their own use, and not competitors, suppliers, or others trying to test the bottom of each marketer's bargaining capability. The host could do this by charging consumer participants a transaction fee to cut down on frivolous "shopping." Also, the host could require statements of good faith from consumer participants and carefully track which items each consumer shops for (presumably, only a competitive car dealer would shop for cars more than once every few months, for instance).

Ultimately, of course, the only genuine insurance for a marketer that he is not quoting his lowest prices to a competitor is to know his customers and most likely prospects from previous exchanges. Providing any kind of dialogue tool to current customers and prospects will enable him to secure a deeper, more profitable, and less competitively vulnerable relationship with each of them. But the deeper each relationship is and the more it is based on dialogue, the less regimented that relationship will be. If it's real dialogue, the marketer won't be controlling it all by himself any more. The customer will be just as much in charge as the marketer is.

The ultimate implication of 1:1 media, using electronic mailboxes and bulletin boards in any form, is that the traditional marketing structure—we make, you take; we speak, you listen—will be turned completely upside-down.

The customer will speak, and the marketer will listen. The customer will ask, and the customer and the marketer will both make, together.

The Support Structure for the 1:1 Future

The technological support structure for the 1:1 future is half in place, and the other half is coming sooner than we realize. By the end of the decade, many major magazines will offer subscribers not only personalized advertising, but personalized editorial content as well. Some newspapers may also offer personalization. Fax machines, already found in 30 percent of Japanese homes, will be found in more than 50 percent of US households (and many of these will actually be fax-modems attached to personal computers).

Already, airplane seat backs come not just with telephones, but with interactive video screens as well, connected by satellite to programming providers and catalog merchandisers. Microwave ovens will soon respond to the spoken instructions. Nintendo sets will be used for homework, connecting televisions by phone to databases that provide encyclopedias, textbooks, and news. Consumers driving their cars will be able to choose from hundreds of customized pay-radio programs delivered over the cellular bandwidth.

Interactive televisions will also be with us before the end of the decade—whether such service is brought to consumers' homes by a cable TV company also offering phone service, or by a phone company also offering TV service, or brought to the home computer via Internet and Worldwide Web services that transmit video as well as text and graphics. Once a true "video dial tone" capability is available, anyone with a phone and a television camera will be able to go into the business of TV "broadcasting" for fun or profit.[8]

These new technologies may sound inaccessible to individuals and small businesses, but in fact just the opposite is true. They are accessible in a way that mass media have never been. In a future of video mailboxes and electronic bulletin boards, of computer sorting and storing and forwarding to individualized communications, the old economics of scale that gave an overwhelming advantage to gigantic marketers will evaporate.

What many of us don't realize is just how close the 1:1 future already is.

If fax machines in people's homes and appliances we can talk to sound too far-fetched, then think back on a world without automatic teller machines, or cellular phones. That was 1980. In 1980 the number of televisions with remote control devices was statistically insignificant. There were no compact disks, almost no videocassette recorders, and no video rental stores. Only restaurants had microwave ovens. Facsimile machines cost several thousand dollars each, took five minutes or more to transmit a single page, and were found only at very large companies. No one had a personal computer.

Every twenty years since 1900 the amount of computational power— machine brainpower—that could be purchased with one dollar has increased by a factor of a thousand. That's more than a million-fold increase just since 1950! If the real cost of manufacturing automobiles had declined since 1950 at the same rate as the real cost of processing information, it would be cheaper today to abandon a Rolls Royce and buy a new one rather than put a dime into a parking meter. Today there is more computational power in a new Chevrolet than there was in the Apollo spacecraft that went to the moon.[9]

Put another way, for what it cost a 1950 marketer to keep track of all the individual purchases and transactions of a single customer, today's marketer can track the individual purchases and transactions of several million individual customers, one at a time.

One Customer at a Time

The mass marketer visualizes his task in terms of selling a single product to as many consumers as possible. This process involves advertising, sales promotion, publicity, and frequently a brand management system for organizing the efforts of the company's marketing department. The marketer's task has always been to make the product unique in a way that would appeal to the largest possible number of consumers and then to publicize that uniqueness with one-way mass-media messages that are interesting, informative, and persuasive to the "audience" for the product.

A 1:1 marketer, however, will not be trying to sell a single product to as many customers as possible. Instead, the task will be to sell a single customer as many products as possible—over a long period of time, and across different product lines. To do this, a marketer will need to concentrate on building unique relationships with individual customers, on a 1:1 basis. Some relationships will be more valuable than others. The best relationships, and the most profitable business, will define a marketer's best customers.

Imagine a florist in a small town, for example, The florist's task can be visualized in two different ways.

A traditional marketing approach would be to calculate market share by counting up a shop's total sales of flowers for any given year. Divide that by the grand total of flower purchases in the town, and the florist discovers she has, say, 10 percent of the total flower business. Using the traditional, mass marketing approach—which inevitably follows from market-share thinking—this florist could run some specials for Mother's Day and Valentine's Day, when a lot of people buy flowers. This might increase her traffic and maybe even her share of the market, providing her competitors don't lower their prices too. But it will cost her some of her profitability. So will the newspaper ads and radio spots necessary to publicize the sale.

Any extra business she gets will be from customers who only come in because she's offering a discount, or running a sale, or giving away a premium, or doing more advertising. All of these customers will defect to competitors the moment those competitors offer similar inducements.

Now imagine a different approach to business. Last year a professional on the East Coast called a local, independent florist in a small Midwest city where his mother lived to have flowers sent to her on her birthday. Three weeks before her birthday this year, he received a note from the same florist, reminding him (1) that his mother's birthday was coming up, (2) that he had sent spider lilies and freesias last year for a certain price, and (3) a phone call to the specified number would put another beautiful bouquet on his mother's doorstep on her birthday this year.

This small, independent florist is working hard to improve her share of her customer's business. Instead of spending just to publicize her products to an entire market, using non-addressable mass media to make the same offer to everyone as if no one had ever bought flowers from her before, she is taking a share-of-customer approach. This florist is engaged in a 1:1 communication with an individual customer, *to get more of that one individual's business.* The information she has about *this* customer—Mom's birthdate—cannot help her get more business from any other customer, but with *this* customer, it gives her a distinct and bankable advantage.[10]

She is performing a service—reminding our friend of his mother's upcoming birthday—and is making her flower shop indispensable and easy to do business with. This doesn't mean the florist isn't also working on acquiring new customers. She just makes sure that she gets every possible bit of patronage from those customers she already has. Her tools? Nothing more than a PC and a lot of common sense.

The company which takes a share-of-customer perspective will build relationships with customers which will transcend the comings and goings of the individual employees in the marketing or sales departments. With a thousand-fold decrease every twenty years in the cost of information processing, today a company can follow, and follow up on, the individual purchases and transactions of millions of individual customers simultaneously, one at a time, for the same cost required to track a few hundred customers in 1970. And every year it gets less and less expensive to track all those customers. This means the possibility of an *electronic* relationship that allows every employee in the company to *remember* the entire relationship and allocate resources wisely to the most valuable customers.

The information tools required to manage millions of such individualized relationships are already available. However, understanding the capabilities of these tools—and knowing when and how to use them—are not trivial skills. For instance, instead of doing research in the comfortable old way—conducting surveys and projecting the results to a broad, undifferentiated target audience—marketers will conduct research by conducting "experiments" with individual customers. In the 1:1 future a marketer might conduct hundreds or thousands of different experiments at once.

The most indispensable element of a relationship with each customer in the 1:1 future will be dialogue and feedback. What do customers really want? What does *this customer* really want?

Clearly, product and service quality will be paramount—to say that quality has always been king sounds trite. But it has never before been possible for most large marketing companies, or even very many smaller ones, to identify and capitalize on individual customer satisfaction, or to detect and prevent individual dissatisfaction and defection. Soon the push for product and service quality will come directly and explicitly from a company's *individual* customers, talking one-to-one with that *company*.

Without a satisfactory product and an acceptable level of service, no customer will be willing to continue a relationship with a marketer for long. But customers do not all experience the quality of a product in the same way. One customer's convenience is another's hassle. Since every customer's quality experience is a subjective event, a 1:1 marketer will be dealing not just with product quality but with *relationship* quality.

The nature of the relationship with each customer in this new environment will be collaborative. Instead of having to be "sold to," customers increasingly will "sell themselves," stepping hand in hand with the marketer through the complicated information exchanges that will, more and more, accompany individual product sales.

As customers, we can already see this beginning to happen. Marketing companies are asking us to collaborate with them in the selling process—whether it's the long-distance company asking us to specify the twenty phone numbers we'd most like to receive discounts on; or a bank asking us to complete money transfers at the ATM machine, or via touch-tone phone, or an automobile company asking us to complete a survey and rate their dealer's service department, or to make a wish list of the options we'd like on our next car.

The more individualized this kind of collaborative interaction is with regard to a particular customer, the more the marketer and that customer will develop a joint interest in the success of the marketer's own marketing effort—as it applies to that customer.

Instead of measuring the success of a marketing program by how many sales transactions occur across the entire market during a particular period, a 1:1 marketer will gauge success by the projected increase or decrease in a customer's expected future value to a company. The true measure of success, one customer at a time, will not be market share, but share of customer.

Interactivity *Requires* 1:1 Marketing

Before being able to take full advantage of the new media and information technologies now becoming available, a marketer has to have a practical set of principles for applying these capabilities. Today's mass marketing paradigm has no *need* for interactive media and computers that track individual customer transactions, linked over time. Tracking customers and conversing with them individually are not tasks that fit into a market-share approach to competition.

But the instant a marketer begins thinking in terms of share of customer, rather than overall market share, new vistas of competitive opportunities will open up. Suddenly, we will see all sorts of ways to employ interactive, addressable media technology, and sophisticated computers. Instead of being overwhelmed by these new tools, we will want more and better tools, *more* interactivity, *more* computer memory and processing power.

The key share-of-customer requirement is to *know* each customer, 1:1. A marketer must know which consumers will never purchase the product at all, so she can stop spending money and effort trying to get them to do something they never will. And she must know who her loyal customers are, so she can take steps to make sure that hers is the brand they choose even more often.

Most companies today are not prepared at all for the kind of cataclysmic change in business competition that is just around the corner. Many, however, are already beginning to apply the principles of the 1:1 future to engage in a totally new and dramatically different form of competition.

Thinking about marketing and communication turned upside-down can be a challenge. Marketers have gotten comfortable with the methods they've been using for the past four decades. Market share. Segmentation. CPMs, GRPs, ratings and shares. Psychographic and geodemographic analysis. These have become the shrines of a religion to the mass marketer. Some say the game is changing. Wrong. The game is *over*, and when we all wake up (tomorrow morning) in the dawn of the Information Age, the mass marketers will be holding their aching heads, trying to figure out what happened to their credentials.

Nearly a hundred years ago, mass production made mass marketing possible. But it was the rise of mass *media*, in the form of radio and national magazines, that *mandated* mass marketing. Likewise, new developments in technology make mass customized production possible, but it is the fractionalization of mass media and the rise of one-to-one (1:1) media that *mandate* 1:1 marketing.[11]

The heart of 1:1 marketing will be a focus on winning a greater share of each customer's business precisely because marketers now have the computational power to remember every detail about a customer's transaction history, and that includes communication. (It's about time. After all, customers have always been able to remember their interactions with companies.) Instead of trying to sell as many packages of product this quarter as possible, marketers will be able to use this new-found memory to satisfy each individual customer's needs. Instead of assigning a product manager the task of trying to sell as many packages of bologna this month as possible, Hormel will task a customer manager with getting Hormel products into Johnny Smith's lunchbox. Instead of trying to sell as many Windows packages as possible to whomever will buy them, Microsoft will instead focus on winning share of disk for many different applications and programs—for each customer, 1:1.

It's obvious that growing *each customer's* business has dramatic implications for the rules of engagement:

- A new emphasis on long-term relationships with consumers (building Lifetime Value, or LTV).

- High-quality product and service, since repeat customers won't happen any other way.

- Differentiating customers, and spending more resources on those who are more valuable.

- Initiating and maintaining dialogues in order to build learning relationships with consumers, and abandoning the old-fashioned advertising monologues of the mass marketer.[12]

Advertising and Dialogue in the 1:1 Future

In the old-fashioned mass-media paradigm, the way advertising has worked has been simple: Figure out the likely prospects and aim standardized messages at that target market using mass media for delivery. If the marketer can win awards in the process for her cleverness and wit, great. But the primary goal has been media efficiency against a specified audience who is likely to see the media vehicle chosen. While they're there, they just might get a glimpse of the ad. The marketer's goal is to penetrate the cerebellum with the message that his gum has longer-lasting flavor or his hotel provides a better stay for the money.

That worked fine when we could make reasonable predictions about where people's attention would be directed. But with a cosmic explosion in media choice, as well as the ability of the interactive customer to *talk back*, future advertisers will have to completely rethink the way they talk with consumers. When marketers talk to customers through interactive radio (cell phones), fax response, electronic mail, interactive TV with 500-channel capability, and other new media, what new rules will govern play?

The nature of "advertising" and promotions face major changes. In the 1:1 future, advertising's role will shift from building awareness and affective response to serving as a broker between marketers and customers, providing an explicit bargain for dialogue participation, and finding new ways to be considered part of the entertainment milieu.

Several new media already offer the technological capability that will characterize interactive television and can serve as an analogy for the video dial tone. Specifically, the Internet offers the host computer necessary to serve as information intermediation that will protect consumer privacy while providing explicit bargains between marketers and individual consumers.

In the past, copywriters and others responsible for marketing communications have based their success on unique selling propositions, positioning, and other creative strategies designed to direct a broad appeal to a defined but mass audience. In the future, copywriters will face the challenge of personalized message delivery as well as the profound implications of dealing with individual feedback made possible through currently available interactive media.

In the 1:1 future, advertising will be *invited, solicited,* and *integral.*

- Invited: Successful advertisers will have to stop their frenetic shouting at customers, and will instead engage in the polite invitation. "We will credit $4.00 to your phone bill if you watch our infomercial and call our toll-free number with the PIN code we've recorded in the middle." The bargain is explicit: Listen to our pitch and we'll give you something you want—a pay-per-view, maybe, or a few minutes of cell-phone time.

- Solicited: Customers will keep marketers honest when they can initiate the dialogue. A customer goes on-line, identity protected by an information intermediator, and sends the following ad: "I want to buy a 15-75mm camera with point-and-shoot capability that also allows manual control. Need auto-rewind-before-shooting feature, and carrying case. Willing to spend $100-$300. Who wants my business?" Responses could appear in the customer's coded video or fax mailbox from local retailers, national electronic mail order shops, manufacturers, and individuals looking to resell a used camera.

- Integral: As customers opt out of advertising per se *because they can,* the advertising will become more and more a part of entertainment and information. Already product placement in movies is big business, with clear distinctions in placement fees for background use vs. handling by the hero. In the future, we will see a greater fusion of publicity, advertising, and careful product placement in nearly every media outlet.

Does this mean mass media, and old-fashioned mass media advertising, will disappear? Is this truly the end of all mass marketing? No—no more than farming disappeared when America left the Agricultural era for the Industrial age. It just meant that fewer people were needed for farming, and more people were needed instead to work in factories in the city. As a minor side effect, all of society changed, but we still eat. So we will still see Michael Somebody advertising Nikes and Pepsi (after all, it's no fun to pay over \$100 for shoes if your friends haven't heard of the brand), but we will also see a lot less mass media advertising.

What this means for marketers is a greater challenge to get their messages to individual consumers. What this means for consumers is more messages that we might truly find useful, and fewer messages that we classify as "junk." New media mandates a new strategy, or we will simply send "junk mail at light speed."

The question is not how we can use the Internet to make products more profitable. The question is how we can use new tools, and old tools, to make *each customer* more profitable, one customer at a time.

References

1. The telegram was discontinued by Western Union in December 1991. See Levin, Gary, "Western Union Not Fading into Sunset: New Services are Added as Telegram Drops," *Advertising Age,* April 27, 1992, p. 54.

2. Daimler story details were discussed with Bernd Harling, manager of corporate communications for Mercedes-Benz of North America, Inc. Telephone interview, December 16, 1992.

   The number of cars on the world's roads is a conservative estimate based on 424,365,795 cars in 1989, with annual net growth of approximately 12 million. Motor Vehicle Manufacturers Association of the United States, *Motor Vehicle Facts and Figures,* 1991, p. 37.

3. Peppers, Don and Rogers, Martha, *The One to One Future, Building Relationships One Customer at a Time,* New York: Doubleday/Currency, 1993, Ch. 7.

4. Peppers, Don and Rogers, Martha, "Let's Make a Deal", *Wired,* February 1994, p. 74.

5. Using the fax machine to bring buyers and sellers together was reported by William M. Bulkeley, "Faxes Prove to Be a Powerful Tool for Setting up Electronic Markets," *Wall Street Journal,* July 28, 1992, p. B3.

6. We spoke to Marcia Linley, V.P. and Director of Technical Operations for GAIN, by telephone, March 3, 1993.

7. Prodigy's William Tobin is quoted from *Direct,* August 1992, p. 36.

8. Paragraphs about the support structure for the 1:1 paradigm are based on current developments, reported widely. For an overview, see:

Personalized ads and editorial: Albert Scardino, "Donnelley Develops a Way for Magazines to Get Personal," *New York Times*, November 20, 1989, p. D8.

Fax machines: *Newspapers and Voice*, "Hot Off the Fax," April 1992, pp. 20-25; Takami, Hirohiko, "Facsimile Diffuses to Home Users," *Business Japan*, November 1989, pp. 73, 79, 81; Judith Waldrop, "Strong Fax Sales will Challenge Postal Service," *American Demographics*, June 1991, p. 12.

Airplane video screens: Larry Riggs, "Catalogues Contacted for a New In-flight Program," *DM News*, June 8, 1992, pp. 1, 2.

Microwave ovens respond to speech: John J. Keller, "Computers Get Powerful 'Hearing' Aids: Improved Methods of Voice Recognition," *Wall Street Journal*, April 7, 1992, p. B1.

VCRs respond to speech: Richard Zoglin, "Can Anybody Work This Thing? New Gadgets Keep Aiming to Cure VCR Illiteracy. The Latest Lets People Simply Talk to Their Machines," *Time*, November 23, 1992, p. 67.

Extended Nintendo: Eben Shapiro, "Nintendo and Minnesota Set a Living Room Lottery Test," *New York Times*, September 27, 1991, p. A1.

Cellular radio: Howard Schlossberg, "Like your Ballgames on TV? Get Ready to Pay for Them," *Marketing News*, April 13, 1992, p. 14.

150 channel to 500-channel capacity: Mary Lu Carnevale, "Ring In the New: Telephone Service Seems on the Brink of Huge Innovations; Baby Bells, and Cable Firms Vie to Win Video Market and Add a Host of Services," *Wall Street Journal*, February 10, 1993, pp. A1, A7; John Markoff, "A System to Speed Computer Data: Compressing Images May Lead to a Variety of New Products," *New York Times*, January 30, 1991.

Interactive TV: Alice B. Cuneo, "The Fine Points of Interactive TV," *Advertising Age*, May 11, 1992, p. 60.

9. Information about fiber optic lines abounds, but we drew from George Gilder, "Into the Telecosm," *Harvard Business Review*, March-April 1991, pp. 150-61, and John J. Keller, "Pacific Bell Tests Fiber-Optic Lines for Home Phones," *Wall Street Journal*, August 27, 1991, p. B4. Of course, many marketers do realize just how close the 1:1 future really is. See Betsy Spethman, "Marketers Tap Into Tech," *Advertising Age*, January 25, 1993, pp. 30. Also see George Gilder (*Microcosm: The Quantum Era of Economics and Technology*. New York: Simon & Schuster, 1989), who suggests that, throughout most of this century, the amount of computational power that can be bought for one dollar has increased by a factor of 1,000 every twenty years since 1900. He suggests that the rate is speeding up and is now probably every ten years. Or less.

10. Peppers, Don and Rogers, Martha, *The One to One Future, Building Relationships One Customer at a Time,* New York: Doubleday/Currency, 1993, Ch. 2.

11. B. Joseph Pine II, Don Peppers, and Martha Rogers, "Do You Want to Keep Your Customers Forever?", *Harvard Business Review,* March–April 1995, p. 103.

12. Learning relationships are introduced in Pine, Peppers, and Rogers, *Harvard Business Review,* March–April 1995.

CHAPTER

2

Maintaining a Customer Focus in an Interactive Age

The Seven I's to Success

Michael Spalter

Michael Spalter's work in interactive marketing has been covered in a range of publications including *Business Week,* the *New York Times*, the *New York Daily News*, *Women's Wear Daily*, *Ad Week*, and the *Journal of Commerce*. Spalter created one of the first interactive multimedia marketspaces, hailed as a "new concept in retailing," for Bloomingdale's.

As many consumers and companies continue to migrate from the physical marketplace to the electronic marketspace,[1] maintaining customer focus will require new management constructs and reengineering of existing structures. This means a whole range of opportunities and threats will emerge. Unfortunately, the vast majority of businesses currently online have neglected or failed to ask several fundamental marketing questions:

- Why would a consumer want to do business in a marketspace?

- What are the key success factors in creating an outstanding marketspace?

- What new competencies will organizations need to successfully compete and involve customers in their marketspace?

- What can marketers do to individualize and personalize customers' experiences?

- What must be done to demonstrate a company's integrity and insure that consumers' privacy and security are safeguarded?

Many forward-looking businesses understand that new electronic distribution channels provide opportunities to expand market reach while enabling consumers to make transactions faster and more convenient. Consumers empowered to control, choose, and help create their own commercial experiences will wreak havoc on rigid, inflexible organizations unwilling or unable to adapt to the marketspace. In a classic domino effect, many marketing practices are falling as networks and interactivity cause a series of systemic changes. This realization has caused many executives to ask, "What makes a company thrive in the marketspace?"

The answer is: *maintaining customer focus.* To do this one must understand two key principles about how and why interactive marketing differs from traditional marketing practices. First, networks and the ability to communicate over them from **anywhere** in the globe **at any time** remove the constraints of space and time associated with physical marketplaces. Maintaining customer focus will require businesses to adjust to the staggering changes brought about by the marketspace.

Second, traditional mass marketing media have consisted of monologues presented to the consumer through print, audio, and visual media such as newspapers, magazines, direct mail, radio, or television. The advent of commercial online services and the far reach of the Internet have, for the first time in mass marketing history, created the potential for a mass interactive **dialogue**. This shift is redefining marketing practices and the businesses that depend upon them. Interactive marketing is rapidly destroying and blurring the traditional distinction between push (as in sales workers) and pull (as in advertisers). How this one issue alone is handled will make or break entire companies and industries. The historic distinctions and professions built around this old paradigm are becoming eclipsed by new modes of conducting business, giving birth to the Age of Interactive Marketing.

Business people are just beginning to understand that some of the most sacred concepts in marketing are being challenged and made obsolete:

- Market research is evolving into market **usership.**
- Database marketing is evolving into database **consuming**.
- The marketing mix is evolving.
- Traditional distinctions between mass media advertisers and salespeople are blurring.

This article offers a construct to aid individuals charged with maintaining a customer focus in an interactive age. Utilizing what I call the Seven **I**'s, marketers can better analyze and prepare for their transition from the marketplace to the marketspace. The Seven **I**'s are:

1. Interconnection
2. Interface
3. Interactivity
4. Involvement
5. Information
6. Individualism
7. Integrity

Interconnection

New marketing approaches made possible by the evolution of large and complex interconnected networks, often referred to as *"information highways,"* and the creation of marketspaces are destroying many sacred cows and forcing dramatic changes in organizations small and large, domestic and foreign. Just as the introduction of railways, highways, telephone lines, and broadcasting of radio and television signals has changed businesses and lifestyles, the rapidly growing information highways will leave no one untouched. Interconnected information highways represent an entirely new distribution channel with as much potential to redefine business and society as the introduction of any technological innovation in history.

Millions of individuals throughout the world are becoming interconnected because of networks—the most famous, of course, being the Internet. Navigating on the networks, individuals can guide themselves to areas that contain information ranging from news services to commercial malls. Once within an area of interest, known as a *forum* or discussion group, they can begin to participate in a *"virtual community."* Inside a virtual community one can communicate with other individuals from around the world. As people travel, or *"surf"* the information highway, many would say they are now in *cyberspace*.[2] The "information" speeding down the highway is anything that can be digitized and transmitted—images, text, audio or graphics, ranging from real-time news feeds such as Reuters to entire inventories of product lines such as the L.L. Bean catalog. Virtual communities formed around special interests, ranging from occupational to social to religious, are uniting millions of individuals as barriers of space and time are lifted.

The era is not far off when networks will interconnect hundreds of millions of people around the globe to use such features as real-time, interactive, full color-video to explore myriad informational resources and entertainment offerings as well as conduct commerce. The private commercial online services and the World Wide Web, commonly referred to as the "Web," on the Internet are filled with examples of businesses that have taken their content and put them into a digital format. These early examples, while primitive, enable students of interactive marketing to see specifically how many old notions about marketing and communications are threatened. As the allure of attracting denizens to these virtual communities grows, businesses increasingly are beginning to move from the traditional brick and mortar marketplace into the electronic marketspace. A business wishing to maximize its profits in the marketspace will want to be located in areas with the maximum accessibility to the largest number of potential customers. Businesses must decide what kind of network to establish a presence on to optimize market reach:

- Should a business be on a commercial service such as America Online, or is a site on the World Wide Web on the Internet more appropriate?

- What about creating a marketspace on all the commercial services that serve as a gateway to a larger Web site?

Where a corporation chooses to establish a presence in the marketspace is as important as in which city and on what street corner a retailer decides to open its doors. Interconnectivity will require many marketers to adopt an international perspective and will accelerate the trend towards globalization. A traditional market segmentation should be conducted to gain a thorough understanding about which networks and sites are attracting target customers.

A key strategic marketing factor is the ease with which individuals from around the world can access one's sites. On the Internet, for example, geographic barriers hold almost no meaning in the marketspace. A thorough analysis of where target market members are deciding to spend their time online will help determine whether a presence should be maintained on one or more networks. A highly focused and targeted network or site might already be attracting and maintaining the very customer groups you are interested in reaching.

Analyzing other sites on a network and their proximity to your "icon" will help pinpoint where establishing a marketspace makes sense for a specific organization. On America Online's main menu, for example, there are fourteen categories of explorable member areas ranging from personal finance to education. Ideally, organizations want to be in an area that serves as an interconnection and focal point for those with desirable buying patterns. Once a business has selected a network on which to establish a presence, the challenge becomes getting users to "click" onto their site—one that may compete with hundreds if not thousands of other areas.

Interface

The interface of a marketspace can make or break a business online. Corporations are just beginning to acknowledge the profound commercial impact and challenge of repurposing their businesses to create digital assets that can be electronically displayed and purchased. Marketing organizations must adopt a new core competence of market-oriented interface development if they hope to capitalize on the interactive age. If a marketer is successful in inducing trial, the consumer will enter the marketspace.

Recent history is filled with examples of how a superior interface can catapult a product from relative obscurity to a position of market leadership. Apple Computer's Macintosh, with its intuitive graphical user interface, helped Apple become the leader of the personal computer revolution in the 1980s. The Mosaic and Netscape browsers are also examples of graphical user interfaces that helped fuel the explosive growth of the World Wide Web and Internet in the mid-1990s. America OnLine emerged as the leading commercial service from out of nowhere to eclipse Prodigy and CompuServe; AOL's interface is regularly cited as one of the primary reasons for its success.

The importance of creating a "user-friendly" intuitive interface cannot be overstated. As networks proliferate and the importance of marketspaces grows, traditional marketing techniques will be fully utilized and exploited to induce trial in order to get an individual to "click" into a site. Building brand awareness in the form of icons online will be a challenge for businesses. When surfing, for example, through a marketspace, would one be more interested in clicking on an icon that represents the Apple logo or on the word *Apple*? As consumers are induced to try a marketspace, the comfort and security of clicking onto a visual icon that represents a known brand will be of increasing strategic importance.

The interface can determine whether an individual wishes to explore the marketspace or move on to another site of interest. Careful construction of a market-oriented interface will assist consumers in passing through the buying process. An intelligent interface will incorporate the "stage models" of the buying process:[3]

- Problem Recognition
- Information Search

- Evaluation of Alternatives

- Purchase Decision

- Postpurchase Behavior

As the traditional distinctions between advertising and sales blur, it will be the interface that increasingly is charged with communicating a company's products and value to the target customers. Assuring that the interface successfully captures the attention of potential customers will require a coordinated multidisciplinary effort that involves the following disciplines:

- Marketing

- Sales

- Advertising

- Psychology

- Design

- Computer programming

- Operations

- Market research

Marketers need to understand how interfaces influence customers. Perhaps the single most important component of successful interface design is an iterative design process that is driven by customer feedback. Thanks to the ability to precisely monitor the "click streams" of users online, it is possible to conduct extensive testing of a proposed interface (more discussion on this will follow in the Individualism section). As a result of database technology, unprecedented measurements are at the disposal of marketers, enabling the desired response to an interface design to be continually improved.

Finally, careful attention must be paid in the interface design to language and cultural differences. Subtle social and cultural differences will have to be incorporated into the various interfaces created to meet customer needs throughout the world. Few examples exist of interfaces that respect linguistic and cultural differences. Unfortunately, this disregard for many consumers reinforces the general lack of customer focus online. The day is not far off when marketers will address this situation and empower users with the ability to explore the marketspace using their native language.

A quick tour of the Treasures of the Louvre on the World Wide Web illustrates how easy it is to translate one or more languages in an interactive setting. English speakers visiting the Louvre online and unable to speak French have the option of reading descriptions in English. By offering this simple language option in the interface, descriptions of the Louvre's holdings are now accessible to tens of millions of additional visitors. The interface, if planned successfully, will induce trial. It is the degree of interactivity of the marketspace, however, that will determine whether a customer's interest is piqued.

Interactivity

Marketers continue to rush like lemmings into the online world, pumping millions of dollars into dozens of ventures. Yet few commercial organizations are attempting to provide new modes for the viewing, listening to, and testing of their products and services. In order to do this, one must understand interactivity: What will and will not work in an interactive medium.[4] Publishing houses, movie studios and others have tried to conquer the interactive market but no clear front-runner has emerged. Many of these marketers encounter frustrations when customers do not respond to their sites as they wish. This new medium seems to offer opportunities to manipulate and navigate through content in innovative and exciting ways, yet many executives who grasp the growing importance of interconnectivity quickly grow disillusioned.

Why?

Many marketers are not maintaining a customer focus. They are not asking what *customers* value in an interactive age. They are unwilling or unable to fully explore a key principle of the new medium—interactivity. Thanks to interactivity, for the first time in history mass media has moved from a monologue to a dialogue. Now customers can interact with content and other human beings, steering their own experience and opening up a new era in business history.

Interactivity includes letting customers:

- control and choose the content they are viewing.

- "chat" or communicate in real-time with one or more individuals.

- e-mail one or more individuals.

- post and respond to posts on bulletin boards.

For those of you completely unfamiliar with interactive services and marketspaces, let's assume that you are interested in buying a magazine for pleasure reading, but have been unable, due to time constraints, to get to a newsstand. Instead, you can visit an area on the Web hosted by Time-Warner called "Pathfinder" that enables you to actually interact with the magazine content being shown. In this site, you will view a screen in which the logos of magazines are displayed, ranging from *Money* to *Time.*

With the click of a mouse, you can decide which magazine you wish to "tour." By clicking on a logo, say *Time,* you can begin *interacting* with images, sounds, graphics and text areas. Within the virtual version of *Time* it will soon be possible to interact with advertisements.

This simple yet awesome capability instantly alters the field of marketing in much the same way that Automatic Teller Machines forever altered the banking industry. The ability of the marketer to interact with a consumer viewing a product or service through a medium similar to TV is revolutionary. This simple step will be as important in the history of marketing and customer service as were the expansion of railroads and the U.S. Postal System. The magnitude and scope of this simple yet profound ability are changing the business world.

Thanks to recent and ongoing technological achievements, products reaching the customer over the information highway offer much more seductive interactive graphics capabilities than an ATM. These souped-up *multimedia* elements (multimedia is the integration of video, sound, music, graphics and text) can make the virtual experience far more fun and stimulating than many have previously thought possible. A key difference between ATMs and Interactive Marketing on the information highway is the ability to communicate and express oneself. Tackling this difference will make or break many businesses hoping to compete in the marketspace. Understanding and then leveraging the ability to communicate with customers online will separate the successful marketspaces from the also-rans. The age-old adage that understanding your customer is the cornerstone to business success will have greater meaning than ever before in the marketspace.

Voilà. With the press of a button in an online magazine ad, you can tour the inside of a car, get information, go for a visual test ride, and review a bulletin board of customer feedback. After you tour the car, you can then return to the magazine or arrange with the click of a button to be put into contact with a dealership. Soon customers will be able to ask any number of additional questions and even make a purchase—including details of optional service contracts and dealer financing. Depending upon the sophistication of the interactive experience, you may be able to order the car without ever speaking to anyone, or the marketer may wish to "pull" you to "push" an icon on your screen. This new ability to interact with media will redefine entire industries.

Many adept marketers and sales executives fail to see that for the first time their customers have a media outlet to express their *emotions*. To some, the idea of a person sitting alone in front of a television typing away as the ABC Evening News or a Honda commercial airs may seem absurd. Yet more and more people are communicating and interacting with each other at their computer terminals. Whether at a TV or a computer terminal, users must be involved in the interaction; by failing to engage customers in dialogue and take their responses into account, many businesses are losing and will continue to lose precious opportunities to maintain their customers' patronage.

We are still in the early days of *new media* (multimedia) usage and people are amazed at the ability to integrate text, audio, video, graphics and animation. Less well understood or contemplated is the *interactivity* of the new media work. The maturation of the interactive multimedia format must be addressed as the market explodes if the marketspace is to reach its potential. The key to an interactive marketing site is whether this new environment dramatically enhances the customer's experience. Many marketers are jumping to the wrong conclusions about this new medium, assuming that traditional media (text, audio, video, photography, animation) will naturally provide an interactive experience when digitized and made into a marketspace. This is a waste of precious marketing budgets.

Most existing content (whatever medium it was created in) was *not* designed to be interactive. An excited marketer tells a techie, "Here is the company's sales catalog, get us online. . . ." The techie says, "Of course," but then the challenge begins: How to take traditional media content and make it interesting and stimulating in an *interactive* format. Note that the CD-ROM market has not been driven by the titans of industry but by individuals like the Miller brothers, creators of MYST, who, through their unique understanding of the interactive environment, engage and involve thousands of customers.

Trip Hawkins, founder of multimedia companies Electronic Arts and 3D0, summarizes the importance of interactive multimedia: "In the sense that audio is the medium of hearing, and video is the medium of viewing, multimedia is the medium of 'doing'."[5] Getting customers to interact with a marketspace is not the same thing as getting them involved. Active customer involvement leads to customer loyalty.

Involvement

Businesses can profoundly influence the success of their sites by paying careful attention to crafting an atmosphere that encourages customer involvement. A key success factor is to decide how one creates new, original customer experiences for an interactive setting, or transfers traditional works into new and potentially enhanced materials that actively involve users by engaging them in forums, bulletin boards, and customer clubs. Ongoing research should integrate traditional products and services in innovative, powerful ways. As with traditional marketing, the answers to what works reside with your customers.

Initially, there are several ways to attract individuals to a particular site. These include:

- Creating an inviting, intuitive interface for content.

- Linking your site to a popular area or site that will serve as a gateway to your site.

- Leveraging brand equity.

- Integrating traditional marketing communication materials such as advertising, correspondence, bills and promotional materials with information on how to access your site.

Like window shopping in the physical marketplace, it will take more than a well-known brand name and compelling interface to engage potential marketspace customers. On America Online with its over 500 databases, content alone does not dictate success at sites such as Military City, Motley Fool (a financial area) and American Express' ExpressNet. It is the ability to express one's emotions and react to content by interacting and communicating through bulletin boards, chat features and e-mail that make these sites so successful. Communicating empowers individuals to become *involved* in their community of interest. Preparing a marketspace that will involve users is a critical strategic task.

As users interact with the content within a marketspace, a cycle of success can be created wherein content attracts users, users create more content, new content enhances the value of the site and more users are drawn to the marketspace. The cycle of success is broken if the subject matter and ensuing dialogue lack flair. Unless customers have a compelling hook that engages and involves them in a site, the peril of losing potential business is high. Involving consumers can be done in a number of ways, including:

- Continually updating and refreshing content.

- Sponsoring and moderating interesting and stimulating chats with guest experts and/or interesting topics.

- Creating direct links with content for customers to voice their opinions through bulletin boards.

- Reviewing and commenting on customer messages or posts contained in bulletin boards.

- Acquiring or aligning with other content providers who might serve as a hook within your site (e.g., Amdahl, a site on the Web, has a number of hypertext links to interesting sites ranging from *HotWired* to the White House Server).

- Offering sophisticated search mechanisms that help consumers pinpoint information. (e.g., Time Warner's Pathfinder has a built-in search feature for topics covered within magazine articles. The search enables someone reading an article on the Supreme Court, for example, to search *Time's* extensive databases for articles on a particular Justice).

The thousands of marketers establishing their businesses in the marketspace must understand the importance of interactively involving customers to maintain their interest and involvement. Marketing organizations must grapple with how digital assets can be enhanced and made interesting, stimulating, and easy to navigate if put into an interactive format.

Interactive marketers capable of producing experiences that appeal to wide audiences will understand that the key to interactivity rests in involving and capturing users' attention by enabling them to control their own experience and communications. Interactive marketers will:

- Like a Ray Kroc, make their sites synonymous with quality and value

- Like a Ralph Lauren, make one want to see their latest offering

- Or, like a David Ogilvy, make the viewer cry, laugh, or smile.

One of the first challenges for traditional businesses in the marketspace is to get people who understand how to transform content to involve users. The best way to do this is to take a product or service and ask why and how its content would work in an interactive format. The most common answer is that it is a more convenient channel of distribution, one that penetrates directly into the home. Many products, however, do not work in this medium, which should not be surprising since many goods rely for their marketing upon consumer reaction to physical sensations such as touch, smell and taste. As these traditional businesses begin to explore what content they wish to market with interactive new media, it would be helpful to include creative multimedia specialists in the process of selecting products and services. Rather than have a seasoned marketing guru dictate that his or her top-drawing product line be the first interactive project because everyone knows and loves the brand, have a creative multimedia specialist detail for you the ways in which the product can become interactive.

The new paradigm is most apparent in the World Wide Web, where individuals can utilize hypertext. The WWW interconnects tens of thousands of Internet servers containing digitized information in a range of formats including text, graphics, video, and sound. Hypertext enables users to control how they view the information presented. This ability transforms the user's traditional linear experience into a non-linear one. A customer, for example, can be reading an article about a company in the *Wall Street Journal*'s interactive edition and then "click" on a search engine known as a briefing book. The briefing book, through a hypertext link, offers (when available) additional background information, a financial overview, stock performance charts and data, recent news and press releases, or a link to the company's home page or a database of related stories.

The Marketing Mix is Evolving

Traditional mass marketing media, as discussed earlier, have been essentially monologues presented to consumers through print—newspapers, magazines and direct mail, radio—one-way audio, or TV—one-way audio and video. The potential for an interactive dialogue forever changes promotion, and therefore customer focus. The distinctions and professions built around traditional notions of marketing are now in the process of becoming eclipsed by new modes of conducting business, giving birth to the age of Interactive Marketing. It is now possible to read online a newspaper or magazine article about an interesting product or service, then click on the name of the company offering the service and immediately be linked to a marketspace. Once in the marketspace, consumers can order the product or service that caught their interest.

Many business people use the marketing mix popularized by E. Jerome McCarthy (consisting of the Four Ps: Product, Price, Place and Promotion) to develop a marketing campaign.[6] Interactive Marketing stirs this mix. Promotion is undergoing a radical change which has not been thoroughly explored, much less documented.

Promotion within the marketing mix has encompassed the two distinct and often complementary sales tools of advertising and personal selling traditionally known as Pull and Push. The advertiser attempts to *pull* you to a product, showcasing it in a *nonpersonal* way that will draw you into the place where the product is sold, while the salesperson attempts to *push* you to the product in a *personal* pitch by bringing product information (and possibly the product itself) to you directly. Think about the difference between a Coca-Cola commercial on TV and the Avon person knocking on your front door.

With the birth of Interactive Marketing, we now see the demise of this dichotomy. Indeed, the distinction between pull and push is becoming increasingly blurred. The blurring of the roles of salespeople and advertisers in the marketing mix means that we must reassess:

- The very nature of advertising and a sales force

- The entire idea of a distribution channel (i.e., what happens to traditional distribution channels when the needs they now fulfill can be met in front of a PC?)

- The ways in which some traditional business processes can be adapted to take advantage of the revolutionary impact of new media.

The dramatic changes underway in the marketing mix will affect all four Ps, forcing marketers and businesses to address one of the greatest changes in the history of modern business. As an example, the information highway enables customers to deal directly with manufacturers, thereby potentially cutting out a number of intermediaries such as salespeople and retail outlets. Cutting out these segments (known as disintermediation) of the distribution channel lowers expenses.[7] Savings are usually passed on to consumers, resulting in lower prices. The recent interest in Barry Diller's QVC is an early and primitive example of the future.

Not only will Interactive Marketing change advertising and salespeople's roles, but it will force many industries to reconsider the other components of the marketing mix.

- If a business can cut out sales commissions, how does this affect the Pricing strategy of a product?

- If a one-person business can reach the entire globe through the Internet what constitutes a geographic market and what does this mean for Place strategies?

Understanding how the marketing mix is affected by interactive marketing can help business people prepare for the imminent changes in their organizations. Those able to grasp these structural changes will be of unique value to their organization by helping it successfully adapt to the interactive age.

Let's turn to the blurring of the salespeople's and mass advertisers' roles and examine what this may mean for the advertising industry (which relies heavily upon pull strategies) and then turn to those industries (such as real estate, retailing, and financial services) that depend heavily upon salespeople and push strategies.

Advertising Age reports that over $100 billion is spent annually on advertising in the United States. Interactive marketing could become one of the best-funded efforts in our society to use interactive information technologies. Marketers ***must*** address the impact that this new era will have upon their profession, when individuals can control and choose when they want to initiate being pushed in real time. With traditional television and radio advertising, the majority of ads leave an impression upon the individual that attempts to *pull* them into a store at some future time period to purchase a product or service—this is about to change.

We have already seen the evolution towards real-time interaction in its most primitive form with ads like those for the Ginsu knife that ask the viewer to telephone for a direct order during a 30-second spot (one-way video—television, and two-way audio—the telephone). QVC and its home shopping network, as well as the introduction of infomercials, are evolutionary steps in this process of getting people to be pulled and pushed in real time. Online services shatter old notions of personal sales and mass media advertising by offering both in real time! Consumers watching an advertisement now can not only control what they are viewing, but if moved to make an impulse purchase can do so.

What is the significance of all this?

In marketing there is a model known as the "hierarchy of effects continuum"[8] which attempts to persuade a customer to purchase an item.

EXHIBIT 2.1 Hierarchy of Effects Model:

Cognitive   Affective   Behavior

Awareness —> Knowledge —> Liking stage —> Preference —> Conviction —> Purchase

---

Until recently, most mass media advertising attempted to build awareness of a product. The less complex the product or message, the more an organization would depend upon advertising to pull customers to purchase a product or create an image. Procter and Gamble, for example, spends over a billion dollars a year to spread its simple messages.

Financial services, real estate, and insurance, on the other hand, offer more complex products with many variations and do not rely on pull-type methods as heavily as consumer product companies. It is not surprising that there are nearly two million salespeople in the finance, insurance and real estate industries or that there are more than six million salespeople in retail and personnel services (US BLS Current Population Survey Annual Average Data 1993).

It has been far more difficult and expensive for these salespeople to use mass media to advertise a specific financial instrument, home furnishing, shoe, or house on Main Street. National chains often attempt to differentiate themselves through mass media by promoting their level of service or the overall quality of their corporation—and, by association, their salespeople. The goal is to pull consumers to their salespeople and then push them into an interactive dialogue to purchase a specific product.

As mentioned earlier, QVC is helping to break the mold. So are Richard Simmons and other infomercial tycoons. These entrepreneurs took a gamble on buying 30 or 60 minutes of commercial time that would enable them to move slowly through the entire hierarchy of effects model, reaching millions of viewers with the hope that there would be a payback. Both QVC and Simmons have successfully coupled one-way video with two-way audio to make the transaction an interactive experience. Unlike the lone traveling salesperson who knocks on your door or cold-calls you (capable in the most wildly successful day of reaching perhaps fifty prospective customers), QVC or Simmons reach millions! And those millions can initiate contact by picking up a phone and talking to a salesperson.

Yet, Home Shopping Network is becoming quaint when compared to marketspaces on online computer services and interactive television. The integration of two-way video and audio is now being realized in a primitive fashion through the use of CD-ROM and interactive multimedia. It is only a matter of time before consumers will be able to determine to what extent they wish to learn about products or services. Today, when you are watching a television program, you have little choice but to sit through a commercial message during an intermission. The rise of online services and interactivity completely changes this paradigm. Mass media no longer has meaning when any individual can interact and control contact with the marketer. Messages delivered through mass media and electronic lines have been exclusively delivered in a linear fashion. It may seem absurd to think that an individual could ask over his television set what a particular knob on an appliance actually did. Equally absurd to some is the notion that one could specify during a commercial message desired product comparisons or image reviews. That is all changing. Now marketer and consumer not only transact but must interact. Those marketers who avoid interaction will undoubtedly lose sales, and even their very companies.

Information

As interactive marketing evolves, the entire paradigm of database marketing is being turned on its head because database *consuming* is being born.[9] Database consuming is the result of customers' using database technology to target products just as marketers have been using databases to target customers. Database "shopping engines" will give consumers access to the same technologies marketers have been using for decades. Database consumers, as a result of the advances in information technology, have access to unprecedented tools that enable them to search out almost instantly vast amounts of information on products and services offered throughout the globe. Imagine having the ability to enter a product name and price in a database and then find every business that carries the particular product and the price at which they are selling it. Database consuming will strengthen the individual's control, choice and empowerment and will heighten the importance of providing useful information to consumers. Database consuming will also increase the importance of advertising in informing, persuading and reminding. Assuming a marketspace is successful in creating an intelligent interface that interactively involves customers, it will be the freshness and variety of infomation offered that will keep customers coming back time and time again.

An example of database consuming is illustrated with a revolutionary new tool of the marketspace—the *key cost*. Thanks to the key cost marketers will better appreciate the critical role of advertising in nurturing and maintaining their brands. The key cost will become the first cousin to the "key word" found in many popular word processing programs and will enable consumers to search out the lowest price for a product. The key cost will make the difference between quality, service and price more distinct in the minds of consumers during the purchasing decision.

Millions of people are familiar with the key word search function in word processing programs that enables the user to scan thousands of entries or pages of text to locate a particular string of letters or numbers. The key word has made finding a needle in a haystack as simple as typing the word "needle." A process that in the past might have taken days, weeks, or even months is reduced to seconds. The key cost search will become one of several powerful functions a customer might use while database consuming.

The adage that "knowledge is power" will have a new significance for those consumers using the key cost function when database consuming. Immediately, they will have the ability, from the comfort of their homes, to comparison shop based upon price anywhere in the world at any particular time. Consumer awareness of what an item costs, coupled with the ability to have it delivered overnight, could potentially force entire industries to change.[10]

CUC International's Shoppers Advantage offers a glimpse of the potential of database consuming. CUC's members can access online, from their homes, over 250,000 brand-name products, enter a series of parameters (e.g., cost, features, etc.) and read about the different products that match their interests. When CUC customers make a purchase through Shoppers Advantage they also receive a low price guarantee and extended warranty. CUC is currently working with Time-Warner in Orlando and Viacom in Northern California to launch two different interactive TV home shopping ventures. America Online's much publicized CD-ROM, 2 Market, also shows the potential of database consuming. It enables consumers to view scores of catalogs while searching for, requesting information about, and viewing over 39,000 products from some of the top retailers in the world including Tiffany & Co., L.L. Bean, Williams-Sonoma and many more. One can enter a product type such as "linen" and immediately see which of the numerous companies on the CD-ROM carry such products. Instead of wasting time price shopping from store to store, consumers will sit at a desk in front of their personal computer, type in the particular product they want, and limit the search to the lowest five prices. Within seconds they might find the same product offered at a store across the street for, say, $180, and also find it on sale by a reputable business in a different state or even country for only $75. Database consumers will cut their costs by searching out the best prices on items ranging from underwear to kitchenware.[11]

Marketspaces that wish to avoid becoming casualties of key cost searches must explore innovative ways to add tangible value to consumers by integrating desirable information into their marketspaces. The World Wide Web, for example, hosts a portfolio accounting and performance measurement firm, Security APL (SECAPL), that illustrates an intelligent use of interactive media. SECAPL offers visitors to its site free stock quotes. The quotes attract users who wish to receive minute-by-minute updated information updates (prices are delayed). After a symbol is entered, SECAPL then offers a hypertext link, when available, to the EDGAR Dissemination project, a site for Securities and Exchange Commission's filings. EDGAR provides a whole array of information required by the SEC pertaining to publicly traded companies.

Another powerful example of intelligent bundling of information is found in Time-Warner's marketspace, Pathfinder, on the Web. Time-Warner has made an agreement with the Reference Press, publisher of *Hoover's Guide to Corporate America.* A reader of *Money* magazine online could read, for example, an article about General Motors, and within the article click on the words "General Motors" to receive a detailed profile with information offered by Reference Press. Both of these examples illustrate a way to differentiate a marketspace by offering consumers additional value. Note that each of these examples provide utility by offering a link to a third-party information source.

Businesses will change prices on products with much greater frequency, in a manner similar to the ever-changing prices we see in the airline industry. Markets will be forced to become more efficient as businesses respond to educated consumers. Distribution systems, in the process, will continue to evolve as delivery times increasingly become a source of competitive advantage. Consumers will expect not only a price in the range of the best key cost price, but also speedy and reliable delivery of their item. Outstanding service guarantees will become commonplace for many organizations hoping to conduct business online. We might even see entirely new forms of distribution arise because of database consuming.

Individualism

As interactive online networks begin to proliferate, market *research* will give birth to market *usership*.[12] Market usership makes it possible for online marketers to pinpoint who is using their marketspaces and what features those customers are using. Market usership builds on the previous **I**'s of Interconnection, Interface, Interactivity and Involvement by helping to individualize the customer's experience. What does market usership mean for the advertiser, the market researcher, and the marketer?

Advertisers should be able to create more effective campaigns because for the first time in history marketers can receive real-time feedback about viewers' choices and reactions. Just as an ATM records every transaction you make while using a system, online services will be able to record and create reports based on your interaction and feedback. It will soon be possible for businesses in the marketspace to statistically record exact usership of their various offerings.

Because advertising has been based on one-way communication, there is no opportunity to exchange ideas between advertiser and consumer, no feedback from consumer to marketer. The old role of market research—to supply feedback from the marketplace to the marketer—has constituted a method of converting advertising from a one-way to a two-way communication process.

Never before have marketers been able to precisely measure the impact of media in advertising. Instead, estimations and polls such as the famed Nielsen ratings have been used to determine the effectiveness of marketing campaigns. Armed with new, exact knowledge and precise measurement tools, advertisers can determine with unprecedented accuracy market reach and frequency, customers preferences and dislikes. Not only will marketing organizations be able to communicate in real-time through their advertising, but, of equal importance, they will be able to know by whom, when and for how long their product or service was being viewed.

The potential for interactive marketers to better serve and individualize customers' needs thanks to market usership will help to maintain customer focus by giving marketers the ability to:

- Mass customize products and services

- Craft more effective advertising

- Better measure the effectiveness of advertising media

- Improve the measurement of the effectiveness of the advertising message

- Make improved decisions in such areas as product development, channels of distribution, media selection, and resource allocation.

Market usership could play as important a role in mass customization as that of the assembly line in the era of mass production. Market usership should enable savvy marketers to individualize their products and services, adding greater value and utility to products and services being offered. B. Joseph Pine II, a pioneer of the mass customization movement, describes in his book the range of companies that can transform information through mass customization:

> Customized services that can be performed on standard information include personalizing, categorizing, generalizing, analyzing, integrating, repackaging, facilitating, monitoring, filtering, locating, and matching, not to mention making the information convenient and readily accessible whenever and wherever a customer wants.[13]

Market usership will force marketers to be more accountable to their clients and provide better customer focus and targeted messages. Marketing and market research will become far more of a science, drawing upon the ability to precisely quantify aspects of a marketing program. When a marketer can sit at a desk and view in real-time the success or failure of a campaign, a new hybrid of marketing, advertising and accounting will be created. Just as the accounting profession has introduced activity-based cost accounting, thanks to market usership we may see the beginning of a new measurement form to be known as activity-based advertising. A campaign's success could hinge upon how much measured activity or interaction consumers have with the ads.

Imagine as a marketer having the ability to know exactly how many people were viewing your ads, or to know immediately what products or services were capturing the interest of your target markets. What would these options mean to your business?

Integrity

The final "I" that is critical to developing a succesful marketspace is maintaining its *integrity*. This includes issues relating to privacy, security and confidentiality. No matter how adept a marketer is at crafting the other Is of the mix, if a marketspace does not provide the customer with peace of mind that their privacy, security and confidentiality are inviolate, all efforts at creating a compelling marketspace are in vain. Many humanists and business ethicists are justifiably concerned about privacy issues in the digital age. The birth of market usership suggests that unprecedented amounts of personal information can be stored and compiled by the proprietors of marketspaces.

Because of the nature of electronic marketspaces and market usership, every "click" that an individual makes online can be recorded.

Detailed and precise personal histories might potentially be created about online users in various marketspaces. The thought of an unscrupulous or unethical marketer gaining such personal information should send chills down consumers' backs. Adding to potential problems will be the lack of regulations currently in place to monitor electronic commerce. What might be considered standard practice in one country might be grounds for suits in another. Some countries, for example, forbid pornography of any type being purchased, but on the Internet there are several areas where such material is sold indiscriminately.

Another area where marketers must be vigilant is in insuring that intrusive e-mail messages are not generated from a marketspace. A key differentiator between traditional marketing and interactive marketing, as suggested earlier, is the consumer's ability to choose and control his or her experiences. When marketers begin to flood electronic mail boxes with unsolicited offers and promotions, consumers are stripped of the empowering aspects of interactive marketing. Marketers who dare to take this risk will find newly empowered consumers who will not think twice about publicly "flaming" the offending company or expressing their displeasure at such blatant and unwelcomed solicitations.

Any electronic dialogue online can be stored indefinitely. What if a customer is having a sensitive conversation about an important personal issue and, to his surprise and horror, a business chronicles the entire conversation online by simply saving the text as a file? Customers also need to be concerned about the level of security afforded their personal information.

There are some individuals who would use interactivity to prey upon unsuspecting people. Insidious electronic practices range from financial frauds to horrific tales of pedophiles frequenting cyberspace to seduce innocents. Those sponsoring marketspaces must consider the full consequences and responsibilities of creating an online meeting place. America Online, for example, offers a parental chat control that limits children's access to areas that might be inappropriate. Careful attention must be paid by marketers to insure that malcontents and potential criminals do not use their areas as a vehicle for illicit activities. Tight editorial controls, coupled with persistent and consistent monitoring of bulletin boards and chat rooms, can help detect and prevent potential problems. Marketers wishing to maintain customer focus should give careful thought to guaranteeing the security of users' information.

While some people may be scared, even outraged that a digital environment allows for easy and infinite duplication of communication, other ethical and socially responsible marketers as well as concerned consumers might have reason to be ecstatic over this capability. It will be much easier to determine when deceptive or misleading sales practices are being used: at the end of any sales presentation in which claims are made about a product or service, the consumer can simply press the save function, thereby documenting who said what and when. Conversely, the marketer can also document consumer misrepresentation of important information such as employment history on a mortgage or job application. Needless to say, there will have to be a mechanism that prevents tampering with saved files.

A basic rule of thumb among business ethicists is that if your actions were reprinted on the front page of a newspaper you should still feel comfortable with what you did. Now the ethicists' words can be taken to heart by all marketing organizations who sell online. The ability to use the "save" function at the end of a sales presentation will guard against those wishing to sell snake oil packaged as perfume.

Conclusion

The Seven **I**'s presented here attempt to provide guidance to marketers in the emerging age of interactive marketing. The tectonic shifts underway in the world of marketing will be sure to change the way we buy, what we buy and eventually the very foundations of commerce. If, as Joseph Schumpeter suggests, "The defining characteristic (of the entrepreneur and his function) is simply the doing of new things, and doing things that are already done, in a new way (innovation),"[14] then interactive marketers will help to define business in the twenty-first century. As businesses begin to establish themselves in the electronic marketspace, a critical and fundamental marketing lesson must not be overlooked—meeting and exceeding human beings' needs and wants. Some executives may focus upon one of the **I**'s more than others, but to overlook any of them completely is risky. In the final analysis, the marketspace will continually change and reinvent itself as adventurous souls attempt to make their interactive impact.

References

1. A term recently coined by Jeffrey Rayport and John Sviokla of Harvard Business School in their article: "Managing In the Marketspace" *Harvard Business Review,* November–December 1994, p. 141.

2. A term coined by science fiction writer William Gibson to describe a virtual spatial representation of digital information and information structures.

3. Philip Kotler, *Marketing Management,* 6th ed. (Prentice Hall, Englewood, NJ) 1988, p. 194

4. Michael Spalter, "Desperately Seeking Artist," *MediaWeek,* July 18, 1994, p. 12.

5. Trip Hawkins, "State of The Media," *CYBERARTS,* edited by Linda Jacobson (Miller Freeman: San Francisco) 1992, p. 13.

6. E. Jerome McCarthy, *Basic Marketing: A Managerial Approach* (Homewood, Ill.: Richard D. Irwin, 1981).

7. Michael Spalter, "Here Come The CyberYuppies," *The Futurist,* May/June 1995, p. 20.

8. Robert J. Lavidge and Gary A. Steiner, "A Model for Predictive Measurements of Advertising Effectiveness," *Journal of Marketing,* October 1961, p. 61.

9. Michael Spalter, "Keyed Up: As Technology Changes the Face of Retailing, Advertising Figures to Play an Important Role," *AdWeek,* October 10, 1994, p. 30.

10. Ibid.

11. Ibid.

12. Michael Spalter, "Interactive Age Will Transform Market Research Into 'Usership,'" *Advertising Age,* May 5, 1994, p. 26.

13. B. Joseph Pine II, *Mass Customization: The New Frontier in Business Competition* (Cambridge, MA: Harvard Business School Press, 1993).

14. Joseph A. Schumpeter, "The Creative Response in Economic History," *Journal of Economic History,* Vol. VII (May, 1947), p. 151.

CHAPTER

3

Customer-Focused Strategies and Tactics

Interactive Marketing Weighs in for Customers

Richard Cross
Janet Smith

Richard Cross is president of Cross World Network, a strategic database marketing company co-founded with Stan Rapp. Cross World Network's clients include *Fortune* 100 companies from consumer, business-to-business, nonprofit, and governmental fields.

Janet Smith is a veteran marketing communications consultant and an associate of Cross World Network. A former marketing manager with Digital Equipment Corporation, she is broadly versed in marketing technologies.

Cross and Smith are co-authors of numerous articles and of *Customer Bonding: Pathway to Lasting Customer Loyalty* (NTC Business Books, 1995).

The year is 1996. Jack P., 33, is an architect who lives on the outskirts of Seattle with his working wife and two children. Their lives are chock-o'-block full of technology-facilitated interactions with marketers. These interactions often add new value to old relationships, giving Jack and his family more choices and more control than ever over their lives.

- Jack starts his day with a breakfast cereal the local supermarket has learned to promote to his family from prior purchase history and quickly scans the news summaries faxed to him during the night by his personalized news service.

- Jack's wife, a telecommuter, settles in to a day at her home office. After checking her e-mail and voice mail boxes, she tackles her day's work of evaluating new software programs. She saves time whenever she can by using fax-on-demand or online bulletin board systems provided by software vendors to get instant product literature and technical support.

- En route to work, Jack drops their three-year-old off at a day care center discovered through their county's online parenting resource, and uses his car phone to reserve a family pass for the visiting circus from a local radio station's automated entertainment hotline. Stopping at his favorite coffee chain, Jack runs his loyal customer card through a card reader and, with the help of the chain's database, is instantly served his latté exactly the way he likes it, in the members-only express lane.

- At work, Jack spends much of the day in online conferencing and messaging, exchanging drawings and specifications for a new theater under negotiation with civic contracting authorities in Miami.

- He stops on his way home at the dry cleaners, where he pays for his items with a debit card linked to his bank's buyers' club, which earns him rewards for his purchases.

- At home, he spends time helping his seven-year-old read "My Daily," the new national kids' newspaper that Jack helped to develop by participating in the publisher's Parent Circle. After supper, the family enjoys a Disney movie rented from Blockbuster delivered that afternoon with the groceries (ordered via the community interactive TV channel). Blockbuster thoughtfully checks Jack's profile and throws in his favorite type of low-fat popcorn.

- After the kids go to sleep, Jack and his wife finish the day paying some bills through their online banking service. Before turning in, Jack uses his local newspaper's online bulletin board to check the weather in Miami, where he is due by late afternoon the next day.

Jack P. is getting to be an average consumer[1] these days. His life is busy and full, and he is increasingly involved with marketers who save him time and effort by offering him what they already know he is most likely to want. Jack and his family get what they want from marketers who care enough to record and fulfill their preferences, anticipate their needs, and reward their loyalty. They are actively engaged in the consuming side of the interactive marketing equation. Interactive technologies have fundamentally altered their relationships with the companies they do business with.

In this chapter, we show how interactive marketing technologies are used to transform and redefine relationships with the Jacks of your customer world. We look at five specific examples—each using a different technology to add value to the buyer-seller equation. In some cases, the added value is inherent in the technology itself. In others, the creative application of the technology provides added value. But in all cases, the marketers have figured out a way to fit the technology into a marketing strategy that focuses on customer benefits. The facilitating technologies in our discussion are magnetic card readers, interactive voice response systems, electronic bulletin boards, fax-on-demand, and the Internet's growing information access capabilities.

Our perspective is customer-oriented. It stems from our view that any marketing technique, technology or process will fail unless the marketer steps into the shoes of the customer and understands the customer bonding process. By understanding how each customer interaction creates and strengthens customer bonds, marketers can develop a *customer- and information-based* framework for defining and executing interactive marketing strategies.[2] Such an orientation, we believe, is crucial to any attempt to create lasting success in interactive marketing. Because, for all the activity and interest engendered by new, technology-aided communications channels—online systems, telemedia, kiosks, CD-ROMs, and the like—the success of interactive marketing techniques and processes will depend entirely on their success in building lasting customer relationships.

Direct Marketing at Warp Speed—With a Twist

Interactive marketing balances the benefits scales in the marketer-customer relationship (see Exhibit 3.1). For example, an online purchase transaction can look deceptively like the traditional direct marketing process speeded up thousands of times. All the fundamentals of direct marketing are involved, but the interactive technology adds new benefits:

1. **Speed, access, and information.** Direct marketing and interactive marketing both use two-way communications channels for dialogue and information capture. Customer interaction provides marketers with the customer information needed to do market segmentation and targeting. Interactive marketing speeds the information capture and expands the marketer's bounce-back options. The consumer also benefits from the increased speed of the interaction and often gains access to broader information sources as well. In fact, online shopping permits consumers to seek information directly from a seller *and* from tens of thousands of the seller's customers who are accessible through discussion forums and e-mail.

2. **Measurable value over time.** Marketers who use databases to track performance over time are used to thinking about "customer lifetime value" (CLV). But interactive marketing gives *consumers* unprecedented opportunity to track the value of their transactions as well. In the new technology-assisted equation, buyers know exactly how much they are spending with a particular business and how much reward and recognition they are due. The buyer can measure new opportunities brought on by interactive marketing in terms of "Lifetime Savings and Rewards Opportunity" (LSRO). If you're accumulating points or miles for your purchases, for example, you can easily quantify which airline gets most of your business. In fact, since most airlines have reward programs, you can readily quantify the value of your loyalty. You also know whose mileage rewards are most valuable to you.

In the new interactive marketing equation, both parties value and measure loyalty: the marketer in terms of each customer's lifetime purchases and the customer in terms of the relative long-term value of the various buying sources at his or her disposal.

3. **Precision demand and relevance.** The traditional direct marketer's ability to deliver the right product to the right customer at

EXHIBIT 3.1 The Changing Market Balance

A. *The Traditional Marketing Balance*

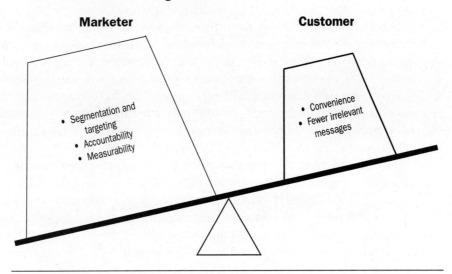

B. *The New Interactive Marketing Balance*

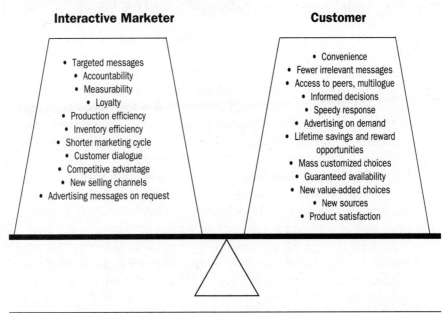

Interactive Marketing balances the benefits scale in the marketer-customer relationship.

the right time is a much sought-after ideal. The potential efficiency of the direct marketing system is a major factor in the decision by more and more marketers to shift resources to database-driven marketing programs. But, while marketers drive that trend, customers derive as much benefit from it—if not more. Personalization, individual treatment, mass customization, and freedom from extraneous advertising messages will soon be expected by every customer. What today constitutes the highest levels of customer satisfaction will be substandard tomorrow, when customers will expect suppliers to fully anticipate their needs and do their shopping for them. In the interactive age, the ability of a marketer to deliver only relevant information will become a key selection criteria in the customer's shopping process.

Let's look now at some examples of actual programs that demonstrate how the buyer-seller relationship changes. Each of the stories that follow uses a different facilitating technology to create new benefits for buyers and sellers. As you read these examples, pay attention to these benefits. At the end of the chapter, we will return to look at the key success factors for creating such results yourself.

Creating Relevancy with Telemedia at U S West

Telecommunications provider U S West stresses *relevance* as a key benefit consumers gain from its interactive marketing programs. In fact, the impact goes far beyond just relevance. We studied one of several programs underway and were struck by how a relatively simple concept, aided by an equally basic interactive technology, allows the company to dramatically alter its relationships with two entirely different sets of customers—business and consumers. U S West achieved this by creating a means for those customer groups to interact with each other and for each to *measure* the value of their relationship in hard dollars.

The program, called *Your Value Card*, is a turnkey relationship marketing service that U S West launched in Omaha, Denver, and Phoenix. The program matches area merchants with consumers, building traffic for the former and delivering savings opportunities for the latter. At no charge, U S West provides each interested consumer household with two plastic cards, magnetically encoded with a unique household identification number. They also provide a thick, indexed guide to participating merchants, each of whom lists specific savings offers for Your Value Card users.

Consumers present their cards to these merchants at the time of purchase along with their cash, check, or credit-card payment to receive the promised benefit. The merchant swipes the card through a magnetic stripe card reader that records the date, dollar amount, and location of the transaction. U S West records the transaction in its cardholder database, which also contains a wealth of demographic and lifestyle data appended from third-party sources. As transaction history builds, U S West analyzes it to determine the customer profiles for each merchant, makes recommendations for specific programs each merchant could undertake to acquire or retain customers, and even executes the communications for those programs.

What's happening here is a total change in the relationship U S West has with its customers. The consumer is getting savings, broader access to information about available shopping sources and, over time, increasingly relevant information from merchants in categories of interest. The merchant builds traffic while obtaining a means for profiling and segmenting its customer base for more targeted marketing in the future. And U S West is building a significant base of information on different segments of its own customer base while acting as a paid mediator between buyer and seller. Wow!

David Downes, U S West's Vice President and General Manager of the Marketing Information Products Groups, says that:

> This kind of service enables businesses that don't have their own database marketing resources to do a better job of delivering relevant communications to consumers. It helps them reduce the marketing cycle time, the time it takes to get to market with a promotion, analyze the results, and get back in the market with a more targeted and efficient approach.
>
> The real opportunity with interactive technologies is to provide both businesses and consumers with opportunities to be more relevant: Consumers are saying, "We want to hear from the businesses we already do business with, and from companies that offer similar services." To respond to this, marketers have to be able to deliver what consumers want, when and how they want it.

How does the program change the consumer's experience? We asked a couple of Your Value Card users in Denver this question. One family of four took to the card instantly, using it for everything from veterinary services and new tire purchases to dining entertainment. "It isn't a credit card. It's a *savings* card," explains Mrs. Eunice Bergen of the

Denver suburb of Thornton. "In the first full week we had the card, we saved $80." The Bergens also feel that the card changes the family's relationship with participating merchants. "Yes, you do start to change the relationship," Mrs. Bergen says. "We took our dog to the vet and discovered that our vet honors the card even though he already knows us. That means a lot. We've also discovered merchants through the program that we wouldn't have known about otherwise. We don't mind these merchants using the program to collect information about us if it means better information and savings on the items we care about."

Bruce Jensen, an assistant school principal in Denver, says that he hasn't been using the program long enough to see targeted offers based upon his purchases. But, he noted, the Your Value Card is now the first place the family looks when shopping for a new service. And he notices that he is frequenting certain merchants more often now that they participate in the program.

Aside from the database and related analysis tools that U S West provides, the key facilitating technology for Your Value Card is the card reader, which is installed in every participating merchant location and is used to capture the transaction data that creates a city-wide consumer

EXHIBIT 3.2 U S West Your Value Card

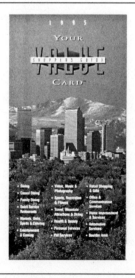 

U S West is building a data-rich customer information base while acting as a paid mediator between segments of that base.

database. In the program's first three months of operation in Denver, 530 participating vendors had installed the readers in 1200 sites.[3] The card readers are pre-programmed by U S West to recognize each merchant's current Your Value Card transaction offer, and to capture the appropriate data. The units also have the capacity to prompt the merchant's staff by asking questions about the transaction; this capability may ultimately be used in expanding the relationship marketing effort.

In Omaha, Nebraska, where Your Value Card was first launched, about *half* of all consumer households now carry and use the card. In Denver, where U S West launched the program in February of 1995, about three-quarters of households had received a card by May.

While U S West is the first of the so-called "Baby Bells" to initiate this type of program, other media companies in the U S are experimenting with them as well. From community-based efforts like that of the *Greensboro Daily News* in Greensboro, North Carolina to Time Inc.'s Pathfinder shopping mall[4], examples of experimentation with new ways to serve and relate to customers are coming along as fast as new technologies permit. The best efforts will be those that, like U S West, affect the equation between seller and buyer by continually improving the consumer's access to relevant information and savings.

Consumers Have a Voice at KMPS Country[5]

Radio has been called the most personal of the mass media. It reaches into the most private activities you do while at home, at work, at play, and on the road. But it is a one-way, non-interactive, broadcast medium. To reap the advantages of interactivity, many radio stations are installing interactive voice response (IVR) systems, sometimes accompanied by fax-request lines and online bulletin boards. Callers who dial into these systems are offered a host of information and interactive options, such as signing up for frequent listener membership benefits, offering feedback or requests to the station or its on-air personalities, getting information about community events, weather, or financial markets, or even shopping electronically with the station's advertisers. In some cases, members are granted access to private portions of the IVR system after keying in their membership number on their touch-tone telephone keypad. Stations typically issue machine-readable membership cards, which are used to record member transactions or other member-supplied information at participating merchant locations or station-sponsored events.

These technology-based relationship enhancements give listeners a way to get more of their individual needs filled from a medium that is not typically customizable. At the same time, they receive access to information and to measurable rewards for their loyalty. The new interactive technologies combine to turn passive listeners into active customers.

A ground-breaking station using *all* of these capabilities is country station KMPS in Seattle, Washington. In mid-1995, the station had 185,000 members in 140,000 households for its *Loyal Listener Club.* Through the benefits of the club—an IVR-based member information line, a monthly glossy magazine, special access to events, discounts on advertiser services, and an Internet site—KMPS enhances the benefits listeners enjoy while expanding revenue-producing advertiser options as well. In fact, the station is the first we are aware of that has been able to completely abandon the Arbitron ratings system.[6]

Fred Schumacher, vice president for KMPS and its sister station, KZOK, began the KMPS *Loyal Listener Club* as a database-building effort in 1991, initially using only an interactive voice response system to facilitate listener communication. He describes the transformative power of technology tools in enacting a customer-focused marketing strategy:

> The IVR system allows us to relate to our customers as individuals and to satisfy at least some of their individual needs. And, by moving some information programming off the air and onto the IVR system, our air time is less cluttered and we can play more music.

Listeners have clearly welcomed the opportunity to access station information and to guide "product" direction by voicing their preferences about on-air personalities, programming options, and ancillary services. They log over 40,000 calls per month (see samples from a single day's input in "KMPS Listeners Talk," Exhibit 3.3). The station uses this listener interaction to guide programming. Each call is transcribed and distributed daily to station management. Listener electronic mail messages from *KMPS Online* are likewise distributed immediately. And, when appropriate, integrated marketing manager Dean Sakai responds directly to individual callers or writers.

According to Sakai, the interactivity of the IVR and online communications channels has strengthened the station's brand identity and its bonds with listeners and advertisers. He believes club members have a high degree of trust in the station, too, noting that they have been very willing to bring friends into the club.[7]

Customer information obtained via these listener interaction channels is added to a detailed base of demographic, psychographic, and purchase intention information provided by listeners at sign-up and at kiosks located at station events. This base of data enables the station to direct programming more effectively at different audience segments and, likewise, to build customized advertiser programs for different segments.

Thanks to the falling cost of database and IVR technologies and the increasing accessibility of online communications channels, even the smallest stations have options for conducting more real-time interactive marketing. According to Rob Sisco, vice president of marketing services at IVR vendor Fairwest Direct, radio stations are using IVR for survey gathering, audience profiling, music research, and for rewarding and recognizing frequent listeners. Stations wishing to develop at-work listening audiences have integrated the systems with enhanced fax technology, he notes. For example, they may broadcast fax messages to consenting workplace club members to announce programs (such as daily workplace listening contests). Some stations also offer fax-on-demand services, so listeners can request information they hear about on-air or on the IVR system.

EXHIBIT 3.3 KMPS Listeners Talk by IVR and E-Mail

KMPS in Seattle has built a database of 185,000 Loyal Listener Club members, and now offers advertisers an integrated system of marketing options including broadcast radio, interactive voice response, IVR, events, a monthly magazine, direct mail, and online. The interactivity has changed the way listeners relate and enabled the station to abandon the Arbitron ratings system.

"We have so much contact with our listeners through direct mail, the phone line, the Internet, and our community events," explains Dean Sakai, integrated marketing manager. "We've created stronger bonds with our listeners than most stations, and grabbed a share of

EXHIBIT 3.3 (Continued)

the most loyal listeners in the market. And we have the capacity to track what's happening with our loyal listeners, to know exactly what they're responding to and how." He shared a sampling of one day's listener input:

- "You are awesome. The best country music station in Seattle. I started to listen to country music six months ago. You guys make it easy to keep listening. You play all my favorite songs, the DJs are really great to chat with, and the Loyal Listener Club is the greatest! I got my card and I am so excited; I am official! I even have a KMPS sticker on my car, so keep doing what you are doing; love you guys!!"

- "I love your station. And I like your Loyal Listener Line. I can call anytime and find out things that I want to know for the weekend and the week."

- "This is my loyalty to KMPS. . . . When the other radio station called me and asked what my favorite radio station was, I lost $1,000 because I said, 'KMPS!' You guys are awesome, keep it up."

- "I went to the concert last night and thanks for providing such good entertainment. Every D.J. I met was really nice. I had a problem with my Loyal Listener Card and they took every effort to get the card working, and then provided me with another way to enter in the contest for the trip to California."

- "I am one of your loyal listeners. I have a problem with your new format during the day. It doesn't let me make dedications. In fact, the format is very inflexible. You can't do anything for customers or anything that involves your listeners much at all during the day. I would really like to see that change."

- "I think you guys like, rock, you know? I just signed up for the club and I think it's pretty cool 'cause you have lots of discounts and stuff. I've like already used it four times and I just got it like two days ago. So, you guys are doing really good . . . Rock on."

Radio consultant Peggy Miles of D.C.-based Miles Marketing notes that interactive technology is changing relationship structures for stations that are using them to create loyalty programs. "You develop a relationship with your listeners and then extend that relationship to include your advertising customers. Your brand then becomes something like a good housekeeping seal of approval."

Creating a Private Online Community: ETEC Delivers Instant Access

New York-based Entertainment Technology Communications Corporation (ETEC), the primary trade publisher, trade show organizer, and de facto trade association for the entertainment event supply industry,[8] is one of a small, but growing number of organizations that are creating private online services dedicated to the needs of a specialized professional community. We predict that there will be an explosion of such communities, each open only to subscribers, but accessible from the public byways of the Internet.

The service, called *Entertainment Technology Online Direct (ETEC Direct)*, is a subscription service that provides access to information and interaction opportunities not otherwise available in the industry. It also serves as a wide area network for companies with multiple locations, enabling employees or associates in different offices to link up and communicate instantly, around the clock, about important projects. Operations director Scott Iverson explained that the network does the same for far-flung networks of freelancers and individual consultants, architects, design, sound, and visual professionals. In its first months of existence, it rapidly became the industry's hottest way to get news and to work out business negotiations, project management, creative development, and production issues. In discussing the benefits to users, Iverson says:

> A local service like ETEC puts you in a community of professionals with similar needs and wants. . . . You have a captured audience. The public highway of the Internet is like a no-man's land. You have to find your niche, which can take a long time. And there's no sense of community except in the places you find that you like to go.

ETEC users are greeted with a graphical menu of options relating specifically to the entertainment industry (see Exhibit 3.4). The system is optimized for the transmission of sophisticated graphics, photographs, moving video images, music, and various interactive tools. Menu options offer everything from job-matching services to *Live Design,* an interactive design tool that lets entertainment professionals collaborate on design or architectural drawings online. Users can also access Entertainment's magazines, *Lighting Design* or *Theater Crafts International,* locate and rent equipment, hire talent, exchange ideas by electronic mail, or participate in one of many discussion forums. About 100 companies signed up as charter advertisers when the system was launched in 1995, and subscribers are signing up at the rate of about 1,000 per month. An Internet gateway also permits ETEC subscribers to send messages and information to Internet users, or to enter the service from an Internet location. And ETEC creates home pages on its World Wide Web (WWW) server for companies wanting to have a commercial presence on the Internet.

The private online service model offers several key advantages over traditional information delivery mechanisms or the public and commercial online services:

1. Users get increased access at greater speeds to more relevant information and more flexibility in how they do business. As a print publisher, ETEC could never provide such instant access to up-to-the-minute information. And Internet marketing options, while improving, are still limited by transmission speed, security problems and the difficulties many users have with access and navigation.

2. The sponsoring company becomes an intermediary among its various customer groups, facilitating their interactions. In return, it increases its value to them and creates new revenue sources.

3. A private network gives all parties maximum flexibility and control over the way information is presented and used.

Such services are naturals for any environment in which the audience shares definable common lifestyle or workstyle interests, including business-to-business, association, civic, and non-profit communities. For example, the city of Alexandria is creating *Electronic Alexandria,* which, when fully operational, will provide area residents and merchants with online access to information on city government, local sports, recreation, and cultural activities, and to dining and tourism

EXHIBIT 3.4 ETEC Main Menu Screen

Entertainment Technology Online (ETEC) has launched a cybermarket for the entertainment industry.

features. It will also permit citizens and businesses to communicate directly via e-mail and discussion forums, and to post useful information or sponsored advertising on the community network. In the process, the relationship between the City and its many constituencies will shift dramatically as *Electronic Alexandria* becomes a source through which constituents can find resources, information, customers, and services.

When Customers Won't Wait: Instant Information Delivery with Fax-on-Demand

The rise of interactive marketing is creating a new era of customer service. Increasingly, consumers expect and demand on-a-dime delivery of information and service. If you make them wait, you may lose them to a competitor who comes through faster. They also appreciate having choices about how they access information. Surveys have shown that many people are still more comfortable getting information by phone or fax than via computer. Fax penetration is still far greater than that of online services. This makes fax-on-demand (FOD) an interactive telemedia workhorse that gives marketers a way of instantly accommodating the precision demands of today's customers.

Long before we became active online users in our own office, for example, we were avid users of fax-on-demand options offered by office products catalogers, publishers, and others. The ability to get detailed product information from a supplier or to retrieve an article from a trade publication with the push of a button has saved us time, money, and frustration on many occasions. The combined benefits of increased service (information) and decreased costs (time) make us appreciate those service providers who give us the option of retrieving information this way. We even conducted some of our research for this book using a daily news digest service, *iNews,* that is delivered to us by fax. When we find a news item of interest to us, we pick up the telephone, enter a request code, and the entire article is faxed to us in a matter of minutes. It's a convenient, easy, and inexpensive way to access a broad set of information resources.

As marketers ourselves, we also use fax-on-demand to distribute information about our articles and books to interested readers. For this, we use a service called MarketFax, based in Irvington, New York, which has even developed the capability to match requesters' fax numbers with names and addresses so that we can follow up on an inquiry.[9] MarketFax works with publishers like *The Wall Street Journal, Golf* magazine, and *Success,* developing custom applications such as interactive reader inquiry services and reader surveys that save time and money for readers and advertisers. MarketFax president Ed Liss also works with associations to develop value-added services for its members. One of these, the National Association of Realtors (NAR), uses fax-on-demand to provide advance information for its annual conferences. It also uses an electronic reader response program in its monthly magazine that pulls about 2,000 responses per issue. Liss explains:

> Every week, MarketFax automatically follows up all incoming information requests with a targeted fax broadcast. Using this combination of fax-on-demand and follow-up fax broadcasting, advertisers are experiencing sales closings in the 50 percent range.

This is increasing advertising revenue for NAR, Liss continued, and is attracting more advertisers to the publication: "Advertisers are placing more of their budget dollars in the magazines," he says, "because it pulls for them and the results can be easily measured."

Today, travel-service providers, telecommunications equipment sellers, publishers, financial services, radio stations, pharmaceutical manufacturers, realtors, and the Federal government are among the many organizations that use fax-on-demand. For some, it is a profit center, used to sell information. Others use it to add value to their relationships with customers. Business-to-business marketers are discovering its appeal as a selling tool for salespeople, dealers, and customers. One telecommunications firm we spoke with plans to put in a reporter's line to keep the media informed.

Fax-on-demand adds benefits to both sides of the marketer-consumer equation. These benefits are similar to those available in an online environment:

- Prospects and customers can enter and re-enter the sales cycle at will and get detailed information at the precise moment they want it.

- In some cases, customers can choose to complete the sales cycle while browsing through the system. Because callers are self-qualifying, the sales cycle is shortened and does not intrude on the customer or prospect.

- The technology permits maximum information relevance and accuracy.

- The marketer gets instant measurement capability to determine how well a marketing program is performing.

San Jose, California cataloger Hello Direct launched an FOD service for its customers in 1994. The privately held company, which markets telecommunications products such as telephone systems, headsets, cellular accessories, fax/modem switches, and even an FOD system, mails four catalogs per year to over 18 million consumer and business catalog buyers. Product developer Ron Becht says that the new system augments the 30 "customer care" representatives in the firm's telemarketing center, providing round-the-clock information access to prospects and customers around the world. Callers use it to get detailed sales and technical information about the company's products. He believes that consumers appreciate having the option of doing some of their buying research this way.

"We average about 1,500 fax-on-demand contacts per month," explains Becht. "The system opens up a variety of opportunities. It lets prospects and customers get more detailed information on products in our catalog. It frees up our service representatives to be on the phone with customers by off-loading from them the time-consuming job of sending technical information to callers. Our new system also lets individuals request a catalog by simply entering a voice-mail message with their name, address, and fax number. It's a seamless, back-end information delivery solution," he continued. "And a nice added benefit to our customer base."

Internet: Attracting Interest over the Ultimate Public Medium

In the rush to create a commercial presence on the Internet, the crazy-quilt network of gateways and connections, many companies are simply transposing traditional advertising and selling paradigms onto this new, most interactive of mediums. Instead of taking advantage of the incredible interactive potential of the portion of the net that supports hypertext links,[10] they spend the consumer's time and patience on image-building text and graphics telling consumers about their products or services, or they alienate whole groups of individuals by being overly commercial in an online chat forum.

The Internet is uniquely suited to developing higher levels of relationships, to establishing dynamic customer communities, and to allowing satisfied customers to become your champions by telling others in the Internet community about your service. Here, the power balance shifts most visibly to the consumer—commercial participants are newcomers in a world that still consists largely of computer-advantaged young men who are justifiably proud and protective of the vast Net community they populate. As access improves and more mainstream consumers come on line, we expect to see a rapid shakeout of the marketers who don't understand that the highest use of the Internet is as a "listening" medium.

One company that clearly understands this is Hanover, New Jersey-based PrePRESS Solutions, a $50 million company that manufactures and sells image-setting equipment, software, training, and services to designers and publishers around the world. The company's new Internet site, *PrePRESS Main Street*, is not your standard amalgamation of company product information. Rather, it feels like a small town community, one that offers you a lot of resources. Among the choices are:

- *Main Street Gazette,* on-screen newspaper updated daily with news stories from around the industry.

- Café Moiré,[11] where mannequin Cynthia invites you inside to participate in news groups and chat sessions.

- The Convention Center, where PrePress presents full reports, complete with digital still images, of products, speakers, and events from major trade shows around the world.

- Classified Advertising, where anybody can place free ads for services or equipment wanted to buy or sell.

- *PrePRESS DIRECT! SuperSTORE,* the Internet version of the company's well-known catalog, redesigned with links to pricing and purchase options.[12]

- A library, with downloadable reference material on a host of prepress issues and PrePRESS products.

- The Print Shop, where browsers can get tips and tools, including free downloadable software utilities to enhance prepress performance.

Company president Robert Trenkamp says that he has wanted to do something like this since the late 1980s. He makes no bones that he wants to sell product through this effort, but he has larger objectives as well. By creating a "gathering place" for the industry, the company hopes to expand awareness, interaction, and credibility. "Our objective is to participate in just about every transaction somebody in the prepress community engages in for the acquisition of goods and services," he explains. "To do that, we need a flow of the entire prepress community through our site."

Trenkamp has a penchant for breaking new, interactive ground in the industry. In 1991, he launched a catalog operation that has become a major part of the company's business and created broad awareness for the firm worldwide. Trenkamp told us that the Internet site is likewise having an immediate, positive impact on catalog sales, as Internet browsers find products of interest and contact the company's catalog operation. The impact is global, too. Translated pages of the catalog are available on the site in four languages to aid overseas viewers.

EXHIBIT 3.5 PrePRESS Main Street Screen

By creating an Internet "gathering place" for prepress production profession-als, PrePRESS Solutions hopes to expand industry awareness, interaction, and credibility.

"We are beginning to accumulate an understanding of what our customers' needs and wishes are," explains Trenkamp. "We're trying to segment our marketing approach down to an audience of one, so that we don't present people with things they don't want to hear." Ultimately, Trenkamp believes that consumers will expect their suppliers to remove the shopping burden from them. "I see a huge change coming in business-to-business marketing, picking up on what's happening in consumer marketing with mass customization," he says. "You're going to see personal shopper relationships, where customers will say, 'You know what I need and what's going on in the industry; keep me supplied with ideas.' We'd love to be the go-fetch person for everybody in our target audience."

The Internet, and other interactive technologies that can monitor and measure every interest of the customer, afford the means for companies to become the "go-fetch" resources for their customers. The ability to "listen," to capture hard data on customer interests and preferences, and to do so with up-to-the-hour timeliness, gives market-ers such opportunities. If database marketing is the wave of the future, then this kind of dialogue between consumers and marketers is the water itself. And the Internet, and subsequent generations of interac-tive network, offer the ideal medium for creating and sustaining true customer dialogues. Consumers will voice their preferences for market-ers who empower them with such access, flexibility, relevance, and time and cost savings.

Conclusion: Working at the Interactive Nexus

The interactive race is on. Companies that fail to get in shape quickly will soon be left in the dust. Marketers are gaining ground when they grasp the subtleties of the changing buyer-seller relationships and are willing to deliver greater power to their customers:

- U S West's *Your Value Card* builds a major information base for a supplier of local telephone services, while delivering savings and new information to customers.

- KMPS radio gains detailed information for its advertisers while its listeners benefit directly with access to events, savings, and an easy means for giving feedback on what they like and don't like.

- ETEC becomes the center for a whole new way of doing business in the entertainment industry, gaining new revenue sources for its creator while its customers get new flexibility and instant information access.

- Hello Direct improves its customer service productivity by giving consumers new information options in the sales cycle for technical products.

- *PrePRESS Solutions* creates an Internet gathering place for an industry and gets the opportunity to learn how to become the trusted information provider for each and every customer and prospect.

For every forward-thinking marketer, of course, there are many more who simply want to be where the action is and don't understand that their role must change. For some, fascination with the technology overpowers common sense and good business judgment. Others seem to have a superficial, product-focused mentality that leads to off-putting programs that quickly collapse from consumer disinterest or disdain.

Here are three simple rules that can help you keep sight of the relationship impact of your interactive technology initiatives:

1. Fit interactive marketing into a larger strategy that continuously creates new benefits for being your company's customer.

2. Strive for a balance between the company's marketing objectives and the consumer's shopping needs and objectives.

EXHIBIT 3.6 Interactive Marketing Technologies Weigh in for Customers

From Marketers' Strategies	To Consumers' Benefits
Lifetime Customer Value	Lifetime Savings and Reward Opportunity
Improved Product Quality	Mass Customization
Targeted Messages	Fewer Extraneous Messages
Loyalty	Rewards and Recognition
Production Efficiency	Lower Prices
Inventory Efficiency	Guaranteed Availability
Distribution Efficiency	Wider Availability
Zero Defects	Product Satisfaction
Information Dissemination	Informed Decisions
Electronic Customer Communities	Access to Peers, Multilogue
Customer Dialogue	Seller Responsiveness
Reduced Marketing Cycle	Speedy Response, Time Savings
Competitive Advantage	New Value-Added Choices
New Selling Channels	New Supply Channels
Advertising Messages on Request	Advertising Messages on Demand

3. Find ways to make each technology-based program provide multiple benefits to both parties.

Interactive marketing is about changing the ability of both marketers and consumers to affect the "relationship" in relationship marketing. Exhibit 3.6 demonstrates how emerging market strategies actually give consumers more power in the marketing equation. Consumers' abilities to choose the relationships they want grow greater as the shopping process is extended and adapted to more interactive channels. Marketers who understand this are using every tool available to give their customers every reason to be their relationship choice.

In short, consumers are no longer the direct marketer's archer's targets in the new interactive marketing paradigm. Instead, they are constantly on the move, like surfers who delight in finding and riding the information waves that interest or amuse them. Marketers who give up their bows and arrows and focus on creating worthwhile waves are the ones who will find them returning again and again.

References

1. We use the word "consumer" loosely; our discussion applies also to buyers of business goods and services.

2. These bonds and the marketing discipline that works with them are described by Richard Cross and Janet Smith in *Customer Bonding: Pathway to Lasting Customer Loyalty* (Lincolnwood, IL: NTC Business Books, 1995).

3. Card readers are valuable tools for building databases. Some offer direct interaction options; they can be programmed to pose specific questions at the time of transaction, for example, or to issue coupons based upon the transaction occurring.

4. Available on the Internet and the major commercial online services: America Online, CompuServe, and Prodigy.

5. Some of this material is based upon an article by Richard Cross, "Broadcast Radio Tunes In To Listeners," *Direct Marketing*, June 1995.

6. Arbitron is a media measurement system that estimates audience size and makeup, which effectively determines station advertising revenue potentials.

7. Sakai estimates that one member-get-member promotion alone grew the club membership by a full 20 percent.

8. This industry is made up of companies providing equipment and services to theaters, arts companies, concert organizers, movie producers, and other entertainment companies. Players include lighting and stage designers, costume makers, tour organizers, promoters, publicists, etc.

9. MarketFax recently added the follow-up capability, which it can provide within 24 hours.

10. Hypertext is a special markup language that allows a text element to become a pointer to another information location. Consumers shopping in a hypertext catalog, for example, might click on the word "alligator" to find out more about the use of alligators in the manufacture of clothing accessories. A growing subset of the computer sites that make up the Internet support this hypertext capability: that subset is commonly referred to as the World Wide Web, or simply as "the Web."

11. "Moiré" is a graphic arts term referring to a repeating pattern in a poorly reproduced color photograph.

12. Because security remains a concern on the Internet, users have multiple choices for ordering, including printing out an order form and faxing it, calling the company's 800 number, or dialing into a secure site.

CHAPTER

4

The Impact of Interactive Communication on Advertising and Marketing

And Now a Word from Our Consumer

Edward Forrest
Lance Kinney
Michael Chamberlain

Edward Forrest is Director of the Interactive Communications graduate program at Florida State University. His ongoing projects include multiplatform CD-ROM and CD-I disc production, and World Wide Web page-site development.

Lance Kinney has worked on both the agency and client sides, including research in affective response and attitude measurement.

Michael Chamberlain is Director, New Media Activities, of United News & Media, plc, London, England. He is also Chairman of OIT Limited, a subsidiary company specializing in the creation of electronic online sites.

What impact will interactive communication have on:

- The role and scope of activities of the advertising agency?
- The form, style and substance of the advertising message?
- Target market segmentation, definition, and strategy?
- Media planning?

Are you ready for:

- The communication concept?
- Interactive advertising-pods?
- Partipulation?
- Technographics?

This chapter will use as an organizing scheme Harold D. Lasswell's (1948) classic communication paradigm:

Who

Says what

To whom

In what channel

With what effect

As an organizing scheme, Lasswell's paradigm allows us to independently address each core component of a mediated communication system. Wherein: *Who* concerns the agent that conceives and controls any given communication. *Says What* refers to the message—its contents and aesthetics. *To Whom* refers to the audience for which the message was produced. *In* What Channel refers to the medium through which the message is transmitted. And, *With What Effect* concerns the nature and magnitude of impact that the message has on the audience's attitudes, beliefs and behavior.

Specifically, we will be contemplating the range of effects that can be expected as the commercial communication industry moves from a mass-mediated to a computer-mediated system.

The Advertising Agency/"Who"

Like so many other instititions born and bred in the industrial age of mass production, mass media and mass consumption, the advertising agency has, in the main, approached the new media with hesitation and skepticism. Advertising has always been an industry that was quick to exploit (if not create) new trends. But, unlike the trends of the past, the new communication technologies have not been readily embraced according to the initial reports by industry observers:

> . . . traditional agencies are woefully behind in mastering technology and getting their clients involved in interactive projects. An August, 1994, *Advertising Age* ranking of the top 29 agencies as to interactive technology use awarded high marks only to Ogilvy & Mather. . . . "The majority of large agencies are doing everything they can to frustrate the interactive movement," asserts Alan Brody, program director of Createch, a Scarsdale, N.Y. company that sponsors interactive advertising conferences.

Interactive advertising means reengineering the way suppliers, producers, and consumers interact. And, as every technology manager knows, reengineering frequently engenders resistance (Wilder, 1994).

It is suggested that the emerging interactive technologies will reengineer the way suppliers, producers, and consumers interact in at least three critical ways.

1. *The agency will evolve: From carnival barker to communication clearinghouse.* With respect to reengineering the the nature of the relationship between the agency and consumer, we will witness the essential character of the advertising agency evolve *from* that of a *barker* on the mass-media midway—of simple slogans and "unique selling points," *to* that of an online *mediator* of comparative and compelling information that will assist the consumer at every stage of the consumption cycle. To date, advertising's most basic charge has been to provide the consumer with a few bits of information in the most direct and entertaining manner possible. For the most part, all that was needed was a catchy headline and/or visual to grab attention, some body copy to describe the products comparative benefits and a logo and slogan to promote memorability. However, we are experiencing an ever increasing array of products and services from which to choose, and coupled with the increasing pace of modern life, we have less time for comparison

shopping than ever before. Moreover, it has always been the case that when it came to "high-ticket" items (such as appliances, automobiles, homes, etc.) and specialty products (such as audio and video components, consumer electronics, etc.) the gap between advertising and sufficient information was filled by the "salesman." It remains that on both fronts—for salesman as well as for commercials—there is room for improvement in the quantity and credibility of information provided consumers. Thus, "instead of cramming the world's airwaves with eye-catching images, clever jingles, and celebrity hucksters," advertising now has the ability to "evolve into a two-way medium in which consumers with PCs and a modem can choose the information they want to access." To wit:

> A PC-based diskette produced by automaker Ford is an example of what sets interactive advertising apart. Called the Ford simulator, the program lets potential buyers compare colors, engine sizes, options, and payment plans for Ford's entire consumer line of 25 cars and light trucks. Information not hucksterism, is the goal, says Larry Dale, a Ford marketing specialist in Dearborn, Mich. "The more information they have," he says about high-tech shoppers, "the better vehicle they will have in mind when they go to a dealership." (Wilder,1994)

2. *The agency will evolve: From working* for *the media and advertisers . . . to working* with *the consumer.* A second function that interactive technology will reengineer will be the nature of the relationship between the agency and the media. Historically, an "adman" was the middleman who bought wholesale chunks of space in magazines and newspapers and then resold parcels to individual advertisers. In turn, the adman received a 15 percent commission ("kick-back") from the medium for his efforts. The advertising agency evolved by adding on the copywriting and design functions to the media placement services of these original "space brokers." In recent years the traditional 15 percent commission has been squeezed by sponsors who want to pay agencies directly for their labor, and not indirectly for the amount of media space or time they consume. Many agencies now place advertising for commissions of 10–12 percent or less. Moreover, the media buying services that were once the sole province of a full-service agency are today provided by specialized media services serving many accounts. And, copywriting, along with print and broadcast production, have moved to so-called "boutiques." Other agencies have moved into specialty areas and niche

services such as promotion and direct marketing. A predictable conse-
quence of this trend of agency specialization is the emergence of the
"interactive advertising agency." As opposed to the advertiser of the
past, the interactive advertiser sees his task *less as a pitchman* for sponsors *than as a consultant* for consumers. To quote one leading interactive
pioneer:

> We see interactivity as enabling brands to create better relationships
> with their customers, said Gerald O'Connell, Modem Media's found-
> ing general partner. . . . Modem Media, Westport, Conn., specializes
> in designing, advertising and promotional campaigns on Interactive
> platforms, ranging from CD-ROM to the Internet. . . .
>
> One campaign Modem Media designed . . . involved a college football
> poll conducted on Prodigy Services Inc. The objective, O'Connell said
> was to "create an affinity between college football and Coors Light."
> Consumers were able to vote for their favorite teams using Prodigy's
> online service, or by phoning to an "800" toll-free number, and win
> such prizes as a trip to the Super Bowl game. The campaign generated
> 10,000 responses in a week. (*Interactive advertising pioneers*, 1994)

At its best, the interactive agency will serve as a facilitator of an ongoing, online conversation between the advertiser and consumer, providing the customer not only with exactly what information they
need—when they need it (on demand advertising), but also additional
venues though which to interact with the sponsor.

3. *The agency will evolve: From the marketing concept to the communication concept.* The fundamental principle on which the advertising and
marketing industries have operated throughout the past decades has
been the *marketing concept* (defined as profit through consumer satisfaction based on the ability of the product or service to deliver the
attributes promised by advertising). While the marketing concept will
continue to be important, the ad agency will increasingly need to pay
hom-age to (what we define as) **the communication concept:** *The process
wherein the ad agency enables, engages, facilitates, sustains and rewards interaction between consumers and advertisers throughout the entire consumption
cycle.*

Future advertising success will be found in giving the consumer the
easiest, most rewarding access to relevant information before, during
and after the purchase. Interactive technology enables the advertiser to

personalize his approach to every customer and exchange relevant information that will prove mutually beneficial. For example,

> . . . when the French edition of *Vogue* wanted to spice up print ads in a perfume supplement, it put a lip-sticked kiosk in the cosmetics area of a Paris department store. The interactive kiosk. . . . didn't dispense fragrance but offered personalized advice. . . . it asked shoppers about the personality of the woman who would use the perfume. . . . Kiosk users could pick up a phone receiver in the kiosk to hear the questions whispered by a female voice. At the end, the kiosk program printed recommendations for the aromas that best matched the woman's lifestyle. . . . (The customer response as described by the sales manager) "it was amazing . . . there was a line from 10am to late at night" (Clark, 1994).

In the future, the bottom line will not only be a matter of marke*t share* (measured by a company's percentage of sales relative to the total sales in a product category) but also *info-share,* measured by the number of clients active in a database that is developed and maintained via interactive technology.

Perhaps the compensation pattern of future advertising will have less to do with the amount of advertising placed or produced, than with the number of inquires any given interactive ad generates. Already this is the system in which direct marketers operate, as do "fulfillment houses" that channel information on consumers back to advertisers via "kickback" cards in magazines and telephone contacts. However, the leads that are passed back for follow-up are often weeks and sometimes months old. Interactive technology simutaneously offers the consumer advertising on demand and the advertiser the opportunity to follow-up any inquiry with additional "just-in-time" promotional materials and purchasing information.

The Commercial Message/"Says what"

The nature and contours of the advertising message itself will undergo drastic change. As we move *from* the mass- *to* - the multi-mediated world of interactive communication at least four predictions can be made regarding its impact on the character and contours of the commercial message itself.

1. The commercial message will become multi-dimensional and transactional. We will move from one-way, truncated 30 second spots, 1/2 page spreads and 7-word billboard blurbs to interactive advertising-pods of product information that can be peeled back like an onion with "tell-me-more" and "show-me-more" buttons, while the consumer provides the advertiser with key facts and data:

2. The commercial message will be move *from intrusive* commercial messages that intermittently interrupt the on-going media experience of the consumer *to invited conversation,* wherein the consumer actively seeks out and requests advertising and promotional materials—defined by Don Peppers and Martha Rogers as *invitational advertising.* The reader might note that this and other original insights into advertising's "one-to-one" future with individual customers were elaborated on by Don Peppers and Martha Rogers in the previous chapter:

> Successful advertisers will have to stop their frenetic shouting at customers, and will instead offer polite invitations designed to initiate or continue individual customer dialogues. Starting a dialogue, either with a current customer or with a potential new customer, will be the primary goal of any marketer hoping eventually to sell products or services. Advertisers will no longer find it beneficial to irritate viewers into remembering their brands. Not only is this a bad way to begin a dialogue, but it is very likely that in the interactive future a consumer who feels irritated with a certain ad or brand will be capable of forbidding that brand from appearing on his own set again. (Schrage, Peppers, Rogers and Shapiro, 1994)

3. The commercial message will be *less ephemeral* (zapped in a matter of nanoseconds; skipped with a flip of the page; driven past at 65 mph) and *more embedded* with information being part and parcel of the program with which the individual is interacting. Indeed, the evolution of corporate web sites (such as the one produced by Modem Media for Zima Clearmalt—described in chapter 17 of this book) is reminiscent of the early days of broadcasting, when programs were wholly produced and controlled by a single sponsor and its advertising agency.

4. Finally, in terms of style and substance, the "commercial" message will move from *glib* and superficial titillation with intangible rewards *to substantive* value-added "infotainment" with immediate and

tangible rewards. No longer will the simple play-on words, funny innuendo or double entendre—with a slice of cheese or beefcake thrown in—be the consumer's only reward for paying attention. The interactive ads of the future will necessarily offer consumers something real and something tangible for their time and attention:

> . . . in the age of interactivity, this formerly implicit bargain between advertiser and consumer is likely to become decidedly explicit. . . . We're talking about deal city, here. Imagine getting offers like these when you turn on your television:
>
> - Watch this two-minute video on the new Ford Taurus, and we'll pay for the pay-per-view movie of your choice.
> - Answer this brief survey from Kellogg and we'll pay for the next three episodes of "Murphy Brown."
> - Push the Tell-Me-More button on your remote at any time during this ten-minute infomercial, and you might win a Caribbean cruise. (Schrage, et. al., 1994)

The very nature of the advertising business has been to inform consumers about "new and/or improved" products in an entertaining way. The expanded frontiers and contours of the new media allow the advertiser to expand the commercial message with much *more "info"* and enables the consumer to *participate in the "entertainment"*:

> Interactive ads can evolve into compelling direct-response environments—informative, intimate, and immediate . . . . It's easy to imagine McDonald's producing an educational video game called, say, Burger Hunt, for its kiddie customers. Ronald McDonald gives the player a random quantity of 'McDollars' and the child has to maneuver, Mario-like, through mazes of Hamburglars and other McDonald-Land obstacles to buy and bring back just the right number of burgers, fries, shakes, and McNuggets—plus change—to win. . . . The point is simple: Games are dual purpose—they create compelling experiences and get customers even more involved with the product. Coca-Cola, Toys R Us, PepsiCo, and Nabisco may all ultimately design games to imprint their products onto the neurons of their younger customers. . . . Similarly, Chrysler or Toyota might develop VR driving games for adolescents and adults to promote their cars. (Schrage, et. al., 1994)

In the 1960s, a prominent political advertising practitioner, Tony Schwartz, spoke of a phenomenon he called *partipulation:Wherein, you could heighten the involvement an individual had with any given commercial if you got them to "participate in their own manipulation."* Certainly, these new interactive ad-games—which in the act of playing consumers will get their neurons imprinted—takes that psycho-behavorial process to heights Tony Schwartz never dreamed of.

The Audience and Consumer/"To whom"

To date, the audience to whom advertising has been directed has been defined in bulk terms—i.e. adults, teens, households, women 18 to 49, men 25 to 34. When dealing with the mass media the mass audience was packaged and sold by the "cost-per-thousand" and by "gross rating points." However, as noted by Paula George Tompkins, president of the SoftAd Group (an interactive ad agency in Mill Valley, CA., with such clients as Ford and Abbott Labs):

> You can't use traditional measurements like cost-per-thousand and cost per response. . . measuring interactive is a lot more involved and detailed. . . . (Wilder, 1994)

Interactive technology will generate a virtually endless stream of consumer information. Instantly a marketer will know what individuals are interested in his product. Within seconds of any inquiry the advertiser can respond to each and every consumer's unique set of questions and needs. The sale can be closed before the consumer ever even encounters a competitor's product on the shelf.

> Of course, that means big piles of new data for marketing experts to sort through and analyze. But this is not the traditional number-crunching variety of marketing information. Detailed buyer profiles present a different information technology challenge than that produced by massaging reams of transaction records from supermarket checkout scanners or telemarketing centers. (Wilder, 1994)

Perhaps the standard demographic descriptors of the audience will need to be supplemented with something like technographics: *combined index of general demographic measures (i.e. age, sex, income, education, etc.) and specfic measurements of an individual's ownership and use patterns of interactive technologies.* Thus, traditional demographic market segments, like women 18 to 49, can be further defined by their access to and amount of time spent with any given interactive technology. Instead of cost-per-thousand we may need to calculate "hits-per-pod" or maybe "mouse-clicks-per-sale."

The Communication Medium/"In what channel"

The real problem with advertising is that there's going to be so much of it. (David Abbott, Chairman and Creative Director, Abott Mead Vickers, one of Britain's top five advertising agencies, quoted in the *Financial Times Weekend*, Apr. 30–May 1, 1994.)

The Internet and World Wide Web, America Online, Prodigy . . . are just some of the online services that we can add to the list. Other new media advertising vehicles include an alpha-spaghetti of acronym platforms like CD-ROM, CD-I, CD-ROM-XA, VIS, DVD, 3DO, etc. Its all online, on demand and brought to you by cable, satellite, fiber optic, optical discs, cellular and wireless technologies. In the emerging interactive media world, mass media will refer more to the number of channels than to the nature of the audience. Tomorrow's audience will order à la carte. In addition to all the various online services and optical disc options, tomorrow's media consumer may have five hundred-plus TV channels from which to choose. It has been estimated it could take up to 14 minutes to survey (zap through) all the channels, lest it be for the intelligent agents ("KnowBots") pre-trained to their master's or mistress's voice that will screen out the excess, and deliver only a limited "menu" of program choices . . . tailored to taste. You like sports? Your "KnowBot" may locate 30 events for your review. Movies? fashions? News? Sitcoms? All there in abundance, and again that is   not including any entertaiment alternatives like movies-on-demand or CD-ROM games. And, how about advertising?

Imagine a television channel devoted entirely to commercials . . . no programming . . . no chatty spots from a shopping network. Only ads. Most people would agree that the station's audience would be a small, eclectic slice of the demographic pie: insomniacs and masochists. Yet, by year's end (1994), 10,000 PC users in four U.S. cities will test an interactive online service that some may regard as the cyberspace equivalant of this imaginary advertising channel. The service called ProductView Interactive, will carry pitches for cars, vacations, stereos, financial services, and sporting equipment. Consumers will be able to comparison shop by clicking icons and hypertext to obtain detailed information about an advertised product. (Wilder, 1994)

With What Effect

Is the ad agency ready for all of this? Are traditional advertising techniques facing imminent extinction? Is an entire industrial age species in danger of becoming "road-kill" on tomorrow's information super-highway? It is becoming ever more apparent that the heady days of the "go-go" 1970's and 1980's are over. Yesterday's advertising campaigns were all about targeting the masses—using mass media to get your (client's) message across. Reach and frequency was the name of the game. One 'good' TV commercial made for up to $ 1-1/2 million—the British Airways "Manhattan" commercial cost that much—could be used time and again to reach the target market with advertisers willing to pay over five times that amount to reach the right audience, such as Budweiser at the "Superbowl." And that's for just one spot. Few and far between are the mass advertising campaigns today wherein a few media purchases generate lots of (easy) commission.

The full-service ad agencies of yesteryear promising global brands, and global marketing strategies to match, have been pummeled by recession, culminating in reduced fees and commissions, and correspondingly dismal levels of earnings. Staffs are smaller, expected to accomplish more with less. The only "innovation" of note has been the growth of specialist media buying "shops" which cudgel media owners into lower-than-rate-card deals. Program sponsorship, product placement and airtime "barter" deals have also grown in popularity. But they are small beer. Clients have become increasingly demanding regarding measurement of performance, with many now coupling agency compensation with market share gain or other performance measures. Large and small agencies alike have been buffeted by the winds of change. They have been forced to reach new accommodations with their clients, and work in much reduced circumstances.

As a result, the agencies claim they are being squeezed so badly on margins that there is little room for maintaining existing services never mind creating or developing new interactive ones. As Martin Nisenholtz, former VP of interactive marketing at Ogilvy & Mather Direct, observed:

> A lot of big consumer product companies had people dedicated to new technologies. . . . but budgets were cut. . . . You have to justify everything you do in terms of short-term value. That's tough to do with interactive technology. (Wilder, 1994)

Meanwhile, the tick of high-technology marches on. The necessity to prepare for its impacts is not entirely lost on the advertising community. By the end of 1994, "the industry's two major trade groups, the Association of National Advertisers and the American Association of Advertising Agencies (also known as the Four A's), formed a joint task force to study the new media" (Maddox, 1994). Advertising executives like Betsy Frank, executive vice president and director of strategic media resources, Saatchi & Saatchi, admits that: "Most of our clients recognize they are going to have to make some pretty significant changes in how they communicate with and motivate their customers" (Maddox, 1994). And, no louder wake-up call could be given than that of Edwin Artzt, chairman and CEO of Procter & Gamble Co., who in a May '94 keynote speech at the Four A's annual convention "exhorted advertising representatives to wake up to the reality of new media technologies" (Wilder, 1994).

Just what exactly that "reality" will be, nobody really knows. There remains a gaping void between the ultimate promise and present performance of interactive technology. Because of this state of affairs advertising practitioners "have shifted from what's possible to what's real." (Maddox, 1994). Until the hardware manufacturers, software programmers and distribution companies narrow the gap, some observers are putting out the "do not disturb" sign for folks like Procter & Gamble's Edwin Artzt. In his petition to "Give Ad Agencies A Break," Al Perlman makes the case to "debunk one of the myths on the state of the interactive market:

> . . . The myth: Advertising agencies aren't doing their share to make interactivity happen. The reality. Bull. . . . Where's the infrastructure? . . . the bandwidth's just not there yet for the video, imaging and audio

> that will enable the type of creative execution clients are expecting
> . . . . The business paradigm for most interactive business is undefined
> . . . . How is fulfillment handled? Billing? Security? Customer Service?
> Advertising comes with many of its own built-in questions. Whom does
> it reach, how many respond, how is the impact of the ad measured?
> Add interactivity to the equation and all of the questions multiply
> (Perlman, 1994).

Indeed, determining the ultimate impact that new interactive technologies will have on the advertising industry is difficult. Moreover, early speculation on the probable applications and initial impact of new media technologies is often off the mark. There is no reason to believe that the prognosticators of grand nature and scope of interactive advertising are any more immune to *media-myopia* than their predecessors; (*with media-myopia defined as a* unique combination of shortsightedness *when it comes to estimating the public's desire for any given technological advance* AND rearsightedness *when it comes to ascertaining its ultimate utility*).

Albeit, the "potential" impacts that new interactive technologies may have on the advertising industry have been recognized. The emerging spectrum of communication technologies will offer the consumer a wide range of options from which to receive information on consumer goods and services. To be sure, the new interactive technologies will allow the consumer greater control and a more central role in how and how much product/service information is accessed. Whether or not the consumer wants to assume a new role and excercise greater control remains to be seen. As Schrage, et. al., observed:

> The fashionable, faux futurism predicts that this time will be different,
> that this time new media technology will guarantee the individual the
> upper hand over the advertiser. Maybe; maybe not. More likely, we'll
> see these new media renegotiate the power relationships between
> individuals and advertisers. Yesterday, we changed the channel; today
> we hit the remote; tomorrow, we'll reprogram our agents/filters.
> We'll interact with advertising where once we only watched; we'll seek
> out advertising where once we avoided it. Advertising will not go away;
> it will be rejuvenated. (Schrage, et. al., 1994)

References

Clark, T. (1994). From Pfeiffer to Perfume: Real Interactive Ads, *Interactive Week*, October 10, 1994, p. 32.

Interactive Age (1994). Interactive advertising pioneers, September 26, 1994, p. 55.

Financial Times Weekend (1994). Quote of David Abbott, Chairman and Creative Director, Abott Mead Vickers, one of Britain's top five advertising agencies, Apr. 30–May 1, 1994.

Lasswell, H. D. (1948). The Structure and Function of Communication in Society. In L. Bryson (Ed.) *The Communication of Ideas* (pp. 37–51) New York: Harper and Brothers.

Maddox, K. (1994). Advertisers seek interactive info, *Interactive Age*, September 26, 1994, p. 45, 55.

McLuhan, H. M. (1964). *Understanding Media: The Extensions of Man.* Toronto: University of Toronto Press.

Perlman, A. (1994). Give Ad Agencies A Break, *Interactive Week*, October 10, 1994, p.23.

Schrage, M. (1994, Feb.). Is Advertising Finally Dead?—part 1 and, Is Advertising Really dead—part 2, AdViruses, digimercials, and memgraphics: The future of advertising is the future of media, with Don Peppers, Martha Rogers, and Robert D. Shapiro, *Wired* magazine, Issue 2.02, Transmitted 94-04-18 to, and cited from, America Online).

Wilder C. (1994). Interactive Ads, *Information Week*, October 3, 1994, pp. 25–29.

CHAPTER

5

Media and Marketing Strategies for the Internet

A Step-by-Step Guide

Tracy Emerick

Tracy Emerick is president of Taurus Direct Marketing, a direct marketing agency and consultancy and president of Receptive Marketing, an electronic mall on the Internet. He is past chairman of the Business-to-Business Council of the Direct Marketing Association and is a director for the Direct Marketing to Business Conference and Business Database Marketing Conference of Dun & Bradstreet. He is co-author of *Business-to-Business Direct Marketing* and *Desktop Marketing*.

The Internet allows for a wealth of interactive marketing opportunities. The opportunities are even more expansive than its interactive predecessor, the telephone. While the use of the telephone as a marketing tool is still active, the Internet's multimedia presentation abilities combined with its inexpensive cost structure provide the ideal tool for direct and channel marketing of goods and services.

The Internet is a method of communication utilizing networked computers as the medium. A variety of different information transfer applications (protocols) are used to facilitate the finding, viewing, and transfer of information. Marketing on the Internet can incorporate a number of different applications.

Electronic Mail

The most widespread use of the network is the exchanging of electronic mail. This application provides a direct electronic communication link between companies and customers or prospects. E-mail employs standardized transfer of text-based messages. In addition, other files of any type (text, graphics, applications etc.) can be attached to an e-mail message, although better methods exist to transfer large files.

A method of sending a single message to a large group of people all at once is referred to as a mailing list. Such a list can be private, limited by mailing list administrator, or public, where any interested party can join the list by requesting the administrator to be added. Lists are best used for a select group with the same interests:

- Professional people
- Customers
- Sales people
- Distributors/Dealers
- Retailers

An e-mail request for information can trigger an automated mail delivery of a file or an e-mail response. This process is called, quite appropriately, an automated response and is analogous to a modern fax-back system.

World Wide Web

Though the Internet's network of computer networks has been in existence for more than 20 years, it is the recent adoption of the World Wide Web that has fueled the rapid growth and expansion of the commercial use of the network. This new application provides a graphical user interface (GUI) between the end-user and server computer being accessed on the Internet. Initially designed as an information delivery method, the Web's graphical and text delivery interface provides the same appearance as traditional printed materials. Along these lines, material on the Web is published on individual, inter-linked pages.

The World Wide Web interface has done for the Internet what the Windows operating system did for the PC in the late 1980s, making the Internet easy to use and navigate by the common untrained person using point and click skills. The World Wide Web provides colorful presentations and the ability to download any digital information to the viewer. Since any information including text, images, sound and video can be converted to a digital format, the presentation opportunities on the Web are limitless. The web employs a hypertext system, which allows designated text and pictures (and portions of them) to be linked to other documents.

Browsers that translate web pages for the end-user can also serve as the interface for less advanced Internet information applications. Though these information and communication mediums are less desirable for marketing efforts, there are appropriate uses for them.

Internet Gopher was the premier information display on access interface before the recent growth of the WWW. Gopher sites provide collections of information in fully indexed databases and are structured by directories/folders and files stored in hierarchical menus. The application provides a document search and retrieval system. Gopher sites can serve in situations where text-only presentations are employed. Gopher's replacement by the WWW as the primary Internet application is inevitable as the interface is available only in black and white.

Usenet and Newsgroups are structured groups compiled over the Internet for discussion of a particular theme. Anyone can post and read a particular newsgroup, which produces near-anarchy. The system works on threads of discussion. An initial posting starts a thread and others comment in a forum atmosphere. Newsgroups can be started among current or prospective customers of a marketing operation to provide user input, profiling, and research. Newsgroups cannot be controlled however, creating challenges for the Internet marketer.

Internet Marketing Strategies

Internet Marketing Strategies can be described, planned, and executed in three steps.

PHASE 1: INTERNET PRESENCE—ADVERTISING AND PUBLIC RELATIONS

World Wide Web Home Page: Developing a presence that serves as the basis for a corporation, division, product group or other entity for worldwide electronic review. The home page can serve several functions:

1. Advertising/PR presentation for channel and end users.
2. Messages to encourage browsers to take further action via phone or fax.

PHASE 2: INVOLVEMENT FROM THE HOME PAGE—PROMOTION

Promotional use of the Internet delivers the information currently delivered using other media ranging from the sales representative to broadcast media. The advantage of the Internet is that complete explanations can be delivered and downloaded locally for use by the customer and prospect.

1. Product/Service offerings—corporate, division, product group.
   A. Electronic pages that can serve the same function(s) as
      (1) Sell sheets
      (2) Specification sheets
      (3) Presentation brochures
      (4) Technical explanations
      (5) Press releases
      (6) Organization messages
      (7) Executive letters
      (8) Utilization suggestions

2. Dealer/Retailer Locator—where to purchase products and services

    A. Linear listings by state, country or other hierarchy, or

    B. Search engine supported by relational database.

3. Presentations for browser review or sales to administer.

PHASE 3: ONLINE TRANSACTION—INTERACTION

The most developed use of the Internet allows for interaction with individual customers and prospects. Interaction can include everything from answers to specific questions to online ordering at the wholesale and retail levels.

1. Dialogue—Real-time discussions with all levels of the channel.

    A. Secure or non-secure channels news group.

    B. End user news group.

2. Research—Decision making information gathering.

    A. Channel information gathering

    B. End user information gathering.

3. Service—Product/service information dissemination and discussions.

    A. Product/service utilization service.

    B. End user and channel service.

4. Support—Product/service explanation and problem solving.

    A. Product/service utilization support.

    B. End user and channel support.

    C. Sales support

5. Lead acquisition—New business opportunities.

    A. Leads for channel sales.

    B. End user leads.

   6. Ordering—Sales to channel and/or end users.
      A. Wholesale
      B. Retail

INTERNET MARKETING COSTS

Internet marketing costs can be divided into five areas:

1. Equipment
2. Connection Fees
3. Development Costs
4. Employee Management Costs
5. Communications Costs

Equipment costs will vary depending on how extensively a company wants to use the Internet in its marketing communications:

- Basic: Desktop computer and modem—$4,000

- Extensive: Server with direct connect equipment—$75,000

Connection fees can include:

- Basic: Dial-up to local Internet Service Provider—$12–$20 per month

- Extensive: Dedicated T1 line direct to Internet—$1,000–$5,000 per month

Development costs generally include:

- Basic: Home Page and three informational pages $1,500 - $4,500
- Extensive: $100,000 +

Additional development is also necessary as the site changes and improves. Employee management involve:

- Basic: Incidental and random use of Internet

- Extensive: Dedicated systems administrator(s), dedicated communicators, manager

Worldwide communications costs—a key benefit of the Internet—are no more than the cost of the connection fees, no matter how basic or extensive the site.

Internet Audience

The Internet audience can be divided into seven segments (an eighth segment is market participants who do not use the Internet) at present:

- Market: Customers, current and past. Prospects, those people who might become customers. Surfers or browsers who are not and will never become customers but still browse your Internet site(s) for entertainment.

- Decision Responsibility: Power to make decisions. Authority is based on job assignment/description. Influence has neither power or authority.

- Internet Involvement: Active uses the Internet as a part of daily activity. Passive has access but seldom or never uses the Internet.

- Off-Line: does not have access.

EXHIBIT 5.1 Reaching Internet Audiences

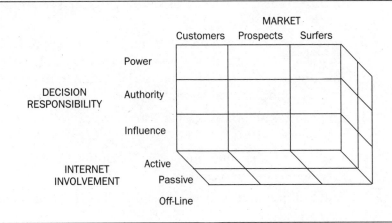

Database and Internet Marketing

The Internet is a communications option that can be used to present database information to users and to capture information for inclusion into a database.

A marketer can maintain a database of simple products/services, descriptions and prices. This database can be put online for customers, prospects, company employees, distributors, dealers, retailers and anyone else who might benefit from the information. A user requests information from the database and it is presented to the user from the database.

This process is accomplished using Gopher for text based information. For the WWW, the information is passed through an on-the-fly HTML generator, which converts the text for transmission and calls up the graphics already in GIF format. If you keep the database current, the user receives the latest information available, in real time.

The Internet can also be used to gather information from a market. The same information you gather using any other media (mail, phone, personal visit) can be gathered over the Internet. The information you gather can be for research, lead generation, selling products/services or any other type of feedback, including customer satisfaction surveys.

Your ability to organize a database is enhanced when the user is doing the data entry. This can also pose a problem, however, if you want information to be consistent. Information gathering over the Internet may use a few basic principles:

1. Limit information requests to a form which can be completed in three to five minutes. It is too easy to exit a site if the user's involvement lessens.

2. Don't ask for information that requires the user to leave their workstation, they will probably not come back. Exceptions to this are if you are registering serial numbers or some other transaction which will benefit the user in some way.

3. Limit response options per question or you will not be able to analyze the results.

4. Use open-ended questions when quantitative response measurement is not necessary.

5. Build in questions which separate surfers from customers and prospects.

Employee Management in Internet Marketing

Logistics of employee management for supporting an Internet site are similar to the logistics of managing a telemarketing or telesales site with one exception, the communicators do not need to be in any particular physical location.

Communicators must be trained in the facets of your business and of customer expectations and demands as they relate to your products and services. Since the Internet allows all users (unless you require a password for entry into all or part of your site) communicators must be schooled in how to determine cranks from legitimate contacts.

The best type of individual for the position of communicator is a person with low aggressiveness and high emotion, often referred to as amiable or affiliator. This type of individual enjoys working with a group and has the ability to deal with various markets with equal ease.

Full consumption of a person's time is always a consideration when staffing any position. An Internet communicator should be monitored the same as all employees. Measurement criteria for this position are yet to be determined. Measurement could be based on number of email messages handled in a day and/or it could be measured in customer satisfaction (seen in re-orders from existing customers). Internet communication may not be a full time position in your company. However, someone should be assigned the responsibility of responding to email and other Internet inquiries.

You can control the flow of messages to answer based on the programs you put on line. If you do not want inquiries, do not provide a way for people to respond to your site.

One way to reduce the need for response is to set up automatic responses for certain types of inquiries. These responses are delivered automatically when an inquiry is received. This can be programmed as an auto function.

You can also set up a FAQ (frequently asked questions) location to answer the repetitive questions, thus reducing the need for increased staffing due to increased inquiries.

One person with some level of understanding of your business and with some pre-written information resources can handle 35 to 45 inquiries an hour. This number is estimated based on the number of inquiries handled in a full workday. A communicator will probably only be online four to five hours per day because of the need to research certain inquiries.

Keeping a site current and interesting also requires an Internet marketing manager. It is easy to put up a site, but keeping it current is more challenging. This function is not defined in most companies since just getting on the Internet is the task at hand. Once active, however, the site needs to be constantly reviewed and updated. Sites that become too big and lack navigation or entertainment value can be cluttered and exhausting for a user. Ease of use and clarity of navigation aids is essential for a site to keep user involved.

Using the Internet as a method of customer and channel contact assumes that customers and channel partners are able and interested in embracing this communications medium. The logistics of working with the market require that you support many skill levels. Until the Internet is more widely used, a great deal of time will be consumed by education and skill development. Skill development can be a strategic tool for you to work with your channel partners. If you provide training and applications which make working with you more convenient and cost effective, you can leverage this in terms of profits through longer lifetime value of customers.

Promotion on the Internet

Promoting your site can be accomplished in a variety of ways both on and outside the Internet. The options available are:

1. Publishing your Internet address in your printed materials and advertising. Like your phone number, your Internet address will be recorded for use by customers and prospects. Surfers may pick up your address from print advertising, but will be excluded when you use targeted media like direct mail to reach your desired audience.

2. Using publicity to reach your marketplace. Getting your address out in this fashion is a hit-or-miss proposition since PR is uncontrollable and may or may not reach your marketplace in a timely fashion.

3. Inside the Internet using announcement locations and search engines.

4. Links from other Internet sites in exchange for links from your site.

As in all communications, involvement, both physically and mentally is a key guideline. If a person is not involved with your message, they are not involved with your promotion. If there is not involvement, there will be no behavior modification-action to take the next step in buying from you. Internet promotion can take on three characters:

1. Information only, a site which only gives information is a dialogue—you to the reader.

2. Custom information, a site where users can gain information specific to their needs.

3. Feedback, a site where users gain and give information.

The custom and feedback Internet sites can build a database for future contact. Each visitor's email address can be captured and used for future contact. It is important that this be done with caution. The culture of the Internet is self-governing and can create problems if a marketer is too aggressive in promoting products and services.

The Internet is governed by general agreement of use called netiquette. This unwritten set of rules allows information to be sought but never delivered unsolicited. Unwanted solicitation of information can result in angry complaints to your e-mail box, called "flaming" or overloading of your server by bombarding it with automated messages from an upset individual, called "spamming."

To avoid getting flaming and spamming, out-bound promotional activities should be in the form of announcements. The announcement provides opportunities for users to visit your site for something that benefits them. Promotional information can include all materials currently available in printed form or in text form used for press releases.

The key to active Internet promotion is to offer something of value to the user you want to visit your site. People are never annoyed with a topic of interest to themselves. Offer development is covered in another section.

Developing Internet Offers

The use of any media to communicate requires a series of steps from the time of contact until the time of closure. A simple model is Attention—Interest—Desire—Action (AIDA). Your Internet promotion will follow these steps, or some steps along these lines, as you reach out into cyberspace to attract people to you and then to do what you want them to do—from simple feedback to online buying. Each one of the steps in the relationship moves a person from a surfer to a customer. Surfers can move through each step more easily if there is something in it for them. You need to develop these "somethings" by developing offers which people will respond to.

Offers can be general or specific. General offers might be taken advantage of by anyone on the Internet regardless of their specific areas of interest. These offers might be information on the standings of professional sports or weather reports in various parts of the country. A general offer is designed to attract a broad audience.

A specific offer is one which is focused on the needs of a specific person. An example might be monitoring and reporting on the migration habits of the North American horned owl. This type of information is of interest only to people interested in horned owl or bird migration. A site where telemetry engineers can discuss the effects of temperatures on wing vibration at super-sonic speeds will certainly only be of interest to this type of engineer.

Offers can be used to move people through three basic steps of relationship building:

1. Attract visitors

2. Involve prospects

3. Sell/support customers

Attracting visitors is the biggest challenge of the Internet. It requires you to have something of interest and that you be known. Using promotion you can deliver your offer. Your offer should be easy to understand. An example might be: Review and download the ten keys to success, URL http://yoursite.com. This offer is such that any person who wants success might drop in for a visit, just to see what you've got. With promotion, this offer could generate thousands of visitors per day.

If you want a specific market you could offer the Five Engineering Tests for Professional Publishing, URL http:yoursite.com. This offer will attract a specific type of visitor.

When a visitor has arrived to take advantage of your attracting offer you have gained their Attention. Now you must involve the visitor in order to create Interest and Desire. If the visitor arrives, copies or downloads your free guide and leaves quickly, you have not taken advantage of the visit. You must engage the visitor in some way to gain the physical and mental involvement. One approach might be to ask for certain information from the visitor, before you provide the download file. As you are asking the information, you could be providing additional information, along the same lines as the attracting offer.

You can embed another offer inside the fulfillment of the first offer. Once a visitor is onsite you can make another, more attractive offer. One that will enhance the life of the visitor in some way. You should ask for feedback at this point and provide enhancements to the offer which will keep the prospect involved. In the case of the success keys, you might have a questionnaire the visitor completes in order to receive a success quotient. This custom report is provided as an additional service, just for taking the time. When the custom report is delivered, you have the opportunity to move to the profitable portion of the relationship.

Action is the step in the process when you receive money for what you are or might deliver. In the example you could have a complete success guidebook for a person for $48.49 which can be billed to their credit card or paid at a later time. The same approach can be used for our engineers, who might receive a special report on wing stress if they will answer a few questions which lead to the $850 desktop calculation software package (billed or charged to a credit card).

Your Action step can also be to gather sufficient information about each other to move to a non-Internet environment—a sales visit or a phone contact. Test the approach of selling online, you might be surprised with the result.

The Internet Mall

Participating in a mall can be a great way to promote and sell products and services to business and consumers. The advantages to participating in a mall are very similar to the advantages of a merchant participating in a retail mall.

1. The mall owner is responsible for the construction of the mall. Design and layout of the Internet mall and merchant participation are costs incurred by the mall owner. This means the cost of entering a mall can be less for the merchant than setting up a site.

2. The mall owner is responsible for bringing traffic to the mall. Promotion of the mall and merchants fall with the mall owner. This reduces the promotional effort necessary by the merchant. Which in turn reduces the need to learn all about Internet marketing so time can be devoted to merchandise and not marketing issues.

3. The mall which has critical mass can be more fun than a visit to a stand alone site. Visiting a mall is a leading form of entertainment in the United States. Visiting Internet malls can also be entertaining if the mall is well laid out and has a variety of merchandise and services.

4. Online ordering is a difficult and expensive process to develop. Mall owners not only provide space; they can also provide online ordering capabilities for the merchant so the merchant does not have to do this themselves.

There are disadvantages to participating in a mall:

1. You may be restricted in how you are presented on the Internet.

2. You may lose some flexibility in how your products and services are presented.

3. If a mall does not do a good job of promotion, you might have less traffic.

4. Mall entertainment can create a lot of visitors with few sales.

5. You may not have direct access from surfers, prospects and customers. They may be forced to come to you by way of the mall home page and not directly into your location.

Mall participation should be one avenue you use to create a presence on the Internet. It is a low maintenance way to gain presence and link to other pages you have in the Internet.

Combining Internet with Integrated Marketing Strategy

As discussed, the Internet is a communications media. Like all media it should be used in concert with other media. The combined effects of multiple media reaching into a market at the same time is generally higher overall than the results of each media added together.

The advantage of the Internet is the relative low cost of the media for worldwide communications. The disadvantage is that not all people in your market are online.

The Internet is generally not coordinated with other media because the medium is so new it does not have a formal link to the marketing communications plan. The Internet is used as a general catch-all for information without regard as to how it ties in with current nonInternet promotion.

An example of using the Internet in concert with other media was the release of "Batman Forever" in the summer of 1995. The producer promoted the movie on TV, print media and online. Supposedly the movie opened with one of the highest grossing first weekends in history.

Combining media can take several approaches as seen in this matrix. The numbers indicate an option and are an index of difficulty in managing multimedia programs.

OPTION 1

This is the simplest form of multimedia. All media being used have the same message and request the same action. An example is an insurance promotion which asks you to call an 800 number or to respond over the Internet. The same message will be delivered on the Internet and in print advertising.

EXHIBIT 5.2 Multimedia Options

	Same Message/ Offer	Different Message/ Offer
Same Action	1	2
Different Action	3	4

OPTION 2

The use of one medium to drive people toward a certain action. The promotion of the Batman movie in all media was designed for the same action, to get you to go to see the movie. The media messages were different, each geared toward the medium being used. In this case the Internet promotion was more involved and expensive than any other media used in the program.

OPTION 3

Using the same message and/or offer to move different people to different actions is relatively easy to promote. The difficulty is trying to determine the results if people can take separate actions. The same message/offer has several methods of action. A manufacturer can offer a set of guidelines for caring for a printer. The action is to secure the guidelines which might be accomplished by contacting the manufacturer or by contacting a dealer. These two options create difficulty for understanding the outcomes.

OPTION 4

Different messages with different actions is the general state of affairs in most companies. One example of a controlled multimedia approach with different actions is used by Publisher's Clearing House when you are instructed to go to your mail box in order to mail in your contest entry. This use of different message with different actions must prove profitable since it is repeated year after year. The next option will be to put this entire program on the Internet and let users subscribe and enter online.

Using the Internet with Channels

The Internet is a low cost, immediate way to communicate with channels. An example of a shoe manufacturer will serve to illustrate:

- Ace Shoe Manufacturer develops a series of pages showing its current shoe styles and general pricing. Each shoe style is given a complete work-up from construction through tips on when to wear the style.

- The distributor can review styles and place orders for stock. The orders can be placed via a privately accessed order form using assigned passwords and account codes.

- The dealer/retailer can accomplish the same as the dealer placing orders with the distributor or with the manufacturer as is the store's method.

- Sales people at all levels can access the Internet presentation for personal education and for presentation to customers. The latest styles and codes are always current so the sales people are not selling old inventory.

- End users/customers can review the manufacturers' styles and general pricing along with all other available information. The site also has a listing of dealers/retailers so the end user/customer can purchase the style or styles they desire—perhaps even order online, a real challenge for the channel.

Manufacturers can provide for end user feedback which can be shared with distributors and dealers in a secure location. This information can provide strategic information for all participants in the channel. The Internet can also be used to complement or supplement existing communication programs ranging from sales people to printed materials and order forms. You can also establish new channels domestically and worldwide using the Internet because of its low cost and immediate information transfer.

Predictions on the Internet

The Internet will revolutionize marketing as it is known today. The revolution will confound marketers, customers and governments trying to regulate and tax unprecedented global commerce. As the tools used on the Internet expand and the speed of data transmission accelerates, the Internet will become a one-to-one marketing medium offering customized interchange between seller and buyer.

Use of the Internet is currently experimental. Surrounded by excessive hype and hyperbola the actual utility of the medium has yet to reach senior executives. Once the utility is known traditional methods of print and broadcast advertising, printed materials and even sales calls will be minimized as part of the media mix. The Internet's capacity for color graphics, sound, text and eventually video will provide the basis for on-demand marketing and sales.

The Internet will also bring about the end of distribution as it is structured today. Combined with rapid delivery systems for goods, the Internet will negate the need for stocking distributors, globally. The roles of distributors and resellers will be replaced with online demonstrations, service and support provided directly by the manufacturer. Only value-added distributors will survive the next decade.

Distribution channels will be streamlined and the remaining companies in the channel will use the Internet as a user-friendly electronic data interchange (EDI). The Internet will be used to support perpetual sales meetings, online trade shows, end user research and feedback vehicle as well as product review, updates and ordering, both wholesale and retail.

Eventually the computer, telephone, and television will become a single unit which multi-tasks between the various information resources for entertainment, business, finances and news. The Internet will flourish as the tools and access become simplified. Cable companies will offer Internet through the cable connection giving the home user every day transmission speed enjoyed only by expensive dedicated lines today.

Any person or business not getting involved with the Internet today will be left on the sidelines within five years. Tomorrow, school children will be using the Internet instead of going to the library. The next generation of business, where employees work from the home, will use the Internet instead of the telephone.

CHAPTER

6

Creative Strategy for Interactive Marketing

10 Rules for Adapting and Winning in the New Marketplace

Carol Nelson
Rocky James

Carol Nelson is Executive Vice President, Communicomp, a full-service direct response agency based in Plantation, Florida. In addition to speaking on marketing and advertising subjects at conferences all over the world, her articles appear regularly in the business press. She also is author of several books on marketing and advertising, including *Women's Marketing Handbook*, which received a 1994 *Choice* award, and *The World's Greatest Direct Mail Sales Letters*, with Herschell Gordon Lewis.

Rocky James is Executive Director, Electronic Media Development and Production for Communicomp. Previously, he was Special Projects Producer for NBC Network News in Burbank and Segment Producer for NBC. James has produced numerous infomercials, including the "Carlton Sheets No Money Down" segment for AMS. His articles on infomercials and TV direct response appear regularly in the business press.

Sure, everyone's jumping on the interactive advertising bandwagon. It's new, it's novel, it's exciting. But it won't ever be a viable advertising vehicle.

We hear that argument—or something very much like it—almost every day. And yet, that's what the newspaper die-hards said when radio surfaced in the early 1920s. It's what radio die-hards said about television back in the 1950s.

Advertising will never fly on the Internet. Why would *anyone* pay to look at advertising?

Sound familiar? That's exactly the argument we heard from the network television die-hards about cable TV back in the 1980s. Yet people not only watch infomercials, they actually pick up the phone and order product.

If you advertise on the Internet, how will anyone see it?

That's one of the first questions detractors ask when they begin to think about interactive advertising on the net or online services. As they exist, they're more like broadcast media (as people "channel surf" from site to site) or Yellow Pages directories (as people search sites by classification) or outdoor billboards (as people speed right past your "billboard" on the info superhighway) than direct response media.

The World's Biggest, Most Confusing Circus

First-time browsers—and they're fewer and fewer, as about 50,000 people each week join the fingertip parade into the netherworld—are stunned by the variety and breadth of offerings.

Who cares if Barnum was right when he said, There's a sucker born every minute? On the Internet, it's as difficult to find Barnum as it is to find the suckers. But Barnum had a virtue along with his vices: He was a spellbinder, and he'd be a strategy-hero on the Internet. Barnum knew that the moment he lapsed into high-flown language, the group in front of his tent would evaporate. He knew that the slightest tinge of un-clarity would create confusion as an unhappy replacement for artificial enthusiasm.

Barnum knew how to sell. He wasn't a technician. He didn't use technical talk. He didn't throw terminology around as a meat-cleaving weapon.

To Internet advertisers looking for maximized response, the clarion call would be, "Go thou and do likewise."

But the Internet and online interactive services have terrific potential for direct response advertising, precisely because they *are* interactive . . . if you know how to use that interactivity to its best advantage.

And the advantages are unique, just as the disadvantages are unique.

Staged Events

The speed with which Internet advertising is sophisticating itself is—well, it can be frightening. Today's brilliant innovation is tomorrow's old hat; and even the most jaded television viewer, who has seen trends come and go in a flash, has to be bewildered when terminology and procedures he has just heard for the first time are already obsolete.

One strategy that does work, although the word *work* has another implication here, is the Online Conference. The huge competitive advantage is that a conference is *interactive*, and interactivity is the key to loyalty—or as much loyalty as the electronically-charged consumer of the late 1990s can muster.

Along with conferences are meeting halls, in which an Internet advertiser ostensibly asks individuals to participate with ideas and suggestions. Here again, implementation demands gradual accretion of a user database to enable the advertiser to contact—whether by e-mail or by mail or by phone—the people who have entered the advertiser's lair and left their names and contact addresses. Careful structuring of what the meeting is about will result in a positive public relations event.

Now, a heavyweight Internet concept: *customer loyalty programs.*

Such programs make more sense on the Internet than in any other medium, not only because—as we've pointed out—the customer comes looking for you instead of your having to prospect randomly for him or her. But also because the Internet isn't free. Oh, yes, it's *virtually* free because the cost-per-hit is insignificant; but it isn't free. This compares to a cold-list name calling you and asking for a copy of your catalog. Treasure that person!

Customer loyalty programs can be as basic as points, such as the frequent flyer programs that have been in place for a generation. But the Internet has an edge over the airlines: The huge, ponderous, and expensive machinery involved in monthly or quarterly contact with members doesn't exist. Members can check their points with a click of the mouse-button. If the advertiser, in an act of supreme benevolence, contacts members by mail (or even e-mail), that's frosting on the cake of a constantly improving relationship.

Technical aside: Those who subscribe to online services such as Compuserve and America Online are instantly accessible because their addresses don't change even if they move across the country. No change of address bookkeeping here!

Surveys aren't quite staged events, because each survey is one-on-one. The advantage to the advertiser is that surveys are structured, while conference halls are unstructured. This gives the advertiser an edge—provided the advertiser knows how to use that edge: Structuring questions to be most beneficial. The best consultants for this type of survey might well be political consultants, who know how to generate questions that cloud the mind and distort actuality.

Like the conference, the survey is apparently 100 percent interactive. If the advertiser follows the survey with a report to participants, score another point for Internet strategy.

The key to staged events is *enthusiastic participation.* Keep the pot boiling. Keep excitement high. Don't lapse into bored sameness, because bored sameness is just about the most contagious disease carried by the Internet.

A New Tool for the Marketing Toolbox

Marketing principles are the same across all media. Only the "toolbox" changes. (Would that more advertising agencies, who exploit one medium because that's the one with which they feel most comfortable, embraced this truism.)

Therein lies a strategic challenge—no, a warning:

> Much Internet advertising is prepared not by marketers but by programmers and technicians. This parallels having ads written by typesetters. Technical proficiency supplants communications skills, and the result may be a technological triumph and a motivational flop.

What's the difference between creating a direct response advertising message for interactive media and traditional media such as mail, television, and print ads? Very little. (A "But . . . " disclaimer is coming up.) Interactive media are the perfect vehicles for your direct response messages. But the interactive age has ushered in a new way to communicate. And as we pick our way carefully through the differences that do exist, we find the communications differences are great enough to warrant an entire chapter in this book.

How to Integrate Your Interactive Advertising into Your Existing Advertising Campaign

The Internet implicitly has superimposed its own set of rules onto the world of advertising strategy. Recognition of these rules may not result in a brilliant campaign, but it should result in a competitively professional campaign.

These are the absolute rules for adapting conventional advertising to Internet advertising in today's volatile marketplace:

1. Passive messages are out. Absolutely. No exceptions. We're fanatical about this because, of all the rules we might impose, violating this one will drive browsers out of your site as though you have the plague. And you do—the plague of dullness.

We put this rule at the top of the list because nearly every one of the nine rules that follow stem from this first rule.

2. Grab and shake the reader instantly. Whoever said television is the medium that generates an instant reaction hasn't hit the Internet. Television is slow-motion compared to a nervous mouse-hand, hovering in limbo and ready to flee at the slightest indication of irrelevance or tedium.

3. Your cover page and the first page of text have to be not only "killers" . . . but have to download *fast.* Slow downloading has destroyed many a bright promotional idea. The "killer" mandate is true of many media, but the fast-to-load mandate is peculiar to this medium because the whole concept had never existed until the Internet existed. That may not seem so difficult, but of all the rules and principles and suggestions in this chapter, it's the one most likely to bite you if you don't follow it. Try it just once and you'll see: This is where many a veteran communicator stumbles.

4. Ask for response—*any* type of response that makes even a little sense—immediately. As the medium slowly matures, another avenue of *intensification* exists. It's one even sophisticated Internet advertisers overlook, perhaps because they are blinded by the glamour of the

medium: e-mail to responders. When you get a response from them, make sure you're equipped to send a response right *back* to them—and *right now*! As one veteran interactive fund-raiser (yes, you can successfully generate response for a fund raising campaign, too), Stacey Switzer says, "Never underestimate the short attention span of your audience. People expect instantaneous response, not a day or a week later!"

Technically, this is easy to do. It also is in keeping, from a strategic point of view, with the state of mind of those who respond to Internet advertising. Certainly, recognizing *who* the recipient of the message is, receptivity will be greater than it would be to a mailed newsletter. You're in the most competitive bazaar ever created, and response is the key to lengthening the browser's gnat-like attention span. Fast, *fast,* FAST have a contest, give away something free, issue an invitation, have a "Today Only!" special. Alertness will pay off. And that leads directly to. . . .

5. Change your message often. Yes, you can run a campaign on television for thirteen weeks and "build" a reaction. You can't do that on the Internet. A browser sees your message, or even your first page . . . says, "Oh, it's one I've seen before" . . . and quickly mouses over to a fresh message by a more astute competitor. Changing your message even every day isn't too often, because your best browsers will hit your surf every time they lurch onto the electronic superhighway. Only once need they say, "I've seen that before." Then they're gone—and it very well could be forever. (If your type of business doesn't lend itself to daily updates, start with a "Chuckle of the Day" or a cartoon or a wise saying. But don't think sameness will sink through layers of apathy, the way it does with a radio campaign. This medium is high-powered. (Exhibit 6.1 shows how one online fund raising foundation has set up its home page to be flexible . . . and easily modified.)

6. Advertise your site in other media (see Exhibit 6.2). If they never see you, they won't buy from you. If they don't know you're there, they'll never see you. (Is this cheating? Certainly not. It's the 21st century application of an integrated campaign.)

To make Internet advertising "visible" within the gigantic morass of information smashed loosely together in this electronic jungle, re-minder advertising in other media is necessary. This is the Internet version of *The Reader's Digest* and Publishers' Clearing House mailings, reinforced by short-term saturation television reminder-advertising.

EXHIBIT 6.1 The Nature Conservancy Page on America Online

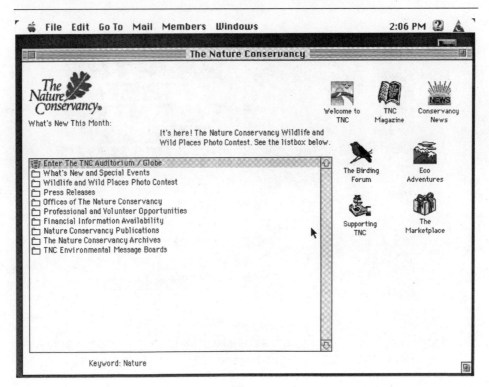

Make it easy, they will come! Make it entertaining and informative, they will come back! says Stacey Switzer. The Nature Conservancy page on America Online makes change . . . and response . . . easy.

7. Establish "links" with like-minded companies. This is what the "Shopping Mall" concept is all about. A financial institution established a Mall, all of whose tenants are linked by a common thread—the bank—as the mall's center. The bank promotes the mall; the tenants benefit from the patronage, just as smaller stores in a conventional mall benefit from the advertising and traffic generated by the mall's anchor store (Exhibits 6.3, 6.4, 6.5). An Internet Solutions company shows off its work by establishing a link to its clients (Exhibit 6.6).

"Member-get-a-member." This venerable technique, as old as book clubs, has found a marvelous home on the Internet. This medium is almost custom-designed for member-get-a-member, not only because

EXHIBIT 6.2 Ad in *Wired*

DO YOU HAVE THE FIBER TO ENTER THE 21ST CENTURY?

FIND OUT ON THE INTERNET.

Stop at the Developers Lab and begin a challenging journey into the future. Along the way, test your knowledge of information technology to make sure you're ready to hit the highway. While you're at it, test those business applications to find out if they have the right stuff.

DEVELOPERS LAB

http://www.mci.com/developerslab/

Space ads in targeted magazines point readers to the advertiser's Internet page. Because this ad appeared in Wired *magazine, the advertiser can assume the reader will already have Internet access.*

referrals don't require any postage nor phone calls nor information beyond an e-mail address, but also because the capability of issuing rewards for referrals is so easy.

9. When you get an order or an inquiry, handle it with lightning speed. That means the same day if possible . . . certainly no longer than one business day. If you don't have this capability, stay off the Internet until you do, because you'll be getting returned merchandise, flame messages, and damaging word-of-mouth (or word-of-mouse).

10. Test. Test. Test again.

How many genuine experts exist . . . gurus who can make (and prove) proclamations about Internet strategy?

As an educated guess: None.

This is because we lack a solid base of testing. Testing has been not just the cornerstone of other media, but their salvation. Testing showed newspapers how emphasis on "Lifestyle" sections and local news could

EXHIBIT 6.3 First Union Corporation Mall Ad

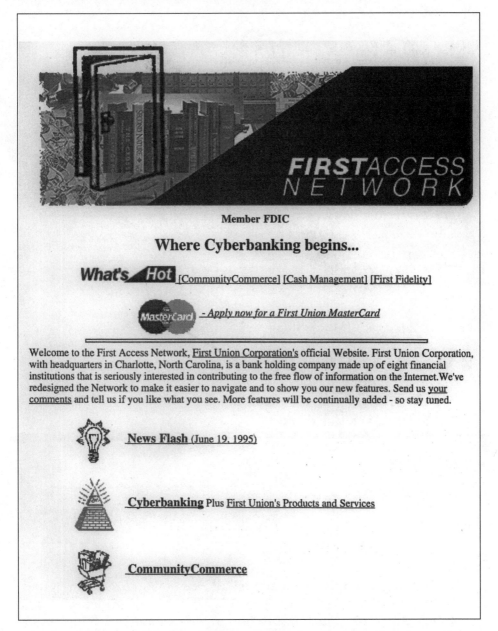

This ad shows how this bank uses interactivity, as well as the shopping mall anchor concept, to its best advantage. Prospects can apply for a credit card online and even leap to sister merchants with the click of a mouse.

EXHIBIT 6.4

7.9% APR

Introductory Rate
Exceptional rate after 6 months: only 5.9 percentage points over Prime*
No annual fee -- ever!

Get the Gold MasterCard value you've been seeking.
Apply online for *fast* response.
*See terms and conditions screen.

Credit Card Application Form

To apply for a Credit Card from **First Union Nation Bank of Georgia**, please fill in the following **4** categories of information: ***Applicant Information, Credit Reference, Review Information, Terms and Conditions***. When all of the boxes are checked below, you may **Submit** your application. The information you enter will be kept in strictest confidence.

1. Applicant Information

2. Credit Reference

3. Review Information

4. Terms and Conditions

Submit Cancel

bring survival in a television-glutted information arena. Testing shows direct marketers which prices, which approaches. which letter length, which motivators, which colors, and which enclosures will turn so-so-results into winners. Testing shows television advertisers which markets are most responsive and which approaches bring customers into stores and automobile showrooms.

EXHIBIT 6.5

CommunityCommerce

Your First Stop on the Information Highway

Community Commerce(sm) is First Union National Bank's vision of the future for community banking. First Union is creating a marketplace on the Internet's World Wide Web. A marketplace designed to offer merchants an opportunity to offer their products and services for sale to a new world market. It is a virtual community that consumers will want to visit again and again to access information, products and services in a feature rich environment.

For the next few weeks, First Union will be presenting merchants with unique products and services. A variety of different payment systems and interfaces will be presented to evaluate efficient mechanisms for encouraging commerce on the web. Please help us evaluate our system by giving feedback on your experiences with each of these merchants.

First Merchants

New merchants will be added to CommunityCommerce during the coming weeks. The first merchants introduced under the trial system include:

- **PCTravel™** - PC Travel - the only real-time airline reservation and ticketing service on the Internet! PCTravel allows reservations and ticketing at travel agent prices with no fees for using the system. Tickets are delivered next-day in the U.S.
- Fountainhead Water Company - Deep artesian wells in the Blue Ridge Mountains release pure, clean water with nothing added, just as nature intended. Fountainhead brings you this taste by bottling it at the source.
- **CBO** - Community Business Online's AutoNetwork® - For those of you shopping for a car, there's no better place to start your search. Go visit a live up-to-date database of dealer inventories all over the country.

How can your organization be a Member of CommunityCommerce?

CommunityCommerce is the perfect site for creating your companies own virtual storefront on the Internet.

EXHIBIT 6.6 Internet Solutions

WELCOME!

Choose one of the links below to find out more about Maxperts, Inc.

| **Networks** | **Client/Server** | **Messaging**

CAL OnLine!. Check out Maxperts client, an adult service that utilizes the latest and greatest in multimedia delivery !

Now featuring full service WWW design and publishing services

THANKS FOR VISITING the Maxperts Home Page! If you have any questions, just drop us a line at info@maxperts.com

Return to the Maxperts home page

If you're a service company, the Internet makes it simple to show what you've done for your clients, just by linking their pages to yours.

The Internet, as of this writing, is itself a test. Results are all over the lot because the medium hasn't settled down, nor have its browsers identified themselves into segmentable groups. The challenge of Internet testing may not be met to a degree at which it becomes useful ammunition on a textbook level, until well into the 21st century. This is because change piles upon change, and fishing for the best approach to any one marketing project puts an advertiser in the position of a football referee trying to dig into a pile of 22 bodies to see who has recovered a fumble.

As the first generation of Internet advertising matures, an imperative to those who read these words and front the second generation:

- Test. Test. Test.
- Experiment.
- Test your messages. Test your sites. Test your techniques.

Then, for the love of heaven, analyze what you've discovered. If you're especially kind, share the results of your testing with those who will follow—the third generation of Internet advertisers, who will assume as a matter of course what we have learned with such painstaking experimentation.

When you have results, analyze them and learn from them. If you're a marketer and not just a researcher—and that's the point of all this— use them for your ongoing promotions until further testing shows you the marketplace . . . or *your* marketplace . . . has changed.

Why might your marketplace change when others remain static? For the same reason singular marketing changes have occurred throughout history. Technology and human desires don't alter themselves in a lump. Fashion might change while breakfast cereals don't. A hot new competitor arises in a single field, and suddenly that industry requires retooling while others sail smoothly across calm marketing seas. Alertness calls for recognition of which factors affect *your* business.

Be on the lookout for changes. Believe us, they'll be there.

The Internet is the wildest, most exciting, and most challenging advertising medium we've ever had the good/bad fortune to encounter. The strategist finds it both exhilarating and exasperating . . . and that's what keeps us alert.

Considerations for 21st-Century Direct Marketers

Focusing on the Basics in New Environments

Richard S. Hodgson

Richard S. Hodgson is President of Sargeant House, a Westtown, Pennsylvania, company that provides direct marketing consulting and catalog development services to companies throughout the world. He is also author of more than a dozen books, including the classic *Direct Mail and Mail Order Handbook*, and hundreds of magazine articles on direct marketing. Dick is a member of the Board of Directors of Foster & Gallagher, Inc., a leading U.S. direct marketing firm, and was formerly a charter member of the Board of Directors of QVC Network, Inc.

As we rapidly approach year 2000, everyone seems to be anticipating dramatic changes in lifestyles and the ways business will be conducted throughout the world. While it's natural to focus on exciting new developments, there's a danger for direct marketers who spend too much time and money on emerging technology, assuming the gadgets and gimmicks of the future will mean replacing most of the techniques spelling success for today's direct marketers.

This rush toward the 21st Century seems to have begun in earnest in the early 1980s. At a direct marketing conference, futurist Alvin Toffler predicted everyone would soon be working at home in their "electronic cottages." A top executive of American Express told us we's better lose no time in molding new technology to suit our own purposes since everyone was going to be sitting in front of their interactive TV sets, doing most of their business transactions by merely pushing a few buttons.

What happened to those confident predictions of a brave new world where everything was going to change, where all of us would sit in front of our television sets or computers to do all of our home and business shopping, where our mailboxes would gather dust as printed media disappeared from the scene?

It seems the direct marketing futurists overlooked one important thing. They forgot to ask consumers if they wanted new ways of doing things. Throughout the world, billions have been spent trying to get consumers to fall in love with the latest in electronic gadgetry and abandon their printed catalogs, direct mail, newspapers, magazines. But consumers keep coming back with the same answer: "Why change?"

This leads to the important issue of "critical mass." While I see this as a major problem today, it could easily become an even larger problem in the future, particularly for companies that already have well-established marketing methods against which the success or failure of interactivity must be measured.

You don't have to look any further than cable home shopping to understand the importance of this factor. Over 100 companies—including many of the biggest marketers in America—have spent many millions trying to get involved in this single interactive medium. Yet, only two—HSN and QVC home shopping networks—have been successful in developing profitable national businesses.

The major problem has been critical mass—getting carriage by enough cable systems so they could reach sufficient homes to develop a profitable business. Not only do direct marketers need to be concerned about total critical mass, but also the number of people likely to be accessing the medium during any given time frame. For example, as the number of marketers participating on the Internet continues to grow, the percentage of consumers willing to devote the time and effort during any given time frame to seek out and "listen" to each marketer's sales message tends to diminish.

Even if every household in the U.S. had Internet-accessing capabilities, the competition for each message offered might be so large there may not be critical mass large enough to serve the requirements of many marketers. And when you add the competition from online services, newly developed interactive cable programs, et al, this problem becomes even more complicated. Of course, the critical mass necessary to constitute a viable business varies greatly. But, at the present time and for the near future at least, the numbers just aren't there for the majority of businesses.

In his marvelous book, *Megatrends,* John Naisbitt observed,

> The gee-whiz futurists are always wrong because they believe technological innovation travels in a straight line. It doesn't. It weaves and bobs and lurches and sputters.

And today's electronic technology is weaving, bobbing, lurching and sputtering. But that doesn't stop the direct marketing futurists from predicting straight line adoption of what is now being called the "Information Superhighway."

One of the hottest subjects at direct marketing meetings and in the trade press has been the imminent arrival of an interactive Information Superhighway, with cable systems offering 500 channels of programming. With the trend toward demassification in direct marketing, multiple cable channels would appear to offer an efficient way to reach specialized audiences. And if it were possible to eliminate the rising costs of paper, printing and postage plus large staffs of human order operators, think of all the increased profit potential! Sound too good to be true? It is. And it is likely to be so for many years to come.

What has stirred up all this interest is a process called "digital compression." The basic technology has been developed. But practical implementation is still in the experimental stage, with many different variations being tested. Digital compression can be compared to instant coffee. Coffee processors remove the water, ship only the solids, and the consumer adds back the water before drinking. With digital compression, redundant information in a digital television signal is removed before transmission, then added back on the home television screen before viewing. By this process, as many as 10 channels can be transmitted within the same band-width required for only one channel today.

But 500 is not a magic number. With digital compression, there could be room for 300, 600 or 1,000 channels or more. But will consumers really want that many channels? And will they pay for them? Thus far, every study I've seen indicates there's no overwhelming demand on the part of consumers for more channels. Consumers' main complaint is not the lack of choices, but the cost of service. And additional channels will mean substantially added costs.

And what about interactivity? A limited audience may not be willing to pay for the devices which will make it possible to interact with a television set and again, it is likely to be many years before homes equipped with interactive TV sets provide the critical mass for direct marketers to consider it a viable market.

Meanwhile, there are a number of services which permit interactive electronic direct marketing via personal computers. However, all of them combined haven't come close to the sales success of QVC, which racks-up annual sales well over $1 billion and keeps growing. QVC founder, Joe Segel, points out:

> Text and non-moving pictures won't satisfy the public. Moving images are more appealing than still images, and listening is more appealing than reading. Those are two powerful reasons why every text-based and still-picture-based interactive television experiment in the past has failed. That's also why no computer-terminal-based service has ever generated anywhere near the volume of retail merchandise orders that the televised shopping channels have achieved. To gain maximum acceptance, the visual appearance of interactive services needs to be more television-like than computer-like.

There's also the matter of what John Naisbitt called, "High Tech/ High Touch." With so many parts of our lives involving "high tech," there comes a time when the majority of consumers want the "high touch" of less complicated things. When they get home from technology-loaded jobs and turn on their TV sets, they just want to become passive viewers. Perhaps this partially explains the success of today's "low tech" home video shopping.

As a charter member of the Board of Directors of QVC Network, I had a first-hand opportunity to observe the vast difference between what direct marketing futurists predict and what the public really wants. Sure, QVC took advantage of the new electronic technology. But QVC founder Joe Segel was astute enough to recognize there were two important elements needed to make home video shopping appeal to the marketplace: it had to be *simple* and *common*. Consumers didn't have to learn anything new. Just turn on a TV set and dial a telephone. No complicated keypads, no special buttons to push, no computer or modem to install.

"The appropriate response to technology," Naisbitt said, "is not to stop it, but to accommodate it, respond to it, and shape it." And that's what Joe Segel did at QVC. By taking the basic principles of direct marketing that he had learned in developing The Franklin Mint, and combining them with today's new technology, he captured the fancy and pocketbooks of millions of American consumers, building QVC into a billion dollar direct marketing business.

QVC programming is simple. Each hour, 24 hours a day, a separate category of merchandise is presented. A friendly show host describes each item of merchandise and often has live conversations with viewers, who have an opportunity to ask questions about the items being presented and to tell why they like it. To purchase, viewers simply pick up their phones, dial a toll-free phone number, and talk to a friendly order taker. Everything is simple and common.

This approach reaps great rewards. QVC logs-in thousands of orders in a single hour. When clothing from upscale retailer Saks was presented, QVC sold the entire $570,000 available inventory in a single hour.

Often celebrities join the QVC show hosts to present merchandise which carries their names. TV personality Joan Rivers sold $10 million of costume jewelry in five weekend presentations, and actress Morgan Fairchild sold some $1 million of jewelry in just three hours.

While celebrity presentations add a little extra oomph to presentations, the vast majority of sales are made without them. And QVC doesn't make the mistake of many would-be home shopping programs which put the emphasis on entertainment, rather than on selling. Viewers are never allowed to forget the reason for the programming is to sell merchandise.

This format has been so successful that QVC adds 100,000 new customers each month and well over 50 percent of them become repeat buyers. Amazingly, thousands actually purchase as many as 100 times a year.

This all happened in less than a decade, and certainly represents one of direct marketing's greatest success stories of the 20th Century. There's a lesson to be learned from QVC's success and other things which have been happening in today's world of direct marketing. During the past 50 years, I've seen direct marketing evolve from simple Multigraphed letters and black-and-white catalogs into a potent multi-media powerhouse destined to become increasingly important in the 21st Century.

There are three key direct marketing developments of the 20th Century which I'm convinced are part of the groundwork critical to the continuing success of direct marketing's future. I feel it's important to understand these cornerstones and how they evolved as we rush toward the 21st Century.

The Trend toward Demassification

Cataloging has become a highly specialized business. Today there are over 10,000 consumer mail order specialty catalogs in the U.S., plus thousands more carrying all types of business products. What distinguishes these catalogs of today is how specialized they have become. No matter what personal interests you may have, there's a catalog to serve your wants and desires. Consider just one field—food. There are mail order catalogs specializing in meats, fruit, cheese, nuts, candy, gourmet specialties, cooking utensils, popcorn, caviar, fruitcakes, wine, etc...

Catalogs have gone through a process which American sociologists call "demassification." There was a time when all telephones were black, all refrigerators were white, and teenagers wore the same outfit all day long. Today, however, people everywhere demand choices. Instead of wanting the same things everyone else wants, they want to express their individuality.

Interactivity

Whenever that Information Superhighway is mentioned, the subject of interactivity is almost always included. It is as if interactivity is something new. Actually, interactivity has long been an important element of successful direct marketing, although direct marketers usually call it "involvement."

Long ago, direct marketers discovered that you could get better repsonse by encouraging the customer to become actively involved in a promotion. We adopted techniques like sweepstakes, contests, paste-on stamps, tokens, rub-offs and other involvement devices to make our mailings more interesting and to encourage response.

We created order and inquiry devices which make it easy to respond. And when toll-free telephone service became available, direct marketers were quick to take advantage of this interactive device. For some reason, the proponents of advanced electronic interactive devices seem to have adopted the idea that there's something magic about being able to push a few buttons on a gadget hooked up to a television set or on a home computer in order to respond to an offer. But listen to what Joe Segel of QVC had to say at last fall's Direct Marketing Association Convention in Toronto:

> Everyone knows how to dial a phone and place an order. So, present-day systems are about as simple as they can be. If a new system requires more steps to do esentially the same things, consumers may resist it. It would be to the peril of creative geniuses to forget that people always gravitate towards doing things in the easiest possible way. Recognize that you ahve a secret weapon. The direct marketing industry as it now exists has a unique kind of interactive system utilizing voice recognition software that is infinetely superior to anything that the most talented software engineers or computer manufacturers can produce. It's called the human order entry operator.

Integrated Marketing

"Integrated Marketing" is another of the buzz words we hear so much today—and for some reason the futurists think it's something new. But it's something successful direct marketers discovered years ago. It's just the term that's new. We call it "multimedia promotions." Probably no direct marketer has been more successful in utilizing multimedia than American cataloger Foster & Gallagher. At one time, all of Foster & Gallagher's direct marketing was done through catalogs. But businesses like Breck's Dutch Bulbs and Spring Hill Nurseries were highly seasonal. Off-season catalogs were uneconomical.

So, Foster & Gallagher pioneered in the use of solo mailings and statement and package inserts to build a year-round business. More recently, they've added an extensive outbound telemarketing program. And their Michigan Bulb business makes extensive use of newspaper and magazine advertising. No medium goes unexplored. While the Breck's Spring Hill and other Foster & Gallagher catalogs continue to prosper, the company's on-going growth can be attributed to a well-balanced blend of different media.

Also pioneering multi-media for direct marketing was Omaha Steaks International, another highly seasonal business selling gourmet meat products which in the U.S. are primarily purchased for Christmastime gifts. But Omaha Steaks was turned into a 12-month success with solo mailings and a highly-effective year-around telemarketing program to supplement Christmas season catalogs.

Of all of the 20th Century media to impact direct marketing, the use of the telephone—both inbound and outbound—has had the greatest impact. But for the majority of direct marketers, telemarketing is not a stand-alone marketing medium. Instead, from the very beginning, it had been most often carefully integrated into a multi-media program.

In conclusion, I see three major hurdles to the full adoption of new media technologies in direct marketing, time, management and critical mass.

Time

Time and again, I hear that the amount of time it takes to initiate a search for information and complete a transaction is the main objection to the use of most electronic interactive marketing techniques. While this may be perfectly acceptable to those who approach interactive media as a "hobby," it is definently a stumbling block for those who are content with present methods.

Management

Most people in top management grew up in a "non-interactive" era, and/or are likely to have heard more about interactive failures than about successes. They may have personally watched funds previously budgeted for interactive ventures go down the drain. Therefore, getting managment approval—and consequently adequate budgeting—to embark on interactive marketing, and being able to continue to secure budgeting through sometimes lengthy trial and error periods, can be very difficult.

I'm constantly seeing examples of companies that have decided to put their toe in the interactive marketing waters, only to abandon their projects when great things don't happen immediately. I suspect one of the main reasons for such actions is that many top managements aren't willing to devote personal time to things whose ultimate pay-off is likely to be far down the road.

There are only so many things that can be given"thinking time" in a busy business environment. Just getting top managment in many companies to spend "thinking time" on the company's overall marketing is often difficult enough without getting interactive on management's "thinking" agenda.

Critical Mass

As I stated in the introduction, I see this as the greatest problem that interactive marketers must face. With more and more companies developing a presence on the Internet and through other interactive mediums, the critical mass needed to ensure a profitable return on investment diminishes greatly. Again, the critical mass necessary to constitute a viable business varies. At the present time, the numbers just aren't there for the vast majority of businesses.

SECTION II

Media Tactics
and Techniques
in the
Interactive Age

With the strategic groundwork laid for understanding cybermedia, it is time to turn our attention to specific tactics and interactive marketing vehicles available. The marketer today who is looking for success can choose from an array of media. The Internet is often the first medium that comes to mind, but there are many other choices available. Marketers can also select from old standbys like the telephone, the evolving platform of interactive television or the use of disks, CD-ROM, and kiosks. The organization, presentation, and promotion of electronic media will vary from medium to medium. This section will provide useful suggestions, ideas, and advice on how to move onto the Interactive Superhighway.

Public relations and promotion play a vital role in cybermarketing. Nancy Ruscheinski and Pam Talbot of Edelman PR Worldwide present many practical examples of how this can be done effectively in "Public Relations and Promotion on the Internet: A Thriving and Profitable Partnership." Public relations is the art of developing well-crafted messages, packaging those messages and conveying that information to a wide variety of audiences including consumers, media, and opinion leaders. The World Wide Web is uniquely suited to this process because it can dynamically add depth and scope to promotional efforts.

Why?

Ruscheinski and Talbot stress the importance of integrated efforts that marry offline and online promotion while exploiting the unique strengths of each. They caution that marketers not fall into the *Field of Dreams* mentality of "if we build it, they will come." The launch of a new web site should be treated no differently than the launch of any new product. Marketers should promote the launch aggressively through every medium and vehicle at their disposal. Traditional media should be employed, but the lion's share of the attention should be given to online promotion and marketing. They provide specific insights into the steps to take in order to capture visibility and drive the existing Internet user to your site.

If you've mastered the challenge of bringing people to your Internet site, you have half the battle won. Now, you need to capture their interest. Herschell Gordon Lewis gives no-nonsense advice and several examples of how to do this in "Copywriting for Interactive Media: New Rules of the New Medium." He presents rules for Internet copywriting including "Knock their socks off . . . immediately." The object is to convert a surfer who bounces from site to site into a browser who is interested in what you have to say. Strong copy is needed to compel that browser to pause long enough to begin to interact with the site. The next challenge is to convert that casual browser into a buyer. This can be done by offering "fast, clear, right-now benefits." Copy must be clear with no jargon and no slang. Lewis's prescription is to use shock treatment in your copy approach because photography still lacks the clarity of other media and purchasing options are currently limited to credit cards. He provides many examples of good and bad copy that will allow marketers to see his credos put into action.

With the current avid interest in the Internet other interactive media cannot be overlooked. The interactive kiosk can be an information "vending machine" and technology's answer to the ultimate salesperson. Customers today are more predisposed to use these because automated teller machines and personal computers have helped pave the way. In "Interactive Kiosks in the Retail Environment: What Do Customers Really Need?" Thomas Hutchison discusses in-store interactive kiosks and uses examples of different systems employed in retail music stores to prove how kiosks can be integrated into a marketing program. Hutchison studied kiosk and record listening booth usage to determine how effective systems are in driving sales, providing sales information, and appealing to various groups of respondents. The results provide insights into how to effectively use this interactive technology.

Kiosks exist in public spaces, but other interactive media can provide a more intimate experience. "The New Disk-Based Marketing Communications Tools: Guidelines for Creating Powerful Electronic Catalogs and Presentations" explores disk-based presentations, electronic catalogs, and fax-on-demand as effective sales and marketing tools. Today, the estimated cost of a business-to-business sales call exceeds $275. Companies must explore innovative methods of delivering their message and increasing customer awareness on a more cost-effective basis. Vic Cherubini analyzes each of these tools in terms of features and benefits and provides steps for implementing them. He provides an outline for sales and marketing managers to effectively incorporate new media technologies into their marketing plans.

Earlier Peppers and Rogers made a cogent case for a change in marketing from mass marketing to 1:1 marketing. The importance of understanding your customer and building a relationship with them is paramount both in the consumer and business-to-business worlds. In "Sales Automation: A Modern Business Imperative" Tony Alessandra illustrates the necessity of finding new ways of doing business. Customers are demanding more of their suppliers; and suppliers must have a greater knowledge of their customers' specific needs. A sales automation system has the ability to get, coordinate, and use all of the information necessary to make relationship selling work. He points out that this is "processing and not technology." Companies who make the investment in databased two-way or bidirectional contact management systems must also reengineer the sales process. Salespeople have been the traditional lone wolves and have often kept most communication with the customer to themselves. More and more salespeople need to bring others into the fold to truly get closer to the customer. Alessandra provides checklists that outline how departments and personnel beyond the sales group must be involved in interacting with the sales database. This results in a more robust and truly effective sales force.

In these days of continuing advancements in technology it's easy to overlook the original interactive device—the telephone. Carol Morse Ginsburg reminds us "anyone who thinks that telephone applications are relics of a past age is mistaken. . . . Remember the consumer has a love-affair with the telephone." There is untapped potential available for those who make a renewed commitment to use the medium. In "Interactive Telephone as a Marketing Tool: Using the Telephone to Promote a Product or Service" she provides example after example of how the telephone is being used in combination with print, radio, television, online services, and the Internet. Beyond its use in tandem with other media vehicles there is interactive potential in adjuncts to the phone including 900 numbers, prepaid calling cards, and audiotex. The challenge for marketers is to capitalize on the convergence of the new electronic media and create cohesive and innovative applications.

Tyrone Lam also talks about convergence: Interactive television was "touted as the convergence of the personal computer, the telephone, and the television which would create the ultimate communication tool." But this has not yet happened. One of the brightest stars was the Time-Warner interactive television experiment in Orlando, Florida. The project dazzled marketers and advertising agencies who rushed to participate. That star has fizzled out with Time-Warner recently announcing they would abandon the broad scope of the project and just focus on video-on-demand. "Interactive Television: Broadcasting to Millions—One at a Time" examines the reasons for the current state of affairs. Instead of being a revolutionary process the move to interactive television will be an evolutionary process. In the not-so-distant future PC-based services will expand and help spawn ITV content. PCs suffer from not having true broadcast capabilities to deliver content, video, graphics, and sound and this is something that television can do with ease. The combination and convergence of the two will provide consumers with power and value.

We must keep in mind that in adopting new technology consumers want that new technology to empower them, give them more control, and also save them time and money.

If the technology is also intuitive and sometimes fun, the consumer gets an added benefit. As interactive TV evolves it will fulfill each of these promises. Each household member will be able to create a personal profile, marketing messages will be filtered based upon these profiles, and ultimately the experience will be more personal than it is today. As Tyrone Lam says: "Stay tuned . . . ."

"Anatomy of a Web Advertisement: A Case Study of Zima.com" is a must-read case study of how an Internet site was developed and designed for the alcohol beverage Zima Clearmalt. Charles Marrelli believes that this was the first national consumer packaged good to have a dedicated web site. He provides cogent commentary on graphic considerations and explains why and how users will be attracted to certain designs and turned off by others. You'll understand the importance of a home page, why a FAQ (Frequently Asked Questions) section should be developed, the strategic use of e-mail, what navigation considerations should be made, why frequent updating of content is of paramount importance, and much more.

Marrelli urges marketers to think outside of the box. A site should have many layers and it need not contain only content created about the company and the product or service. He explains the value of hyperlinking or hotlinking to content on other sites. This approach expands the richness and relevance of the site. His insights are invaluable reading for anyone who is thinking of launching a web site or who wants to see if their current site is up to snuff.

CHAPTER

8

Public Relations and Promotion on the Internet

A Thriving and Profitable Partnership

Nancy Ruscheinski
Pam Talbot

Nancy Ruscheinski is the Director of Interactive Solutions at Edelman Public Relations Worldwide, the world's largest independent public relations firm. She created the agency's rapidly growing home page production and promotion business.

Pam Talbot is the President of Edelman Consumer Worldwide, the agency's global consumer marketing practice in more than 30 offices. She is also the chief strategist on the agency's Microsoft consumer business in the U.S.

Here's our utterly biased opinion: if the Internet hadn't come along on its own (with the help of the government and academia), the PR industry would have invented it.

Think about it: public relations is a discipline that specializes in communication. More specifically, it is the art of developing well-crafted messages, packaging those messages and conveying information to a variety of audiences, including consumers, media and opinion leaders.

Never before in the history of communications has there been a vehicle better-suited to this process that the World Wide Web. The ability to customize information for a wide range of niche audiences, the immediacy and currency of the Net, and, most importantly, the democracy of the information on the Net (remember, now everyone can be a publisher as well as a subscriber) demand that it be embraced by the public relations industry as perhaps the most efficient tool we've ever had to get the job done.

Frankly, public relations professionals should be better at communicating on the Internet than anyone else. After all, we're used to communicating complex, layered messages to different audiences. This is not a medium that lends itself to the quick fix, the 30-second spot, the half-page ad—no matter how compelling that spot or ad might be. This is a medium that is fueled by information, and the public relations business is, quite simply, the information business.

PR & the Internet: New Challenges for Today and Tomorrow

At the same time, the Internet has dramatically altered the playing field in terms of how information is disseminated. Several trends have emerged:

First, an increasingly chaotic news and media environment: With the proliferation of "off-line" media (24-hour broadcasting, more magazines, more television channels), audiences are becoming more and more segmented and de-massified, leading to the rise of media grazing. Consumers seek specific pieces of information in the pastures of their own special interests.

Media analysts agree that the Internet has exponentially increased the chaos, breaking down the order of the existing system, but history has shown us that people seek order in chaos. Just as talk radio and talk TV exploded only to be reevaluated by the public, we believe that the

Internet will develop its own sense of order. The truth is, we all want some editing and structure, and we believe that the Internet, too, will develop its own structure, allowing clear roles for influencers while allowing for greater participation. Just as people currently respond to multiple influences in their decision-making—from the experts to their next door neighbors—people will continue to evaluate both the sources of the information and the quality of that information on the Internet.

For public relations, the challenge is to identify the new influencers and the new ways of reaching those influencers in a "Net society," as well as to insinuate ourselves more forcefully into the ongoing Internet dialogue. And, we contend that people will eventually gravitate toward the organized sites like Microsoft's Slate e-zine, HotWired, and others. That's where the influencers—and the ongoing Internet dialogue— will manifest themselves, and that's where we need to be on behalf of our clients.

Second, the impact of the Internet on "traditional" media: With consumers now able to gather exactly the information they want when they want it, new problems face general interest magazines and newspapers. Each consumer can now be his or her own "editor" and choose only the pieces of information that are of particular relevance. But remember that, historically, new media does not replace old. It simply adds another layer; thus, we believe that these traditional information sources will remain, but that people will draw on the information in different ways. For public relations practitioners, the challenge will be to create information that is highly desired or to integrate existing information with other highly desirable content.

Third, the unreachable consumer: If the consumer is able to structure his or her media diet, how does public relations reach that individual? How does it "force feed" information to a public that doesn't care enough to seek it out or doesn't know enough to actively search for something that might be of interest? Our challenge is to create opportunities and environments that stimulate interest, enthusiasm, and relevance, propelling a consumer to seek out more information either on or off the Net. Just as we've learned in recent years, companies and their products need to be where their consumers are, versus expecting consumers to come to them.

Where does all of this leave public relations? Clearly, the way we do our business is changing, but we believe that the role of PR is becoming more rather than less important. Just as we changed the way we did business when television came along, the Internet offers PR another realm—potentially a more exciting realm—to interact with and to convince consumers. The hunger for information on the Internet and for rich content and dialogue make it the ideal medium for public relations, with our role expanding from that of "intermediary messenger" (with the message ultimately filtered and delivered by the media) to the primary messenger.

New Roles

As we see it, there are two clear-cut emerging roles for the PR professional in the Internet Age, two new ways of doing what we've been doing for decades: communicating client messages.

The first role is to become the *content creators* for our clients. Developing marketing-driven web sites for clients is the logical next step in the communications continuum. In the eighties, the solution to a client marketing challenge might have been the production and distribution of a value-added consumer brochure that showcased the product in a positive light and also provided a wealth of related tips and techniques that a consumer would need and want. We can take that solution to the next level on the Internet by creating brand-specific web sites that engage the consumer and offer the opportunity to interact with the brand, while obtaining value-added information.

The second role that PR practitioners should be carving out for themselves is to do public relations and promotion for client web sites that already exist. A favorite saying in the Internet industry is, "If we built it, will they come?" meaning, does creating a compelling web site ensure that consumers will visit it? And the answer is a resounding "no." A web site simply cannot succeed without an ongoing aggressive marketing and promotion campaign behind it, and PR is the discipline that's ideally suited to do just that.

If public relations professionals seize the above two opportunities, they'll find that not only are their clients' overall business and marketing needs being better served, but also that the Internet can be an extremely profitable and rewarding business "partner."

Creating Content for the Web: The Role of the PR Professional

We'd like to walk through a few examples of web sites that respond to the new marketing and public relations environment. The goals of these sites have been diverse, with target audiences ranging from children to veterinarians to professional photographers to cooking enthusiasts. One element that these sites have shared, though, is an understanding of the tremendous potential for relationship marketing on the World Wide Web.

A Native American saying is especially apropos here: "Tell me and I'll forget. Show me and I may not remember. Involve me and I'll understand." That, in essence, is the beauty of the Internet: Like no medium that has come before it, the Internet has the ability to truly involve the user and to help the user reach new heights of understanding that simply aren't possible with a brochure or a television advertisement.

Smart marketers recognize this fact and know that the World Wide Web is the ultimate platform for engaging consumers and involving them directly with a brand or a product or a corporate service. Because it facilitates two-way dialogue and one-to-one communication between a consumer and a corporation, the Internet can truly be relationship marketing and brand-image building at its best.

VISA

The first example, Visa site (http://www.enw.com/visakids), shows how a successful "off-line" public relations program—a contest encouraging children to artistically depict an Olympic sport of the future—can be re-created as an online extension of that program.

The target audience for this online version of "Visa Olympics of the Imagination" was children, their teachers and their parents. The goal of the site was not only to drive entries for the contest but to post multilingual contest rules (click on your country's flag to receive the rules in your native language) as well as profiles and artwork from previous winners. The site was an extremely effective way to communicate the excitement and logistics of the contest to a worldwide audience. Doing the same task "off-line" with printed materials in multiple languages would have been cost-prohibitive.

The Visa example is particularly useful for the public relations industry because it demonstrates the wealth of opportunities for taking traditional public relations programs like contests, brochures, and educational programs and bringing them to life on the Internet. While Visa already had an exceptionally well-done corporate web site, the company saw the value in creating a separate, dedicated site (hyperlinked to the corporate site, naturally) targeted to children to enhance a specific marketing campaign.

BAYER ANIMAL HEALTH

Public relations has always been instrumental in generating awareness of and demand for new products. The World Wide Web is a particularly dynamic tool for adding depth and scope to a new product launch, as the launch for Bayer Animal Health's new flea control product, Advantage, shows.

Because of the potential for interactivity on the Web, a new product launch supported online can become much more of an aggressive outreach program. With Advantage, a product sold exclusively through veterinarians, the plan was to create a place where consumers could not only learn about flea control in a fun and entertaining way (no small challenge), but could also educate themselves about the product attributes, enabling them to ask for the product by name at their veterinarian's office.

Along with all of the expected product FAQ's (frequently asked questions) about efficacy along with information about how to get the product and a section exclusively for veterinarians, we added some unexpected extras designed to engage the consumer and create a memorable experience with the brand: an interactive Flea Index enabling users to pinpoint when flea season starts and ends in their city; a "Flea Free-For-All" section featuring a Flea I.Q. Test and a "Find the Flea (and Zap Him!)" game; a "testimonial" from a dog who uses the product; and an "Ask the Bayer Vet" e-mail component.

Because Bayer understood the importance of a strategic, totally integrated marketing campaign to launch both the product and the site, including prominent advertising and promotion of the URL (which, incidentally, is http://www.nofleas.com), exhaustive registration of the site with online directories and search engines, and postings to numerous pet newsgroups on the Web, the site was extraordinarily successful within even the first twelve hours of operation, during which it netted 30,000 hits and 600 e-mail inquiries from consumers. That's the power of interactive marketing.

Marketing and Promoting Client Web Sites: The Role of the PR Professional

The single most critical element in determining the success of a web site has nothing to do with graphics, VRML or Shockwave programming, or high bandwidth. It has to do with marketing and promoting a company's URL as creatively and extensively as you market a company's products or services. In fact, launching a new web site should be treated no differently from launching a new product. Although it's now relatively easy to do a search on the Internet to find a site of interest, companies shouldn't fool themselves into believing that consumers will simply find their site and come flocking to it.

After all, it's easy to find a product in the supermarket—but would you leave it to consumers to seek out your product on their own? Of course not. You market and promote your product aggressively through every medium at your disposal so that consumers will seek it out. Web sites are no different and should be marketed in much the same fashion.

An effective web site marketing campaign requires a two-tiered approach, utilizing both online and off-line marketing techniques. Online marketing consists of a variety of tactics designed to drive the existing Internet user universe to your site. This is a vitally important audience and shouldn't be overlooked. After all, you're preaching to the converted when you're talking to users already on the Net, and all the off-line advertising in the world might help lead your horse to water, but it won't necessarily make it drink. This may seem obvious, but it's an important fact that many companies have learned the hard way. Users who are already on the Internet are the people most likely to access your web site, so don't overlook them in your zeal to target the more traditional universe of consumers who read magazines and newspapers. They may come to the Net eventually, but it's the current online audience that should receive the lion's share of your attention.

What opportunities are there to promote your web site online? Lots of them, beginning with newsgroup postings. Newsgroups are special interest groups that congregate on the Web to share questions and advice about a particular topic, whether it's pets or food or animal rights or AIDS research. Now numbering more than 19,000, these newsgroups, which post messages to online "bulletin boards" that can be viewed by just about anyone surfing the Net, can be a powerful adversary or a formidable foe to marketers.

Newsgroups have special protocols and rules for participation and woe betide the marketer who brashly attempts to infiltrate a newsgroup to promote a product. The best approach is to learn about a newsgroup of interest by observing quietly for awhile, reading posted messages and responses, and learning about the "Netiquette" of the group.

Once you've done that, it's perfectly acceptable to post messages that have a legitimate place in a newsgroup, for example, messages to food newsgroups on behalf of web sites like the Butterball Turkey Company (http://www.Butterball.com), Land O'Lakes (http://www.landolakes.com) and the American Dairy Association (http://www.realbutter.com). Newsgroups are hungry for information on particular topics, so if companies have recipes on their web sites that would appeal to, for example, the alt.fatfree newsgroup or the alt.food.ice-cream newsgroup, we post messages to those newsgroups accordingly, incorporating live "links" to web sites within the posted messages. This is an extremely effective way to drive traffic to a web site, yet it's surprisingly overlooked by most marketers.

Other online marketing techniques include registering your client's URL with Internet search engines and directories. With more than 250 of these indexes now on the Web, it's no small task to do so, but you'll be richly rewarded if you go through all of the necessary steps (and each directly has its own protocols for inclusion) to submit your URL to at least the most significant ones, including Yahoo!, Netscape, Infoseek, AltaVista, and Lycos. The majority of Internet users find their information and identify web sites of interest through these search engines and directories, so you can't go wrong by ensuring your URL is prominently featured.

Another tactic for driving traffic to your web site is via strategic hotlinks to other sites. Look for sites that attract audiences that appeal to you, then e-mail the Webmasters of those sites to see if a mutual hotlink to/from each other's sites is viable. When the Visa Olympics of the Imagination web site (cited earlier) was established, links were provided to some 25 other sites for children and 40 other sites for teachers. Most were happy to oblige us with reciprocal links, again, driving desirable, targeted traffic to the Visa site.

One of the most effective ways to market your web site to the online community is via online promotions, contests, sweepstakes and give-aways. The Net culture is one that flocks to the "freebie," and free offers or the opportunity to win prizes are enthusiastically sought after on the Web. When the Butterball web site was launched in early November, the site's theme was "How to Prepare a Picture-Perfect Turkey." To create excitement around the launch of the site and drive immediate traffic, it was important to publicize the fact (via newspaper "blurbs" and postings to newsgroups) that the first 1,000 visitors to the site would receive a free disposable camera from Fuji Film USA for photographing their picture-perfect birds. The response was swift and thorough; the prizes were gone within the week.

As effective as online marketing can be, off-line marketing is also needed to round out an effective web site promotional campaign. This is where traditional public relations tactics come into play, such as mass mailings to media (a simple postcard featuring a URL is often sufficient), pursuing site reviews in trade and mainstream publications, and staging high-impact launch events. When Bristol-Myers Squibb's "Women's Link" online cyberclub for women was launched, it was important to get the buy-in of women's health, beauty and fashion media, since those topics were prominently featured within the site. The web site was literally brought to life at a memorable launch event at Bristol-Myers Squibb headquarters, with real rooms depicting each of the cyber-rooms and a variety of experts on hand to teach journalists how to navigate the site. Some 60 journalists from 40 publications came by for "surfing lessons," and the resulting site reviews in the traditional women's publications were superb.

One caveat: remember that in today's uncluttered Web environment, simply launching a new site is no longer news. A year ago, simply announcing the fact that Company X had a web site ensured that a lot of journalists would visit the site and mention the URL. Today, though, new web sites are launched by the thousands each month, and capturing the attention of the increasingly jaded media with news of a new web site requires a more creative approach and, of course, compelling content.

Last Gasp

PR, promotion, and the Internet: it's a dynamic and evolving relationship that can be profitable and rewarding for PR practitioners and clients alike. Learning the new rules (which at times don't even seem to be in the same language!) can be daunting, but it's a necessity. This is where the communications industry is heading, so anyone who believes the World Wide Web is simply a fad is wearing blinders that can be extremely hazardous to one's career. Our advice to the novice? Jump in and learn—or better yet, ask your kids to show you how. The opportunities for using this vehicle to enhance your current marketing campaigns are simply enormous, and you can't begin to take advantage of them until you're comfortable with the medium. Remember, no one knew what to make of the funny-looking radio that became known as the television, either—and look at the kind of marketing communications victories we've been able to achieve with that medium. Now imagine consumers being able to interact with the TV—to talk back to you right through the TV, in the middle of your advertisement—and you've begun to grasp the awesome power of the Internet.

CHAPTER 9

Copywriting for Interactive Media

New Rules for the New Medium

Herschell Gordon Lewis

Herschell Gordon Lewis is regarded as the world's leading authority on writing copy that sells. He has written more than a dozen books on the subject, including *Selling on the Net* (with Robert Lewis), *Sales Letters That Sizzle,* and *The World's Greatest Direct Mail Sales Letters* (with Carol Nelson). He is a regular columnist for such publications as *Direct Marketing Magazine, Direct, Catalog Age,* and *SELLING.* He is President of Communicomp, a full-service direct response agency based in Plantation, Florida.

As the twentieth century draws to an end, a new challenge to advertising creative teams defies previous rules of communication.

Advertising on the Internet is a mutant. It combines the targeting specificity of classified advertising . . . the need for aggressive seeking-out of Yellow Pages . . . the instant visual excitement of television . . . the quick-change potential of radio . . . the taut copy discipline of catalogs . . . and the romance of space advertising.

Correction: It combines those elements if it's done properly. If it isn't, advertising on the Internet combines the arrogance of an egomaniac . . . the dryness of an unwanted sermon . . . the frustration of pay-TV when you realize the movie is dull or one you've seen before . . . and the hard-to-find whereabouts of a master spy.

I'll explain that last reference: Reaching an advertiser through one of the on-line services marketplaces isn't difficult. Reaching an advertiser who has a "home page" can be a test of determination and skill. For example, the Internet address of one printer is:

http:/www.ais.net/dppc

Not quite as mnemonic as 1-800-FLOWERS, is it?

The point, and the reason the Internet at this point is closer to the Yellow Pages than to television: To reach an advertiser, the prospective customer has to:

1. Pay a monthly time-limited Internet access fee.

2. Have at least a passing familiarity with computer use.

3. Keep at hand a strange, arcane combination of letters representing the specific Internet address.

If you conclude that the copywriter also should be adept at creating a *referral* message (to familiarize prospects with the Internet address) in other media, you're right. If you conclude that the very nature of a referral in a newspaper or magazine ad or on a CD-ROM or even a refrigerator magnet means we have a "two-step" conversion instead of a simple transaction, you're right.

An additional flusterer: The image of the Internet walks the tightwire between wild "hype" in publications dedicated to the supremacy of electronic media and total disdain in publications dedicated to their own self-preservation. In fact, the medium deserves neither.

Logical Limitations, Logical Expectations

The Internet sprang upon public consciousness so suddenly that some advertisers replaced their usual dour skepticism with awestruck idol-worship. They fell victim to the self-devouring *"That which is different equals that which is better"* cult. Because it was new, they felt *any* message would shake the cosmos. They were wrong on three counts:

1. Their cosmos was too small.
2. Their browsers weren't valid buyers, but "groupies."
3. They didn't know how to combine medium and message.

The copywriter who assumes what works in other media will work on the Internet *may* be right. Chances are, if it's a classified ad that pulled and pulled and pulled, it will work on the Internet. Chances are, if it's a rewrite of a four-page direct mail letter, it won't pull on the Internet. I'll tell you why.

The Cardinal Rule of Internet Copywriting

One of the venerable rules of force-communication becomes the primary litany of a copywriter who wants his or her message to accomplish the three sequential goals that cause the cash register to ring:

1. The reader has to find the message.
2. The reader has to comprehend the message.
3. The reader has to respond to the message.

The three goals are simple, you say? Obvious, you say? Truisms, you say? Wonderful.

Explain, then, the deadness of this copy—the first that meets the eye—when a browser fights his way (and that's what he has to do, with the delays in graphics and staggering multiplicity of sites) to an advertiser's nest:

Welcome to The Sony Electronics Consumer products. We are pleased to present over three hundred of our products to you, and provide a comprehensive listing of features which you can use to familiarize yourself with our products. We plan to expand upon our offerings in the near future to make your visit even more enjoyable, as well as to provide you with additional information. In the meantime please feel free to browse our digital catalog.

This copy exemplifies the difference between a salesperson and a clerk. Copywriters who know what motivates readers are salespeople. Describers who say, "Here it is . . . you decide whether you're interested or not," are clerks.

So we have The Cardinal Rule of Internet Copywriting:

Specifics outsell generalizations.

If we bother to analyze why the message—*the very first message we get from this advertiser*—is flat, colorless, and with a zero impact-quotient, we have lots of ammunition. The first sentence marches in place. "We are pleased to present over three hundred of our products to you" suggests work on our part, sorting through a pile. " . . . Provide a comprehensive listing of features which you can use to familiarize yourself with our products" is slide-rule writing, analytical instead of inspirational, without a single motivator in its multisyllabic innards.

You may think "We plan to expand upon our offerings in the near future to make your visit even more enjoyable, as well as to provide you with additional information" isn't execrable copywriting. If that's what you think, I hope you're my competitor. In fact, the copy is worse than execrable, because it suggests that whatever we see now, we ll have better pickings later on.

And this leads us to. . .

The Second Rule of Internet Copywriting

Second only to The Cardinal Rule is this one, just as logical, just as profound, just as significant, and just as easy to implement if you're a salesperson and not just a clerk:

Offer fast, clear, right-now benefits.

Obvious? Not to this marketer, who apparently doesn't even know a far more primitive rule of communications . . . one so old it goes back to the abacus, let alone computers:

Present tense outsells future tense.

The Second Rule of Internet Copywriting and the ancient Present Tense rule are congruent, because dealing in the future is Micawber-like—good things are going to happen tomorrow. Prospective buyers have had their cynicism hardened by generations of wild claims by television advertisers and politicians and by "once-you're-out-of-the-store-it's-out-of-date" obsolescence of computers and software. They don't want to wait until tomorrow. Why should they? Tomorrow they may not be here. Tomorrow *you* may not be here. Tomorrow a competitor might make a better offer.

(This is another reason why the promise of fast delivery increases response and the disclaimer "Allow 4-6 weeks for delivery," however valid, depresses response.)

The Third Rule of Internet Copywriting

The Third Rule of Internet Copywriting, like the first two, separates salespeople from clerks.

Salespeople know how to generate and stimulate the buying impulse. A key generator/stimulator is:

> Knock their socks off . . . immediately.

Direct marketing copywriters know that subtlety doesn't work. They know that sneaking up on the reader doesn't work. Multiply that by ten times and you have the Internet ambience, where the combination of an impatience-potential and unrelieved co-existence of competitors will have that mouse popping away in another direction before you get to your much-delayed point. Fire a big gun to start the battle and you might score a hit. Waiting until you see the whites of their eyes might have your own eyes rolled back in your bloodied head.

WHAT MIGHT BE A PROPER HEADING?

So a proper heading for an Internet advertisement might be one of these:

- Today only: $50 off our best-seller!
- Price slashed for browsers only: 28.8 modem, $119!

- Call this private number for Internet customers only and get our current issue free!

- *Today's closeout superbargains—first come, first served.*

- 5% discount for each mispelled word you find in this message.

That last one misspells *Misspelled* deliberately, to get them started. Remember, the reader wants benefits now. She's already seen and recognized one, so how difficult can it be to find the others. While she's finding them, she's not only reading your message, but she's actually enjoying herself because you ve transformed a hard-boiled sales pitch into an interactive game.

What do all those samples have in common? No, it isn't that so many of them use final exclamation points, although many "Benefit right now" headings are (and should be) exclamatory.

(A parenthetical point: One exclamation point at a time, please. Two exclamation points are not only sophomoric; they actually weaken each other, because the reader becomes aware that they're a device and penetrates our ploy.)

What these headings—and the hundreds you'll discover as you fight for position on the Internet have in common is immediate gratification, the "Open Me Now!" cry that gets an answer when mild pleas or quietly dignified logic goes not just unrequited but unnoticed.

If They Can't Set the VCR Timer, Can They Surf with Us?

A 1995 survey points up two problems marketers face when establishing a presence on the Internet. First, 80 percent of respondents answered "No" when asked if they want to surf the Internet. Second, among women 88 percent answered "No." This makes the medium questionable as a logical target for many, many items that find comfortable homes in traditional media.

As this book is published, we still can generate an excuse: The medium is new, and those who use it for shopping are computer superliterate. As a few years roll past us, the level will drop to the computer literate . . . then the semi-literate . . . then everybody.

Except: It hasn't happened with videocassette recorders. And whether the density of 28,800-baud modem-equipped computers will ever equal the market penetration of VCRs is a question it's simply too soon to answer.

The astute copywriter gears his copy for clarity, no matter who the target is. That way, more people might be tempted to dip a toe in the surf. The "digit-head" approach to copy, loaded with arcane and unexplained initials and jargon, will kill off the timid, the less-than-enthusiastic critics, and the first-timers whose own uncertainty doesn't need reinforcing.

The Communicator Arrogance *Syndrome and Its Conqueror:* The Clarity Commandment

Even in its infancy the Internet has spawned an unpleasant cadre of copywriters—totally computer-literate and contemptuous of those who aren't. They succumb to The Communicator Arrogance Syndrome: "If you don't understand what I'm saying and how to respond, the hell with you."

A caution: If you're tempted to aim your message in a narrow direction, first ask yourself whether your ideal target matches that direction. A successful commercial message *of any type* conforms to this Great Law:

> Effective force-communication reaches, at the lowest possible cost, the most people who can and will buy what you have to sell.

(The "lowest possible cost" inclusion isn't a suggestion to underproduce a message; rather, it's the suggestion to avoid *over*producing a message.)

So if what you're selling is computer-related—as so many early Internet offers are—you're on reasonably safe ground assuming that most people who can and will buy what you have to sell are your confrères. If you're selling flowers for Mother's Day and ignore that great law, you're costing yourself some orders you otherwise would have had.

The move to a point at which Internet advertising can be, to hybridize a computer term, reader-friendly is a logical anticipation. More exciting is the Internet as the best and easiest way to establish an international marketplace. And an international marketplace means the writer has to pay extraordinary attention to The Clarity Commandment:

When you choose words and phrases for force-communication, clarity is paramount. Don't let any other component of the communications mix interfere with it.

The moment your message has the opportunity of reaching beyond the bounds of your own country, take the vow: No jargon. No argot. No slang.

Some of the phrases I've seen on the Internet—obviously attempts to project a casual, reader-friendly image: "You'll be a happy camper if . . ."; "Yes, Virginia, there is a Santa Claus"; "Don't be jerked around by. . ."; "A Grand Slam Home Run!" To browsers in other countries, these can be as indecipherable as "Yes, we have no bananas."

Closer to Classifieds than to Catalogs

Catalog companies are prime Internet advertisers, and with good reason. Not only must they be aware of what their competitors are doing, but they also logically embrace a medium that allows them to make copy and price changes in an instant.

Traditional printed catalogs generate orders from two sources:

1. Those who chance upon the catalog, see something they like, and order;

2. Those who, while ordering one item, page through the catalog and decide to order a second item totally unrelated to the first.

Both these advantages are "iffy" in the Internet because the Internet more closely parallels classified or Yellow Pages advertising than catalogs. The browser has to enter a key word. It parallels looking for homes for sale or classic cars or office equipment in the classified pages. If I'm looking for a loft to rent and you're offering a terrific bargain on Jeep Grand Cherokees, we'll never see each other.

That's why headings and greetings are crucial not only to the success of Internet catalogs but to their basic visibility.

How Does Internet Catalog Copywriting Differ?

In theory—and, usually, in practice—Internet catalog copy doesn't differ at all from its paper cousins.

But this might be a mistake based on the oversimplified rationalization that a catalog is a catalog, in whatever medium it appears. It isn't, and I'll start a major argument with the "Different = better" cult by telling you why.

Let's suppose you're browsing or surfing or for that matter gawking. Are you truly in a buying mood? . . . Or are you enjoying the novelty of the medium, the way new television owners watched wrestling and Frankie Darro movies in the 1950s because the medium was the message?

The gap between browsers and customers is ocean-wide in the world of printed catalogs and planet-wide in the universe of electronic catalogs. To convert an Internet browser to a customer, shock treatment is in order, for two reasons:

1. Photographs, at this point, in no way parallel in clarity even a coarse 85-line screen.

2. Orders, except for "pay when you're satisfied" offers, demand a credit card. No checks. No company purchase orders. Because abuses can be rampant, often a call-back to verify the order gives the customer's creeping case of Buyer's Remorse the opportunity to cancel.

Enthusiasm and the Electronic Edge

So enthusiasm has to permeate the copy. Here s the copy for an attaché case, offered by a well-known cataloger. I wasn't able to check it against the printed catalog, but I assume it's identical because it typifies copy in the printed catalog:

Lighthouse Attache

The Lighthouse Attache is our lightest and sportiest, yet it's still plenty tough. Made of rugged vinyl-backed nylon cloth, it weighs just 10 oz. We sew it with bound and welted seams that won't give out on you, and the fabric gives, unlike hard-sided attaches. Whatever your line of work, its 10 almost infinitely adaptable interior pockets are sure to provide a place for most all your portable office needs. Its roomy exterior pocket has space for important last-minute files. Useful umbrella and key holders; carrying strap, luggage tag included. Made in USA. 17 _" x 13 _" x 3 _".

Colors: Dark Burgundy, Black, Charcoal, Hunter, Classic Navy, Olive Khaki, Regal Navy.

SKU #2869-9M99

$42.50

For a holiday (Father's Day) promotion, the company changed the pitch entirely, four weeks before the holiday to introduce and play up personalization that gives cachet to a gift:

> FREE MONOGRAMMING on the [NAME OF COMPANY] Original Attaché.
> A great gift for Dads and new Graduates!
> Our Attache is made of rugged 18 oz. cotton canvas that ll handle all the rough stuff you put it through. For extra durability we bind the inner seams. Inside are a bunch of pockets for stashing your essentials—files, books, calculator, pens, you name it!
> It's made in our own Midwest shops. But lately it seems, we've been making them a little faster than we're moving them . . .
> Have we got a deal for you! For a limited time, we'll monogram our attaché with your name (maximum of 10 letters) or initials (maximum of 3 letters) free of charge. Made in USA. 17-1/2" × 13" × 3-1/2".
> Monogram styles available: Script initials, Side Block Initials, Diamond Initials, Block Name or Initials, Circle Initials, Greek Letters, Double Diamond.
> Colors available: Charcoal, Hunter, Dark Burgundy, Stone Brown, Classic Navy, Black, Olive Drab
> SKU #2915-3M9x
> $42.50

See the difference? And while you're at it, see the edge an electronic catalog has over a printed catalog? No printed catalog can change copy "on a dime" to fit a short-period selling opportunity. While they were at it, this creative team also eliminated that blah phrase "all your portable office needs." They can't decide whether *attaché* and *initials* should be capitalized or not. And why they keep "you," as they should, but abandon "Dad" and "the Graduate" as possible targets for a gift-buy is a mystery, but they adapted their copy to the four-week period before Father's Day, adding a factor that injects logic to a gift-buying decision.

The category heading became more salesworthy, too. Instead of "Attache Case," it was "FREE MONOGRAMMING on Attache." (No accent marks or fractions yet in this marketplace.)

A coffee company faced a different problem. This was one of their Internet product descriptions:

> THE BETTER BLADE GRINDER
> Our exclusive blade grinder grinds evenly with its unique sloped chamber that spins beans throughout the chamber, resulting in a uniform grind.
> Applicable sales tax will automatically be added to your order.
> SKU #111186
> *$19.95*

What was the problem, aside from using variations of the word "grind" three times in one sentence? One of being able to show the item properly. The "sloped chamber" remains a mystery. So does the size of the item. So does the whole concept of "blade grinder," which might have a science-fiction overtone to those who don't know the terminology.

Pros, Cons, and a Not-Too-Cloudy Crystal Ball

Because an Internet browser has to use a "mouse" to reveal copy longer than a handful of lines, and because illustrations aren't as yet remotely comparable to those in conventional printing processes, the Internet marketer is best off promoting items that lean on (a) timeliness; (b) huge bargain; (c) quick availability; (d) closeouts. Every one of these—especially in a gigantic marketplace with many thousands of addresses—demands copy that shouts, not whispers.

A more profound reason to shout is the time-factor. Most Internet access sources charge a flat monthly fee against a specific number of hours. If the first impression doesn't generate a "Wow!" response, your offer—no matter how attractive you think it is—encounters the danger of browser-abandonment. (As advertisers develop ways to circumvent the cost factor—the way a furniture store will pay taxicab fare to its premises—this problem will diminish.)

The best service a copywriter can provide for the entire medium is to help the Internet develop an image of hot deals . . . right-at-the-moment offers that have just come up and will disappear before they could make their way to other media.

This opinion may distress writers whose view of their profession is more exalted than realistic. It may annoy Internet-hypers who believe the entire world shares their spirit of adventure. It may outrage disciples of the "That which is different equals that which is better" cult.

But—again, in my opinion—it will please advertisers who keep score not by their personal ego-satisfaction but by the number of times the cash register rings.

And getting the cash register to ring is what effective copywriting is supposed to do, isn't it?

Interactive Kiosks
in the
Retail Environment

What Do Customers Really Need?

Thomas W. Hutchison

Thomas W. Hutchison is currently a faculty member in the Department of Recording Industry in the College of Mass Communication at Middle Tennessee State University. His research and consulting efforts include consumer analyses for Geffen Records, including projects on the artists White Zombie, Peter Case, Billy Walker, Jr., Sonic Youth, Weezer, Hole, and many other acts. He has also conducted bounceback card and focus group research for Polydor/ Nashville Records and Sony Music/Nashville.

The latest rage in automated retailing is the interactive information kiosk, strategically placed in high-traffic areas of retail stores and accessible to consumers. This information "vending machine" is technology's answer to the ultimate salesperson, armed with a depth of product knowledge and information that overshadows even the most knowledgeable of sales clerks. Multimedia kiosks are designed to offer an increased level of customer service, replacing sales clerks for some tasks and thus reducing overhead. Additionally, kiosks have shown some success in generating incremental sales which would not be achieved through traditional marketing efforts. The kiosks must provide one or both of these services to be cost effective and meet with success in the marketplace.

Instrumental to the success of these systems is whether the presence of the machines will save enough money on sales help or generate enough incremental sales to offset the cost of the machines. Achieving this goal has been made easier by the reduction of initial costs for installation as the price of the technology falls.

Additionally, acceptance of the machines by consumers provides the vital link in determining ultimate success. Early pilot projects met with mixed success as lack of attractiveness and complexity of the machines discouraged all but the most technologically inclined customers: response times were too slow, touchscreens broke, the kiosks were not maintained and updated, and the graphics were lacking. Kiosks were also misapplied in situations which were not suitable for the service, such as placing travel information kiosks in hotels after the travelers had completed their travel itineraries. There were other problems as well. A real estate kiosk called "HomeSight" was tested and abandoned in 1986 due to high costs of entry and lack of customer interest (Wiesendanger, 1991). In 1989, Sears tested and scrapped a project involving 10 "Gift Sender" kiosks in its Chicago-area stores. That same year, Proctor and Gamble tested and then abandoned computerized information kiosks in supermarkets. The success or lack of success is tied to return on investment. The cost of installing the kiosks must be offset by cost savings or incremental sales (Bredin, 1993). Current costs of kiosks are estimated at about $10,000 apiece (Bredin, 1993), however, some estimates put the costs from several thousand dollars to $100,000 or more (Wiesendanger, 1991). Other estimates range from $4,000 to $16,000 each (Muldoon, 1985).

The early failures have prompted firms to re-evaluate the role of kiosks in the retail environment. The acceptance of automated teller machines and personal computers lowers the barriers and predisposes consumers to rely on computer-operated machines for business information and transactions. "To be successful, in-store media must develop new technologies designed to make the shopping trip easier and more enjoyable" (DeNitto, 1993). Reduction in development costs and vastly improved technologies make the kiosks once again attractive to retailers. As competition increases, "retail will likely be one of the most technologically leading industries of the next decade as it becomes increasingly information-intense" (Bob Martin, Executive VP/Information Systems, Wal-Mart).

In-store Interactive Kiosks

Kiosks are simply electronic information centers (Muldoon, 1985). Each has a television screen which displays graphics and menus. Kiosks have either a self-contained computer with multimedia capabilities, or may be online with a mainframe computer. The stand-alone kiosks, which are the most abundant, are personal computers (PCs) with videodisc or CD-ROM disc systems providing the graphics and database information (*Chain Store Age Executive,* 1992). A one-videodisc system can hold the equivalent of a 108,000-page catalog (Muldoon, 1985). In most cases, the user interacts with the system via touch-screen technology that IBM and other companies have been refining since 1980 (Hume, 1992). The cost of the touch screen has decreased to about $1,000 (as of 1992), down several thousand dollars from just a few years ago. The overall decrease in computing costs and increase in multimedia capabilities have transformed the once-mundane black-and-white text kiosks into a pleasant interactive entertainment experience.

As the problems have been addressed, acceptance of these user-friendly kiosks by shoppers has increased. Schwartz (1992) remarks: "Americans are ready to retrieve information and order products via computer kiosks" (p. 122).

The goal of such kiosks is to provide an increase in level of service at a reduced cost to the retailer. Reilly (1993) states that the biggest complaint of consumers buying in a traditional in-store environment is a lack of knowledgeable sales help. "Kiosks are very often much more helpful than salespeople" (Muldoon, 1985, p. 23). The sheer volume of product categories and brands has made it difficult for salespeople to keep abreast of all product information, as workers can only memorize a limited amount of product and pricing information (Hume, 1992; Schwartz, 1992). In today's market, consumers are more sophisticated and informed. "They want as much information as possible before making a buying decision" (Wiesendanger, 1991, p. 42). Since the kiosk, with its enormous database, has all the answers, the customer's frustration level is reduced (Muldoon, 1985). Imperative in developing the kiosks is the need to anticipate the realm of possible consumer questions and requests for information and to provide that information in an easily accessible manner.

Diffusion Level of Interactive Kiosks

In 1985, Muldoon (1985) estimated that 4,500 electronic kiosks were then in use by retailers. Muldoon forecasted an installed base of 113,000 by 1990. More recent estimates of the diffusion level figure 62,000 kiosks operating at the end of 1992, with 40,000 new units being installed in 1993. By 1996, it has been estimated that 2 million systems will be in use, making them more common than gasoline pumps (*Business Week*, 1992). The latest estimates, however, predict a more realistic installed base of 358,000 by 1997 (Weiss, 1995).

Two-thirds of the interactive kiosks are in retail locations, with the other 33 percent serving tourists in hotels, airports and convention centers. Retailers have been some of the first major users of multimedia projects (Chandler, 1992). Exposure to automated teller machines (ATMs) in the 1980s has predisposed customers to accept the use of the systems (Muldoon, ibid, Weiss, 1995). Research conducted on the users of one kiosk system reveals that more than 80 percent of the users said they would recommend the systems to others (Chandler, 1992).

Examples of the use of such systems include Sears, which is spending $7 million for 6,000 kiosks to handle customer catalog orders and inquire about credit. K-Mart is testing interactive "Information Centers" for home electronics and automotive departments (*Chain Store Age Executive*, 1992). Minnesota Twins baseball fans are lured to a kiosk showing game highlights on a video screen. Once drawn in, the fan can use the screen to order tickets to the games, even previewing the view of the field from the selected seats before purchasing the tickets, all of which is handled at the kiosk (Higgins, 1993). The BrowseStation™ allows video rental customers to preview clips from 700 videotapes before making a selection from the automated vending dispenser

(Higgins, 1993). MusicSource™ operates a database kiosk loaded with sheet music data for 23,000 songs (Greenleaf, 1993). The "Instant Sheet Music Kiosks" print sheet music on demand, saving inventory and shipping costs.

Kiosks in Retail Record Stores

Interactive kiosks serve several functions, from product information, to media previewing, to actual ordering and delivery of the product. In retail record stores and record departments in discount stores, interactive kiosks are projected to serve some of the information functions of:

1. Song or artist identification
2. References to other works by the same artists
3. Music previewing opportunities.

The market share of recorded music sales by retailers has been diminishing in recent years (Silverman, 1993), dropping from nearly 89 percent of the market share in 1988, to 84.9 percent in 1992 (RIAA report, 1993). Meanwhile, direct market sales account for 14.6 percent of the market share, up from 10.3 percent in 1988. In an effort to regain market share and lure customers back to retail stores, the record retailers "have moved aggressively to entertain customers by installing live deejays, or listening booths and kiosks" (Silverman, 1993, p. 116).

EXHIBIT 10.1 Record Store Kiosks

Name	Text reference	Music sampling
MUZE™	Yes	No *
Source™	Yes	No *
K-Mart	No	Yes
Robot Music Store	Yes	Yes
Telescan™	Yes	Yes
i-Station™	Yes	Yes

* Some newer models contain the sampling function.

Several competing interactive kiosk systems currently are in testing and use in retail record stores. Some retail chains (such as Wherehouse and Tower) have been testing more than one type of system to determine which system best suits their needs. Exhibit 10.1 illustrates the types of kiosks currently available.

THE MUZE™ SYSTEM

One such interactive information system is the MUZE™ system, developed by Paul Zullo and Trev Huxley (Leinfuss, 1993). The MUZE™ system is a database of music information that includes identification of songs (or recognition) by "title, a keyword in the title, or an alphabetical list of a performer's songs" (Leinfuss, 1993, p. S-13). MUZE™ will identify which album the song appears on, who the artist is, and other information about the album, such as additional musicians and reviews. The system also displays a graphic of the album cover artwork for many of the selections.

Access to the information is made possible through an IBM "customer membrane keyboard" and a touch-screen monitor. The hardware for the system includes an IBM 386-40 CPU (central processing unit) with four megabytes of RAM (rapid access memory), a videocard with one megabyte of memory, a 212 megabyte hard drive and an IBM CD-ROM (compact disc-read only memory) drive. The hardware system costs $6,000 and monthly software updates run about $1,150 per year (Jaffe, 1993). As of September 1993, there were 135 systems in operation in major retail stores such as Tower Records, Musicland, Virgin, and others, and another 135 back-ordered systems (Jaffee, 1993; Leinfuss, 1993). More recent estimates (source: MUZE™ marketing department, March 1994) place the installed base at about one thousand units.

Research (unspecified source in Leinfuss, 1993) indicates an average of 700 to 800 "lookups" per day with about one-fourth of those resulting in printouts of the information. The survey showed that 34 percent of the users made incremental purchases as a result of using the system and that 81 percent agreed "that the presence of the system encourages them to return to the store" (Leinfuss, 1993, p. S-13).

Elements that are absent from the MUZE™ system include: (1) the ability to search using keywords from the lyrics, and (2) the ability to audibly sample the music. MUZE™ is experimenting with a limited number of audio samples, but developer Huxley is opposed to converting the system into a "free jukebox" for fear of overuse by users not intending to purchase recordings.

PHONOLOG'S SOURCE™ SYSTEM

In competition with the MUZE™ system is the "Source," an interactive CD-ROM-based reference kiosk from Trade Services Corporation, publishers of *Phonolog*™ reference books found in record stores (McGowan, 1993). The Source, which is an electronic version of the *Phonolog* book, lists more than one million song titles and 80,000 albums on the CD-ROM discs which are updated monthly. The system costs about $3,000 and is available through leasing plans.

K-MART'S VIDEO AND MUSIC KIOSKS

K-Mart discount chain has been testing a music preview kiosk containing the top 50 songs accompanied by video clips whenever possible. The kiosks are located in a newly designed Music and Movies department, aimed at attracting the teenage market (Crump, 1992; *Discount Store News*, 1993a, 1993b). In addition to attracting customers into the store, the kiosks are intended to help the customers make the correct music selections, to encourage add-on sales and to curtail returns. The first prototypes used laser disc technology (Pemberton, 1993), but have recently been updated to CD-ROM systems, thus reducing the costs (*Business Wire*, 1993). Designed by PICS Previews, the new systems had been installed in 600 locations across the country as of June 1993.

THE ROBOT MUSIC STORE

In 1989, The Robot Aided Manufacturing Center (RAM) developed a prototype Robot Music Store. The computerized self-contained automat provides retail services for music customers through the use of interactive kiosks and robotics. The 140 square-foot cylinder kiosk is designed to be located in the open court shopping areas of malls (*Washington Times*, 1989). The circular glass enclosure houses 5,400 compact discs, about 36 discs per square foot, compared to a traditional record store which carries 10 CDs per square foot (Murray, 1990). Loss of product (shrinkage) due to employee theft and shoplifting is virtually non-existent as the kiosks are serviced by just one person (*Chain Store Executive Age*, 1990).

Customers are serviced through four interactive listening stations (Fox, 1989), which play 30 second samples of the most popular song on each album (*Washington Times*, 1989b), take orders, accept payment by cash or credit card, return change and receipts, and through the use of a large mechanical robotic arm, dispense the product to the customer through a drop bin (Murray, 1990). The listening station at each quadrant contains an ATM-style keypad and screen at chest level and speakers overhead—after the company scrapped plans for including headphones at the unmanned booths (*Chain Store Executive Age*, 1990).

The entire system costs $130,000, much less than the cost of setting up a conventional retail outlet (Murray, 1990). A prototype system was placed in a Minneapolis shopping mall (*The Washington Times*, 1989a). The company expected to have 150 stores in place by 1991, yet has met resistance from malls that already contain a conventional music store (Murray, ibid).

The limitations of the system include the fact that the kiosk only stocks 2,000 of the top selling titles, far less than a conventional store. And a customer who is "unsure of a title cannot, for example, whistle a tune and get help in finding what he wants" (Murray, ibid).

TELESCAN™ LISTENING POSTS

In 1992, Telescan, Inc., developed an in-store listening post designed to boost music sales and reduce returns of unwanted merchandise (Russell, 1992). The interactive kiosk listening stations contain selections from 150 albums—the 100 top-selling pop titles and a few top titles in various specialty categories—in 20 to 30 second "snippets," with up to three songs per album. All major record labels are participating in the system.

The hardware features a CD-ROM drive, a telephone style keypad and headphones, and costs $1,495 per unit. Monthly updates cost $25 per month for the disc, which includes accompanying artwork and liner notes. In July of 1993, Telescan, Inc. announced an arrangement made with *Billboard Magazine* to build a database of the publication to include in its instore kiosk (*Editor and Publisher Magazine*, 1993). The enhanced version will enable users to compare sales data for particular artists.

THE I-STATION™

Perhaps the most technically (but not mechanically) advanced interactive music kiosk system is the i-Station™, developed by Intouch Group,

Inc. The i-Station can store music, graphics, text and video for over 30,000 albums on its multi-disc CD-ROM system (Ross, 1992). The system uses a UPC code scanner to allow customers to approach the machine with a disc in hand, scan the UPC code from the disc, and preview up to five songs from the album. The system also includes reviews of the album, concert information, cross-reference to other albums by the same artist and similar albums in the same music genre, and allows dispensing of coupons for other products (Miller, 1992). In addition, the customer is asked to rate the songs on a one-to-five scale.

In late 1992, the company placed test machines in three Wherehouse (retail) outlets in San Diego, three in Streetside (St. Louis) and in Tower Records in New York City (Miller, 1992). In addition to serving as a previewing station for record customers, the dual-purpose design of the machine also enables record companies and retailers to compile data on usage of the system and correlate that data with scanner data collected on sales at the cash register (Ross, 1992). Customers are required to obtain a customer identification card, at no charge, before using the system. The card application includes demographic and product interest information and enables the system to build customer profiles based on the kinds of selections a user makes. During the test period, the company compiled a database of nearly 100,000 households from the seven systems. Intouch plans a massive roll-out of the machines to retailers in 1994 (Emerson, 1993). Under the financial plan devised by Intouch, both the store and the record companies fund the system. The retail store rents the kiosks for approximately $300 per month. The record companies must pay $28 annually per store for the inclusion of one new title and twenty catalog (older, previously released) titles (Keel, 1992). For each new album released by a record company during the year, the cost of adding the new title to the system is $28 per store, but includes the addition of twenty more catalog titles.

Limitations of the system include the fact that the product must be identified and located in the store by the consumer before accessing the machine. In the case of out-of-stock albums, the store clerks possess a catalog with the bar codes of most titles, and this UPC code for the particular product can be scanned in from the catalog. While the system does allow cross-referencing by artist, song or title identification based upon lyrics or the artist is restricted to speculation. Confirmation by sampling the music may confirm or deny the customer's assumption. To enhance the song identification capabilities of the system, Intouch arranged with *Billboard Magazine* to include the *Billboard* weekly charts for display on screen (Miller, 1992). The user can browse the charts and listen to samples of the top albums from each chart.

Survey of Record Store Customers

GOALS OF THE RESEARCH

The present study was designed to measure kiosk and record listening booth usage by record customers and how information needs are being served through kiosk use and use of store personnel. The study involves retail record stores and measures attitudes toward sales personnel, use of these personnel, and ties these needs to music preferences. Kiosk use is related to information need, demographic characteristics of the consumer, music preferences, product involvement and the desire to preview new music before purchase.

SAMPLE

For the present study, six retail record stores were selected and surveys were conducted on a total of 374 consumers. The study was limited only to stores which contain one of three types of interactive kiosks, the Telescan Source™, the i-Station™ or the MUZE™ system. Four of the stores are located near the West Coast and the other two in the Southeast. The age groups for the sample closely correlate with the known age distribution of record consumers according to the RIAA statistics. Also, consistent with RIAA figures, the gender ratio for the sample was 61 percent male, 39 percent female. The following are some of the more significant findings:

- **Use of (Reliance on) Store Clerks for Assistance in Identifying Recorded Music:**

  More than 44 percent of the respondents rely on sales help to identify a song title on at least a sometimes basis, compared to the less than 30 percent who indicated that they rely on the clerks to identify songs based upon a piece of the lyric. More than 42 percent indicated that they rely on sales clerks for artist identification at least sometimes.

- **Use of Clerks and Perception of Clerks:**

  Significant correlations were consistently found between the measures of knowledgeability of store clerks and use of these clerks for identifying (1) artists, (2) song titles, and (3) songs based upon some of the lyrics. Significance for the relationship of rating store clerks as friendly and use of these clerks for assistance was found only for the measurement of assistance with *song titles*.

- **Kiosk Usage:**

  Thirty-eight percent of the sample have used a record store kiosk. Kiosk use varies by both kiosk type and by store, indicating that there are factors other than type of kiosk which determine popularity and contribute to the rate of kiosk use.

- **Use of Kiosk and Purchase Rate:**

  Kiosk users purchase significantly more CDs and make more visits to the store than non-kiosk users.

- **Kiosk Use and Listening Booth (Station) Use:**

  Listening booth users are more likely to also be kiosk users than are non-users of the booth. Among stores which contain an interactive kiosk, use of the kiosk is more widespread among customers than use of the listening stations.

- **Music Preferences and Use of the Listening Booth and Kiosk:**

  Fans of alternative, rap, club/techno/house and world music are more likely to use a listening booth than fans of other music genres. Also, fans of alternative and rap are more likely to use the kiosk, and fans of country music are less likely to use the kiosk.

- **The Need to Preview New Music Before Purchase:**

  The group of respondents who use the listening booth, and the group of respondents who use the kiosk, rate the importance of "being familiar with most of a new album before buying" higher than do non-users. Therefore, kiosk developers should incorporate music previewing capabilities into kiosk applications.

- **Use of New Technology:**

  People who are more familiar and comfortable with personal computers are more likely to use the kiosk for a greater number of tasks than noncomputer users.

- **Kiosk Use and Demographics:**

  Kiosk users are generally younger than non-users. Significant differences were found for gender: a higher proportion of males use the kiosk than females.

- **Reasons for Using the Kiosk for the First Time:**

  Usage of the kiosk at the present time is based much more upon curiosity than actual need or by recommendation from a store clerk.

- **Services Provided by the Kiosk:**

  Nearly 72 percent rated the kiosk as informative and helpful. For ease of use, more than 79 percent agreed with the statement that the kiosk was very easy to use.

The Bottom Line

Customers report that they are first attracted to the kiosk system out of curiosity, not by the sales clerk recommendation. More efforts should be made to encourage kiosk recommendation by retail sales personnel.

Kiosk companies should cross reference songs by hook, not just title—especially for new music and commonly mistitled songs. Who can tell you what those songs might be? Sales clerks. In other words, know your potential customer's needs down at the store level.

References

Anonymous. 1993. "Telescan, BPI deal." *Editor and Publisher Magazine* (July 31): p. 19.

Anonymous. 1993. "Teen consumers are music to K-Mart's ears: K-Mart Corp's Auburn Hills, Michigan prototype store's Music and Movies department." *Discount Store News* 32/3 (February 1): p. 49.

Anonymous. 1993. "Latest K-Mart prototype pushes limit of discount retailing: K-Mart Corp's prototype store, Auburn Hills, Michigan." *Discount Store News* 32/3 (February 1): p. 29.

Anonymous. 1989a. "Robot on the job in music store." *The Washington Times* (November 22): Section B, p. 8.

Anonymous. 1989b. "Robot store fetches customers' selections." *The Washington Times* (December 8): Section B, p. 7.

Anonymous. 1993. "Digital video technology helps customers preview products on in-store kiosks." *Business Wire* (June 28).

Anonymous. 1990. "CD kiosk tests retail appeal of robotics: robot music store brings factory technology to shopping mall." *Chain Store Age Executive* (April): pp. 60–62.

Anonymous. 1992. "Nontraditional POS." *Chain Store Age Executive* (July): pp. 14–15.

Bredin, Alice. 1993. "Touch-screen technology handles credit functions: Mervyn's tests kiosks." *Stores* (March): p. 36.

Chandler, B. 1992. "Multimedia" multifaceted retail tool." *Discount Merchandiser*, 32(10): p. 40.

Crump, Constance. 1993. "K-Mart kiosks help, welcome shoppers." *Crains Detroit Business* 8/46 (November 16): Section 1, p. 28.

DeNitto, E. 1993. "Brave new world for in-store media," *Advertising Age* (November 1): p. 52.

Emerson, Jim. 1993. "Intouch groups complete testing of interactive multimedia kiosk." *DM News* 15/19: p. 6.

Fox, William. 1989. "Robot sells compact discs." United Press International (November 20).

Greenleaf, Vicki D. 1993a. "MusicSource U.S.A., Inc., in final stages to complete joint venture agreement to provide 100 kiosks and services to China." *Business Wire* (December 3).

———. 1993b. "MusicSource U.S.A., Inc., holds annual shareholders' meeting, announces extensive catalog database updates." (Company press release).

Higgins, S. 1993. "Executive update: computers and automation." *Investor's Business Daily* (September 29): p. 3.

Hume, Scott. 1992. "Retailers go interactive: Blockbuster kiosks hype films, gather data." *Advertising Age* (February 24): p. 29.

Jaffe, Larry. 1993. "Record store kiosk helps in customer service and tracking." *Direct Marketing News* (October 25): p. 2.

Keel, Beverly. 1992. "Computer could hike disc sales." *Nashville Banner.* Section D, p. 1.

Leinfuss, Emily. 1993. "Music-loving duo creates inquiry kiosk that's selling albums in record stores." *MUZE, Inc. Computer Pictures* 11/5 (September): Section S, p. 13.

McGowan, Chris. 1993. "'VideoHound' bow-wows on CD-ROM: potential seen for resource, promo use." *Billboard* (September 25): p. 75.

Miller, Trudi. 1992. "Intouch i.stations to use Billboard charts." *Billboard* (October 31): p. 8.

Muldoon, Katie. 1985. "The brave new world of interactive kiosks." *Direct Marketing News* (March 15): pp. 22–24.

Murray, Chuck. 1990. "Roboclerk in tune with service industry." *Chicago Tribune* (May 28): Business, p. 1.

Pemberton, H. 1993. "Retail kiosk favors CD-ROM, PICS: Preview contract with Horizons Technology, Inc., kiosks for previewing audio and video products." *Laserdisk Professional* 6/6 (November): p. 212.

Reilly, Patrick M. 1993. "Music stores grow larger and livelier, adding previewing posts, apparel, pizza." *The Wall Street Journal* (June 18): Section B, p. 1.

Recording Industry Association of America. "Industry yearly sales statistics, 1993."

Ross, David M. 1992. "Try before you buy—in-store music preview system." *Music Row* (December 23): p. 1.

Schwartz, Evan I. 1992. "The kiosks are coming, the kiosks are coming." *Business Week* (June 22): p. 122.

Silverman, David. 1989. "Name that tune: campaign to back-announce songs hopes for some record success." *Chicago Tribune* (March 4): p. 2.

Weiss. 1995. "Multimedia hits the streets." *New Media* (February).

Wiesendanger, Betsy. 1991. "Kiosks: automated wonder or lead balloon?" *Sales and Marketing Management* (August): pp. 40–43.

CHAPTER

11

The New Disk-Based Marketing Communications Tools

Guidelines for Creating Powerful Electronic Catalogs and Presentations

Vic Cherubini

Vic Cherubini is founder and president of the E.P.I.C. Software Group, Inc., a specialized advertising agency that develops computer-generated sales presentations for its clients. Mr. Cherubini has spent over 15 years in industrial sales and marketing.

Sales and marketing professionals are now exploring the use of the computer as a new sales medium. It is estimated that well over 100 million computers are being used worldwide. The application of computer technology continues to spread into areas not traditionally thought of as computer territory. Marketing professionals are using the interactive nature of computers to involve prospects in their message. If used intelligently, the computer can demonstrate product information in ways never before possible with traditional media like print or video.

Why have sales and marketing lagged behind other fields when it comes to utilizing high-tech tools? Because using the computer as an air-cooled calculator for automating spreadsheets is far more intuitive than using it to sell your products or services.

The idea of using the computer as a sales tool is new to most people. For many companies, the sales department represents the last major business area to be given computer support. But why? Consider for a minute that no other department has such a strong potential to affect a company's bottom line. Although increasing productivity in other areas may result in reduce costs, an increase in sales productivity will translate to an increase in revenues.

When sales and marketing managers are asked, "How do you intend to integrate electronic media into your direct marketing strategy for the next one to five years?", the response is often silence. Most managers feel that they should be doing something, but are unsure about how to effectively incorporate new media technologies into their marketing plans.

The question is particularly relevant to those in database marketing. Today, market is experiencing a revolution. Mass marketing is dead, and to be successful, a company must tailor its message to a select target audience. Database marketing provides a support structure for direct marketing campaigns centered around computer powered demonstrations.

While many new media technologies are available to sales and marketing people, this chapter will focus on three that are widely used by industries to call attention to their products and services. They are:

- Disk-Based Ads

- Electronic Catalogs

- Fax-on-Demand

It should be noted that the following observations are presented from the viewpoint of a practitioner, not as a scientific approach to the subject.

Disk-based Ads

When faced with communicating a message, most sales and marketing professionals will turn to traditional mediums such as print, television and direct mail. With the explosive growth of personal computers, a powerful new medium can now be considered, *disk-based advertising*.

What is a disk-based ad? Imagine for a moment that you are the marketing manager of a company manufacturing industrial valves. You have a great new product with a unique design and your mission is to get your target market—piping engineers—to notice, specify, and buy your product. You must find the most direct route through the scores of competitors' ads to reach your target audience.

You consider running a print ad in the trade publications, but the ad will most likely get lost in the crowd. Even a full page ad wouldn't be enough to thoroughly explain the benefits of your new "pressure release port." The ad would need to be broad because you have no way of focusing on the specific need of an individual customer.

You might consider producing a video tape of the valve in action. Although video tape players are simple to use, unlike a computer, they may not be sitting, readily available, on your prospect's desk. Additionally, the video does not involve the viewer in the presentation, and cannot print what it displays. It is "static" in that the prospect watches it passively in a linear fashion. No interaction is required, and it assumes that everyone learns at the same rate.

Contrast those traditional methods with a disk-based ad. A single floppy disk can hold the equivalent of several hundred pages of information. The program can include graphics and sound to illustrate how the valve works. The disk-based ad will be designed so the prospect can "open" the valve (using the up arrow key). The prospect watches as water enters the valve. The sound of water is added to enhance the effect.

To really add value, an intelligent selection guide may be built into the program that allows an engineer to pick the best valve configuration for a given application. With one keystroke the valve spec can be transferred electronically to their CAD program and be used in a specific project design. Another keystroke prints the valve along with detailed technical specifications. Disk-based advertising saves the company printing and distribution costs while providing the client with specific information needed to make an informed decision.

When should a company consider using a disk-based ad? Ask yourself these questions. If you answer yes to all, a disk-based ad should be on your list.

- Does your sales information change frequently?

- Does your sales pitch need to be customized for each prospect?

- Does your target market have easy access to computers?

- Do you need a way to differentiate yourself from the competition?

Interactive Electronic Catalogs

Since the days of Gutenberg, anyone faced with producing a printed catalog knows the problem. No sooner than the ink dries, something changes. The information in your new catalog is outdated even before you have a chance to put it in the mail. Reprinting is out of the question, so you learn to live with the limitations. Every company has a horror story about a misprinted catalog or brochure. Just think of the last catalog you printed. Wouldn't you love the flexibility to be able to go back and make "just one more change"? In the world of database marketing, static information is the exception and change is the rule. Keeping a printed catalog up-to-date is an ongoing battle. Consider a high-tech alternative . . . the interactive electronic catalog.

Imagine placing your entire printed catalogue on a single floppy disk. Specification sheets, photographs, order forms, reference materials, and many of the items you have in that 3-ring binder will fit on a diskette. Using the latest advances in compression technology, an amount of information can fit on a 3.5" high density disk. Now, when something in your catalog changes, it is simply a matter of overwriting the old information with the new. From that point on, your catalog is current. Does this mean that every time you update the information on your interactive electronic catalog you have to send out a new disk? No. Because your new catalog is in a digital format, you can send it by modem anywhere in the world for the price of a phone call.

If you had your digital catalog on an electronic Bulletin Board System (BBS), any of your customers could call in and "download" the latest catalog information whenever they want. Although it may sound like a page out of Flash Gordon, many companies are taking advantage of this technology to boost sales.

If you're looking for a way to provide high-quality information and reduce production and distribution costs, an electronic catalog might be the answer. The good news is that the prices of electronic catalogs have dropped over the past two years. Nowadays, an interactive electronic catalog may cost less than its printed predecessor and will definitely reduce expenditures when it comes time to update catalog information.

Common Applications of Interactive Electronic Catalogs

- *Product Guide*—Help your customers determine which products or services are best suited for their specific needs. By linking in an Expert System (a software program that acts like an "expert") you can help a customer select the best product for a specific application.

- *Diagnostic Guide*—The electronic catalog can help your customers determine the cause of a problem, then recommend a solution.

- *Configuration Guide*—Let the catalog help your customer place an order that is complete. When one item is ordered, the program will automatically remind the customer about companion items.

- *Resource Tool*—Provide your customer with a glossary of industry terms, a conversion calculator, or any other useful tools that will help them with their work. Every time they refer to the program, your company's name will be prominently displayed on the screen.

Much of the sales and technical literature an engineer receives is quickly discarded. The environmental and economic impact over time, can be significant. Few people will throw away a diskette, since it can be immediately and easily recycled.

The Evolution of Electronic Catalogs and Disk-based Presentations

In the beginning . . .

For many years disk-based presentations have been used by software companies to market and sell their programs. A demo disk allows a potential customer to experience a software program prior to making a purchase. These software companies used the computer as a natural platform on which to demonstrate their offerings.

With the introduction and widespread acceptance of the IBM PC in the early 1980s, computers began appearing on the desks of professionals outside of data processing departments. It is estimated that over 100 million computers are now in use and that more than two-thirds of all white-collar professionals use them in their work.

Computing power became more affordable to large market segments. This trend continued to increase as computers became easier to use and costs dropped. It was not long before business executives realized the power of this device for sales and marketing applications. Using a floppy disk to communicate information is now a powerful tool for those businesses with customers that have access to personal computers. A disk can hold hundreds of pages of sales and technical information. Unlike printed sales technical literature, which may quickly become dated, digital information can be easily updated or completely overwritten. Sound, animation, and attractive graphics can be used to entertain while informing. Interaction involves the viewer in the presentation, creating a lasting impression. The advantages of disk-based catalogs and sales tools have become too important to ignore.

For companies with very large volumes of sales and technical data, the CD-ROM disk (Compact Disk-Read Only Memory) is proving to be a viable alternative. A single compact disk can contain the equivalent of 250,000 printed pages.

Once a CD-ROM disk is pressed (mastered), the information on it cannot be changed. Even so, the cost of creating, duplicating and distributing a master disk makes CD-ROMs a feasible alternative to traditional methods. It is estimated that more than 20 percent of computers in the home have CD-ROM drives installed. As more computers come equipped with CD-ROM drives, the proliferation of electronic catalogs and disk-based ads will increase.

Computers will increase in power and functionality as will interactive disk-based sales and technical presentations. Multimedia catalogs that integrate text, graphics, video and audio components in one system will become a highly effective way to sell. The use of interactive electronic catalogs will move from being interesting curiosities to mainstream sales and marketing tools by the turn of the century.

Case Study—Shell Chemical Company

Shell Chemical Company produces a wide variety of Kraton Polymer products used by chemists to manufacture pressure sensitive tapes, sealants and adhesives. In 1993, Shell was faced with finding a way to provide hundreds of pages of sales and technical data to the adhesive chemists it serves.

Shell's marketing department, led by Bruce Toig, was looking for an alternative to traditional printed sales literature. They needed an effective way to distribute the large amounts of sales and technical data that comprised the line. Toig said: "The computer turned out to be the perfect medium to bring together elements of our printed sales literature, video, and presentation graphics." Packaged in an attractive mailer, the single floppy disk contains an interactive computer program designed to promote the company's line of elastomers.

The program, called SAGE (Shell Adhesive Guide for Everyone), works by simply loading the disk into an IBM-compatible computer and typing the word SAGE. Colorful graphics, animation, and sound are used to inform and entertain a chemist seeking information. All technical documents can be quickly printed if a hard copy of the information is needed.

The main advantage of the program is that it contains a lot more than just technical information. One part of the program contains a powerful Adhesive Design Guide. The user can simply enter the design parameters they'd like the adhesive to have, and the computer immediately calculates the results. Lab experiments that may take weeks to perform can now be accomplished in seconds.

Other sections of the program contain video animation of KRATON Polymer molecules in action pulled directly from a Shell educational video. Incorporating this video segment in the program enables a new user to step through the production process at the molecular level. Shell also included an entertaining, information packed game in the program. The game, the SAGE Challenge, pits the skill of the user against the computer on industry specific questions.

The SAGE program was developed to provide Shell with an alternative to printed sales literature. "When you print the traditional catalog and the information changes, you can be stuck with reprinting and disposing of the old catalog," said Toig. With electronic sales literature, you simply copy over the old file with the new information. Another key advantage of Electronic Catalogs is that they can be sent anywhere in the world via modem for the price of a phone call.

Shell Chemical Company distributes the program to its key customers by direct mail and leaves a copy for prospects to review after a sales call. The Shell sales reps also have the SAGE program loaded on their notebook computers and use it to give interactive sales presentations and demonstrations at trade shows. "We have included a survey in the program for users to complete and return to Shell," states Toig. "This will help us determine what new features we may wish to add to the next version of the SAGE electronic catalog ."

A Summary of Features and Benefits

Why are vendors turning to the computer to sell? The estimated cost of a business-to-business field sales call now exceeds $275. The average technical person receives over 90 pounds of direct mail each year. With these figures, sales and marketing managers are challenged to find alternative, innovative methods of delivering their message and increasing customer awareness.

ECONOMICAL

While the cost of a four-color printed catalog in a three-ring binder may exceed $50, the same information can be placed on a floppy disk for a much lower cost. Mailing the disk is also considerably more economical than the expense of sending a printed catalog.

EXHIBIT 11.1 Seven Steps to Creating a Disk-Based Presentation

Step	Action Required	Time
1 Project Definition	Identify and quantify goals and objectives. Determine users' needs, including customers.	Week 1
2 Prototype Design/ Development	Create project team to determine how to maximize company image. Create a flow chart based on needs. Produce storyboard showing design and action. Present to management for approval.	Week 3
3 Produce Rapid Prototype	Create a skeletal structure for review. The most difficult and intensive part of program.	Week 5
4 Produce an Alpha Version	At this stage the program has been thoroughly tested and debugged. Only minor changes should be needed. Production of collateral materials should begin.	Week 12
5 Presentation of Master	Master presented for sign-off. The disk should be scanned for viruses and put through a series of quality control tests prior to sign-off.	Week 14
6 Duplication/ Distribution	Disks are duplicated and distributed. Follow-up on user response begins immediately.	Week 16
7 Maintenance/ Updates	Changes made on ongoing basis	Ongoing

EXHIBIT 11.2   Additional Costs Associated with Disk-Based Presentations

Budget Item	Description
Media Style	Disks can be provided in a number of formats, from black and white to color or silk-screened or with photography.
Packaging	Options range from a plain package to an elaborate mailing package that includes sales literature.
Software Support/ Fulfillment	This can be handled internally or outsourced.
Program Maintenance	Well-designed programs include the ability to update information easily.
Training	Materials are—or should be—designed to be used by novices. Since the program will go unused if the salesperson fears being embarrassed in front of a client, training should be easy to implement and complete.

EASY TO UPDATE

If information on a printed piece of sales literature changes or is incorrect, in most cases the only practical option is to reprint the entire piece. For product lines that are rapidly evolving, having the information in an electronic format allows for immediate changes. With an interactive disk-based catalog there is never any reason to distribute obsolete information.

INTERACTION

Printed sales literature is static and involves no interaction on the part of the reader. Computerized sales presentations require the user to become involved in the demonstration.

CALCULATIONS

The promotion of a product that requires calculations can be enhanced by including a number-crunching feature in the program. Error checking can also be included to ensure that correct values are entered.

ANIMATION/SOUND

Colorful animation and sound can also be included to increase the impact of the demonstration.

UNIQUE FORMAT

Distributing a presentation on a floppy disk enables a vendor to differentiate their company from the competition. Imagine getting a floppy disk at a trade show. Although you may return from the show with a large amount of printed material, the disk will surely get more post show consideration than most of the printed literature.

CORPORATE IMAGE

A skillfully created disk-based catalog gives vendors a high-tech image while providing its sales people with a powerful tool. It also builds loyalty by satisfying customers' needs for accurate, easy-to-find information.

CONSISTENT

The computer can help even the best salesperson improve the quality of a sales call. After demonstrating a product or service on the computer, the sales professional can leave the disk behind for further review. Sharing knowledge and expertise enables customers to feel more confident in their buying decisions and leads to repeat purchases.

REUSABLE

Floppy disks are the ultimate recyclable resource. Unlike printed information which requires the use and eventual disposal of valuable resources, new information can be repeatedly written over old data.

INCREASED RETENTION

Studies show that people retain 20 percent of the information they hear, 40 percent of what they see, and 60 to 70 percent of the information they interact with. Since individuals learn at different rates, computerized sales presentations make excellent training tools. Psychologists have determined that the more senses you involve in a learning experience, the greater the levels of retention.

ELECTRONIC TRANSFER

By using a modem, an electronic catalog can be transferred over the telephone lines for the price of a phone call. For companies with overseas operations, this can represent large savings in courier costs. Linking your firm electronically to the companies you serve may create a strategic advantage that will be difficult for your competitors to overcome.

The age of computerized sales literature is upon us. While we are flooded with information, the computer can be used as a filter to collect only the information we need. Using tools like expert systems, animation, and sound will not only ensure a more informed purchase, but will make the product selection process more enjoyable.

Fax-on-Demand

Virtually unheard of ten years ago, the fax machine has taken the business world by storm. While even in the smallest companies, the fax has become the de facto standard of instant communications, it's about to become even more important with the introduction of a new technology called, "Fax-on-Demand."

Fax-on-Demand provides a customer with the information needed to make a buying decision, 24 hours a day, 7 days a week. It will have a profound effect on the way sales and technical information is communicated by database marketers. Let's contrast the way business is conducted today versus the possibilities with Fax-on-Demand.

Advertising appearing in trade journals usually includes a "reader response number" at the bottom of the ad. If you want additional information about a product, you circle that ad's number on the bingo card. The card is sent back to the magazine, combined with other responses for the same information and returned to the manufacturer for follow-up. Unfortunately, it may be weeks before the requested information gets back to the customer.

In contrast, Fax-on-Demand, provides an immediate response to a customer's information request. The magazine ad now contains a phone number to call and a product information number. Your knowledge-hungry customers call your Fax-on-Demand system, enter the number in the ad, and the information is immediately delivered.

Implementing Fax-on-Demand

There are two ways to implement Fax-on-Demand:

1. **Use a Fax-on-Demand service bureau.** A host of companies are providing Fax-on-Demand services, and most applications can be installed in less than a day. Most services charge an initial set-up fee and bill by the minute for access to the system. Set-up charges vary with the size of the application, but typically range from $500 to $3,000. The cost to access the system ranges from $.30 to $.35/minute. A page of text with a simple graphic on it will take 45 seconds to transmit and a three page document with a cover sheet will cost the sender about $1.00 to transmit.

2. **Set up your own Fax-on-Demand System.** An in-house Fax-on-Demand system is recommended for those companies that have information that changes often or must remain confidential. Although Fax-on-Demand is an exciting technology, it has a way to go before it becomes "plug and play." Even small systems can be daunting to those who are new to the technology.

A popular way to ensure success is to work with a Fax-on-Demand VAR (Value Added Reseller). VARs specializing in these systems can install the system, load your data, record the voice prompts, and train your people in less than a week. Simple systems can be set up for less than $5,000.

What are some recommended applications for Fax-on-Demand?

- Specification Sheets
- Sales Literature
- Newsletters

- Material Safety Data Sheets
- Article Reprints
- Pricing & Inventory Information
- Media Packets

Suggestions and Conclusions

With over 100 million computers now in use, database marketers may be missing some excellent opportunities if they are not exploring alternative media such as computer powered sales tools. Although it takes time for people to accept and adapt to new technologies, we will soon see the proliferation of CD-ROM catalogs with full-motion video, high-fidelity sound, and software that is transparent to the user. While other advanced technologies like artificial intelligence and virtual reality are on the horizon, marketers need to focus on developing applications that utilize existing technologies.

CHAPTER

12

Sales Automation

A Modern Business Imperative

Tony Alessandra

Tony Alessandra, Ph.D., is a leading sales speaker, trainer, and consultant based in LaJolla, California. He has co-authored numerous books, including *Collaborative Selling* and *Idea-a-Day Guide to Super Selling*. His most recent book is *The Platinum Rule*.

The days of "hit and run" "spray and pray" selling have been gone for a long time, though you might not think so from the way some companies have continued to sell. As recently as 1991 a survey of 4,000 advertisers and prospects by Cahners Publishing, a publisher of business magazines, reported that as many as 41 percent of a sales rep's customers had not been contacted at least once during that year. Furthermore, only 16 percent of sales reps made it a point to contact their accounts at least once that year, with only 37 percent indicating that less than half of their clients had been called on at least once. The main reasons for poor follow-up cited were: illegible paper records (due to infrequent updates); volume—the difficulty of going through hundreds of records to determine account status; and lost files.

A New Way of Doing Business

Customers—especially in the business-to-business arena—are demanding and getting more from their successful suppliers. Call it what you will—nonmanipulative selling, relationship selling, collaborative selling, one-to-one marketing—for the past decade or more both buyers and sellers have come to learn the benefits of ongoing business relationships built on a set of shared values and interests. For buyers this has meant fewer suppliers and less emphasis on shopping for and buying solely on the basis of price. Service—based on needs—has become paramount. For sellers this has meant taking the time and energy and expense of untargeted cold call selling—whether by face-to-face, phone, mail or other means—and directing it to greater knowledge of specific customers' needs.

This kind of relationship is only possible when each party knows the other's business—its objectives and goals, its problems and capabilities. And this kind of knowledge is possible only with consistent contact and sharing of information.

Traditionally the biggest obstacle to relationship selling hasn't been desirability. It has been *ability*—the ability to get, coordinate, and use all of the information necessary to make relationship selling work.

That has been the argument for automating the sales force. Until relatively recently, the cost of automating a sales force and connecting it to everyone in the company who has contact with the customer—in order to build a total business relationship—has been quite expensive.

That has changed. The cost of computer systems has decreased even as their sophistication has increased. The result is that, first, it is practical for the vast majority of companies to automate their sales forces now; and, second, it is or soon will be virtually imperative to automate one's sale force. It will be the way business is done.

None of these reasons—the need to get closer to one's customers, the power of computers and their declining cost—is new. Everyone in sales has heard them before. An additional reason is that, as implied by the Cahners survey, some sales people have been slow to adapt to new technologies. It's behavioral. Sales reps aren't accustomed to all of the procedures needed to develop customer relationships more effectively. This is a less obvious way in which sales force automation is contributing to sales force effectiveness. The speed and power (as well as the lower cost) have made it possible to put relationship-building activities at the fingertips of sales reps, thus eliminating the need for changes in behavior that had been previously required.

It is interesting to note that the year of the Cahners survey was 1991—at the start of the last recession. Many of the companies in that survey are no longer with us. And the futures of companies that survived the recession but continue to operate in the way reflected in the Cahners survey are not bright. In the words of Warren MacFarland of the Harvard Business School, "[In the future] there will be two types of companies: those using computers as a sales and marketing tool, and those facing bankruptcy."

Process, Not Technology

You will soon notice that I have not mentioned a specific piece of hardware or software and haven't used the term *database*. For one simple reason: it doesn't matter—at least not at first. A database is, first of all, a state of mind. There are companies—successful companies—around that don't own a single computer and yet have well-developed, effective "databases." How? Pencil and paper. They keep all customer information on paper.

I don't recommend that approach. Computers can handle and process information quickly and efficiently. But the point is that these companies know their customers. And if you don't know your customers, you don't need a computer or a database—though you might need a bankruptcy attorney. Companies can only benefit from sales force automation when they know who their customers are. If they do, the benefits can be truly dramatic.

The Basics

In the following pages I will discuss the process of automating a sales force. I will start at the beginning level and show how databases can be integrated into a system that makes all contacts "sales contacts" and makes the entire company customer-focused.

CONTACT MANAGEMENT/DATABASE MANAGEMENT

Database management is a general term that traditionally has involved tracking inventories, people, numbers and other information. From a sales automation perspective database management deals with client record management. It usually involves the tracking of customer contacts and activity, which can include the tracking of direct mail, calls, and face-to-face contacts.

Basic contact management software is an example of personal database management—on the level of the individual sales rep. This is the first and most personal level of sales force automation. It involves a salesperson using a computer system to replace file folders, cards and handwritten notes. Contact managers are usually set up to track all customers, whether they have bought or not. The information typically tracked includes call and appointment entries, reminders, "to-do" lists, client notes and other useful user defined information. Some contact managers can be networked allowing multiple users working in a single location. Some now have the ability to combine stand-alone databases to a central location *as long as the communication is only one way*. After such communication, it would be necessary to re-transmit the entire database to each remote location. Transmitting data from the company out to salespeople or reconciling changes to the same customer by two different people at two different locations is not possible in the contact management environment.

When fully developed, this kind of database contains full customer histories that can be made available to all members of the sales force. This information includes initial contact (and source), purchase history, service history, and preferences. More sophisticated users track and include "soft" information, such as an individual buyer's contact preferences (e.g., "prefers a mailing piece to phone call" or "prefers to be called before 10:00 a.m."). Such information is the basis for developing strong relationships with customers, and this level of development is the launching pad to the next stage, companywide sales force automation.

COMPANYWIDE SALES FORCE AUTOMATION

The Sales Force Automation kernel is formed when all the salespeople's stand-alone databases, contact management functions and the company's database systems are merged. The SFA kernel tracks *all* database marketing targets, buying and prospective customers' needs, and sales activities into a single system.

To do this effectively, a *mandatory* technical element is the ability to update all internal and external databases from any location. This is called *bi-directional data synchronization.* This allows involvement of outside salespeople, regional offices, support or outside technicians, or any others with telephone access and appropriate security level. This is a required capability for companies that have users operating in the field or in remote offices.

Reengineering the Sales Process

Two basic reasons contribute to failure in automating a sales force. Both have involved process.

First, more companies than one could imagine have spent thousands upon thousands of dollars on hardware and software without knowing anything about their customers. For them a "database" was a silver bullet that would increase sales automatically. The opposite is true, and the reason should be obvious: you need to know something about your customers' needs and objectives—their business—before you can benefit from sales force automation.

Second, some companies automate because competitors are doing it. In other words, they automate to avoid a competitive *disadvantage.* This, without a compelling positive reason for implementing a program, will inevitably lead to failure.

Most companies that have been successful in automating their sales functions have done so because they had a clear objective: to create a powerful competitive advantage by getting closer to their customers. Key is including everyone who has contact, direct or indirect, with the customer. Exhibit 12.1 outlines the six steps of collaborative selling, with a description of the individuals involved.

Six Steps to Sales Success

There are six steps or stages to any successful selling process. The following is adapted from *Collaborative Selling,* by Alessandra and Barrera.

THE "TARGET" STAGE

This step helps you understand exactly what you have to offer that is unique and exactly which target audiences can best use what you have to sell. It takes some time, but your success ratios will be much higher because you will be focusing your efforts only on those prospects who have a high probability of buying. Then you will work to see that these prospects have a positive image of you *before* you call on them.

The information most companies already have about existing customers is a gold mine of lead generation and targeting. And both sales and marketing should work together to identify best opportunities, which might include identifying new needs of existing customers, new needs of new customers within existing accounts (i.e., increased account penetration through in-house client referrals), and the development of new business whether by referral or by matching profiles of existing customers with prospects.

THE "CONTACT" STAGE

Making contact with your prospect is the first critical test. Apart from product knowledge, no other facet of the sales process makes a greater impression on the customer. The first few minutes of contact often makes, or breaks, the sale. During that time your prospect sizes you up and decides if you are the type of person he would like to do business with.

This contact may be in person, over the phone, or by letter. Each has its advantages and disadvantages, but the key, regardless of the approach, is to build credibility and trust. When prospects sense you have their best interests in mind, the rest of the sales process should follow more easily.

THE "EXPLORE" STAGE

The purpose of the Explore stage is to get enough information to know the prospect's needs and what it will take to fulfill them. To do that, you need to listen to what your prospect says, but you also must know how to

EXHIBIT 12.1: The Six Steps of the Collaborative Selling Sales Cycle

Sales Cycle Phase	Description	Department and/or Personnel Involved
TARGET	All efforts to develop leads and sales opportunities	❏ Advertising, ❏ Marketing, ❏ Telemarketing, ❏ Inside Sales, ❏ Primary Sales (Cold Calling, Prospecting, Networking, etc.) ❏ Other personnel — Who? ————————————
CONTACT	Starts with the first contact or conversation after an inquiry	❏ Phone Personnel ❏ Inside Sales ❏ Primary Salesperson ❏ Other personnel — Who? ————————————
EXPLORE	Profiling the customer's needs	❏ Inside Sales ❏ Primary Salesperson ❏ Other/on-site fact-finding personnel — Who? ————————————
COLLABORATE	Partnering with customer on feature and benefits that meet the customer's needs	❏ Primary Salesperson with help, information or guidance from: ❏ Other Personnel — Who? ————————————
CONFIRM	Reaching an agreement and closing the sale	❏ Primary Salesperson with help, information or guidance from: ❏ Other Personnel — Who? ————————————
ASSURE	After the sale service and continued account penetration	❏ Primary Salesperson ❏ Customer Service/Technical Support ❏ Training Support ❏ Other Personnel — Who? ————————————

ask questions. Automation can help because it provides a basic structure or sequence of questions that can be asked.

What you want to look for are the prospect's problems and opportunities. The problem, or need, is the gap between what a customer wants and what he or she now has. This gap already exists. An opportunity, on the other hand, is something extra that can be added—for example, a new market, a better avenue of distribution, or an untapped promotional vehicle. A resourceful sales person can create an opportunity. And remember, customers do not form relationships with self-serving salespeople. Fully exploring a customer's needs properly is the only way to build a solid relationship.

THE "COLLABORATE" STAGE

The goal at the Collaborate stage is for you and your prospect to find a solution that meets your prospect's needs. You do this by combining your and your prospect's ideas to arrive at a mutually beneficial solution.

Rather than using a monologue, the best salesperson engages in a dialogue to keep the prospect involved in a give-and-take exchange. As you discuss a solution, explain how it will work in your prospect's environment. Most customers don't care how something works, they want to know how it will work for *them,* how it will solve *their* problems. So the collaborative salesperson speaks the language of benefits rather than features.

THE "CONFIRM" STAGE

Top salespeople are always in step with their customers by making sure there's agreement every step of the way. By the time they ask for the sale, it's a matter of *when,* not *if.* But the ultimate goal is gaining a truly committed customer, not just closing the sale. So the Confirm stage is critical to building a long-term partnership. It requires trust, respect, and open communication on each side. A savvy salesperson sees an objection as a "midcourse correction" that, when addressed properly, can steer him or her toward a sales destination, not as hurdle that can be overcome by using a manipulative closing technique.

One of the most powerful benefits of proper collaboration and confirming techniques is minimized price negotiation. A "dump" of irrelevant features and benefits that do not apply to a customer's needs actually *causes* price negotiation. Customers make the logical assumption that a product without unimportant features would be less expensive. At this point they have two choices: find a product without those features or "negotiate out" those features that are unimportant. Sales software that focuses on proper documentation of a customer's product, situational, and decision needs provides support for relationship building and profitability because it minimizes, if not eliminates, price as a part of the decision process.

THE "ASSURE" STAGE

This is where most salespeople drop the ball because they think the job is over when they get the sale. But for the collaborative salesperson, this is when the real job starts—when the customer says *yes.* Assuring customer satisfaction is indispensable to exceptional sales success. If you make sure that the customer is satisfied, you are more likely to get repeat business.

You can solidify your relationship with buyers, first, by being absolutely clear about their expectations. If you conducted the earlier stages well, you should have a pretty good handle on those standards.

Monitor the criteria by staying involved with the customer. If there are problems with the product or service, see those not as setbacks but as changes to show how much you care about your customers. Think long term. All future sales and referrals depend on your ability to reaffirm your commitment to quality and service.

How important is this? A study reported in the *Harvard Business Review* indicated that 60 percent of customer defectors were satisfied with the current product and current level of service. They left because they felt that the supplier was indifferent to their future needs. And, also according to the *Harvard Business Review,* a 5 percent decrease in customer defections can produce as much as an 85 percent increase at the bottom line.

COMPANYWIDE INVOLVEMENT AND MANAGEMENT

Once the sales force has been automated, you can move to involving the entire company in the process. The involvement of all aspects of the company in customer contact makes it possible to develop customer relationships to their fullest extent. Exhibit 12.2 identifies the stages of companywide involvement. The columns identify the level of contact needed.

EXHIBIT 12.2   Account, Opportunity and Pipeline Management

Contact, Account, Opportunity and Pipeline Management	1	2	3	4
1. *Basic Client Management* Tracking all activities (calls, letters, appointments), "to-dos," notes and next action with each client. User definable fields and unlimited information gathering capabilities. Ability to access information, generate reports or query the database varies greatly depending on the software.				
2. *Basic Account Management* Tracking unlimited clients/contacts and all activities within one company history. Multi-product opportunities and flexible marketing/mail needs examined and matched to your business.				
3. *Pipeline Management* Involves tracking clients and accounts through the sales cycle. Includes: • PROSPECTING new contacts in the TARGET and CONTACT phase of the selling cycle • SELLING existing contacts (EXPLORING, COLLABORATING and CONFIRMING phases) • PENETRATING existing clients (ASSURING phase of the selling cycle)				
4. *Sales Cycle/Pipeline Analysis* A Pipeline analysis by selling phase can give a much clearer picture as to the relative strength of future sales—especially to avoid the long droughts that are typically created after terrific months.				
5. *Opportunity Management* Account Team access to action tracking, notes, planning, pursuing, measuring, forecasting				
6. *Opportunity Analysis* Action priority lists, drill down / roll up reports, cycle analysis, etc. Example: CONFIRMING sales projections.				
7. *After the Sale Customer Assurance / Service* Automatic activity management - thank you's, check up calls, referral and testimonial calls, anniversary of sales letters, etc.				

1 = Absolutely Essential **2** = Required **3** = Nice to Have **4** = Not Required

BASIC CLIENT MANAGEMENT

At this stage sales reps develop, manage, and use the information needed to work with individual buyers within a company account on a day-to-day basis. Such information includes calendar, next-step procedures, and related support information, such as client-related activity reports.

BASIC ACCOUNT MANAGEMENT

This stage involves all activity within a client company. For example, information here can be used for account penetration. Satisfied purchasers are generally the best prospects for additional purchasers of other products. They also are among the best leads for additional business within other parts of the client company.

PIPELINE MANAGEMENT

This involves tracking the development of the relationship through the sales cycle, from prospecting to the assuring phase. When this view of a salesperson's business is integrated into basic contact and account management, the computer will help the salesperson "meter" his time and activities to manage the flow of business better. Specifically, the sales person will be able to avoid or at least temper the sales peaks and valleys that often occur, especially in industries where the sales cycle is longer than a few weeks.

SALES CYCLE/PIPELINE ANALYSIS

This phase involves account-by-account and companywide analysis of sales opportunities. The primary issue addressed here is account management and customer management in all phases of the sales cycle. Contributions from all individuals who have contact with customers should be coordinated here. For example, a customer service rep may note a service-related problem The sales rep needs to know about that problem before making the next contact. Alternatively, the customer service rep might have discovered a potential customer need during a service conversation. The rep should know about that also. He can be prepared to discuss that need during the next contact.

OPPORTUNITY MANAGEMENT

Much has been written and discussed about teamwork in selling. Opportunity management is where it can work very well. By drawing together the resources of the company in one place—from account management to sales to technical support to customer service and so forth—the team can look at special opportunities presented by an unusual customer or groups of customers.

AFTER-THE-SALE CUSTOMER ASSURANCE/SERVICE

This is where customer defections can be cut. Regular contact that supports sales can be used to reassure customers and to help identify needs. It also can be the place where one identifies what one is doing right. Testimonials from satisfied customers can be generated here.

Summary

The selling philosophies described here aren't new. Neither is the methodology. But the means of developing long-term business relationships has. The difference is the computer and what it can offer. It has the speed and capacity to manage the enormous amounts of information that true relationship selling demands. But more important, its strength in repetition and reinforcement can perform 90 percent of the behavior that sales reps must change. It enables them to increase their effectiveness by eliminating repetitive tasks. And greater effectiveness translates into greater efficiency.

CHAPTER

13

The Interactive Telephone as a Marketing Tool

Using the Telephone to Promote a Product or Service

Carol Morse Ginsburg

Carol Morse Ginsburg is editor and publisher of *Audiotex News*, a monthly newsletter for the communications industry. She also is author of *The Directory of 900 Service Bureaus, Promoting Your 900 Number,* and the *Audiotex News Resource Guide.*

The telephone as a high-tech interactive marketing tool? Absolutely. In these days, when new electronic wonders seem to appear almost daily, it's easy to forget about the original interactive communication device—the telephone. The phone's basic function and benefit—communication between two parties—is the essence of interactivity. And as devices continue to proliferate, marketers will continue to incorporate the telephone into their programs.

What Makes a Good Telephone (or Telemedia) Promotion?

The basic response to this question is simple: It depends on you. You might want to build a database of customers and prospects, sell more product now, make it easier to order, cross-sell related products, and/ or enhance your company image. Telephone or telemedia promotions can accomplish all of these marketing objectives if they are structured to respond to basic customer motivations. Here are a few: the ability to get better service, the chance to express an opinion, the chance to participate or to contribute, the opportunity to be entertained, and the chance to get a "good deal."

Customer Service

J. Patrick Herold is president and CEO of Federal TransTel (FTT), an Atlanta-based company that provides financial processing for enhanced products and services and offers nationwide transport for 800/900, 1+, 0+, calling cards, and point-to-point data lines. It also provides billing and collection services for telecommunications services. When Herold looked at the back office expertise his company had honed in the telephony industry, he quickly recognized its applicability to the Internet.

The product Herold developed, NetGAINS, uses the telephone bill as an invoicing vehicle for services procured on the Internet. The invoice enables commercial online services, content providers, and Web site hosts to bill for services and information on users' local telephone bills. To use NetGAINS, Internet Service Providers (ISPs) simply add it to their list of customer billing options. Users' phone numbers are then provided to FTT, which places the itemized charges on customers' telephone bills. FTT collects the charges from the LECs and reimburses the ISPs.

The phone bill is a natural because it is so familiar. It is a universally accepted billing platform with a high incentive for users to pay their bill. This system provides access to new customers, especially those who are not credit card holders or are apprehensive about divulging account information online.

Convenience: The Telephone and Prepaid Phone Cards

The Prepaid Phone Card provides a potent tool for the marketer. When Atlanta-based Landmark Communications realized they had a gap in the services they were providing, they used prepaid phone cards to close it. Callers to their 900-Weather line had access to 24-hour forecasts in more than 600 U.S. cities and 225 international cities, but were unable to access the service from blocked, cellular or pay phones. Many in the target audience were travelers, and for them the prepaid Weather Card was the answer. The station printed an initial run of 10,000 30-minute cards costing $19.95 and 2,500 five-minute promotional cards to reward their "good" customers.

The five-minute promotional cards co-branded with AT&T were a mechanism to reward customers by offering them free time on the service through the mail. Additionally they were used as a way to resolve billing disputes by offering complainants free time and mailing them a card. One way to reach customers with a critical interest in the weather was to hand them to people waiting in line at ski slopes.

The linking of the telephone and prepaid phone cards presents marketing opportunities. In the wake of a merger between Pharmacia & Upjohn, employees were invited to a morale boosting festival. SmarTel, a Boston communications company, was called in to motivate attendance by polling employees on their perspective on the merger. Each employee received a prepaid phone card worth 30 minutes of long distance. Callers heard a personal, 2.5-minute message followed by a six-question survey focusing on employee perception of the company.

The promotion enjoyed a 65% response rate, and 90% of the employees said they liked being surveyed by phone card.

When Intel wanted to educate LAN managers and resellers, and reward people for their knowledge of Intel products plus build a database of qualified leads, they called in SmarTel, which used a phone card and a mailing to create a marketing campaign.

Recipients of the card called a toll-free quiz line, entered a PIN which was printed on the back of the card, and using their touch tone keypad, answered five multiple-choice questions. The questions were based on product sheets and introduced four suites of software/hardware products. Essentially callers were rewarded for reading the product literature. Users received 15 minutes of free calling time just for playing and entering a sweepstakes for one of 500 prizes worth up to $9,000.

Another SmarTel Communications promotion was "How to Succeed in Business Without Really Trying." This promotion involved the distribution of 8,000 brochures with a five-minute phone card. Group sales agents could connect to an application that enabled them to listen to the play's reviews, the play's original cast album, and then connect to the ticket office to place an order. The play's production company reported that the resulting ticket sales represented a six-fold return on its investment.

Audience Participation

Everybody has an opinion, and most people like to express theirs. That has been the cornerstone of the success of many call-to-action promotions. For example, when the viewers of the 1995 Miss America pageant's telecast voted in favor of the swimsuit competition, they used 1-900 numbers to cast those votes. Omaha-based West Interactive was set to handle 100,000 simultaneous calls per minute. But even with that capacity, there were "busies" when some three million people attempted to call during the first 13 minutes of voting.

The pageant's 900 number voting brought a lot of advance press and added excitement to the television show. The 900 numbers, one for "Yes" votes, the other for "No," began several minutes into the telecast and remained open between 9:00 P.M. and 10:30 P.M. Each call cost 50 cents, and the net proceeds were donated to charity. An example of the enormous possibilities of interactive television, this was at that time one of the largest interactive television events.

Increasing Viewership and Listenership

Hermosa Beach, Calif.-based Interactive Marketing Communications, a division of SOFTBANK Interactive Marketing, produced an interactive radio game to promote the television show *Melrose Place.* This unique promotion featured the telephone and radio to promote the television show. Radio listeners could call a local number to answer multiple-choice trivia questions about the television show and win a trip to a *Melrose Place* party. The answers triggered appropriate responses recorded by *Melrose Place* actors. The promotion enabled the FOX television station to collect accurate and immediate feedback about the effect of each radio station's participation. The episodes following the promotion drew the highest ratings ever for the show.

Combining radio, television, and the phone to promote radio stations was begun by Massachusetts-based Impact Target marketing who put together a "Get on the Phone" interactive television project to enhance ratings for radio stations. The TV campaign was consistent, fun, and fair for audience. The potential existed to develop database and promote forced listening. The promotion generated the immediate involvement of listeners and potential listeners. In each of four distinct creative spots a different/greater incentive is provided, as well as a call-to-action asking the listeners to call a special 800 number and leave their name and birthdate from which a viable listener database could be generated. They are then told to listen the next morning at a specific time in order to hear their name announced for a chance to win cash and prizes. In essence, the campaign fully utilized the audience from the television buy. Passive viewers were converted into active listeners. Participation was immediate and the next day's sampling was impressive.

During a six-week-long promotion, Nickelodeon received more than 20 million call attempts for a Kids Choice Award show. Interactive Marketing developed a promotion for kids whereby they could cast their votes for their favorite show, entertainer, etc. via an interactive 800 number. During six Saturdays an 800 number was given informing kids to vote for their favorite movie actress, movie, etc. The goal of increased awareness, interest and viewership was more than met.

In an effort to promote NFL Football games, Interactive Marketing developed an ESPN Football Phoneatic Sweepstakes to promote the Sunday night games. Viewers call an interactive 800 number, enter their name, home phone number, address, age, and answer a question relating to the ESPN Sunday Night NFL Game they were watching.

Questions specifically relating to each game were written during the first quarter and faxed to the voice talent who, through a sophisticated backend system, phoned in the questions and multiple choice answers. The system was preprogrammed for correct/incorrect responses. When entrants pressed in their answers they were told whether they had answered correctly and what prizes they were eligible to win.

The 800-number remained open during and after each game until 30,000 calls were accepted. Viewers were encouraged to log onto the Internet, and all entrants were eligible for the grand prizes as well as various other prizes. In addition, a separate affiliate program utilizing a prepaid phone card was set up. Participating ESPN affiliated working in conjunction with local retail outlets gave away the cards. Each card included an 800-number, a PIN number and two minutes of phone time to enter the sweepstakes, 100,000 cards were distributed, with each affiliate being assigned a specific batch of cards. Prizes included a trip for two to the Super Bowl, 100 ESPN NFL sweatshirts and 100 ESPN NFL hats. The Sunday Night promotions increased awareness, interest and viewers of the football games.

Product Promotion

Check out the advertising on television today. Most of it carries an 800 number and increasingly a web site address. It is estimated that some 30 percent of all commercials on television invite the viewer to pick up the phone and place a call. Clearly, in launching a new product or establishing customer loyalty, or just gauging consumer interest, using the telephone is a primary tool in the marketer's box.

Silhouette Books launched a 900 line for callers to hear excerpts from new and upcoming releases. A call cost $2 and the callers who left their names and addresses received two complimentary novels.

Warner-Lambert Co., makers of Lubriderm skin care and other health care products, conducts an automated consumer education program. Their public relations agency promoted the project to editors at daily and weekly newspapers and to sports, gardening and other special interest magazines.

To participate, consumers dialed an 800 number and answered a series of automated questions on lifestyle and skincare. Once all the questions were answered, callers recorded their names and addresses to receive, via mail, their personalized skindex analysis, additional information on skin care, and of course a coupon for 75 cents off their next purchase of a Lubriderm product.

In 125,000 grocery and liquor stores nationwide, a life-size display of Elvira announced the new Coors Light Elvira Haunted Hotline. For

$12.95, callers heard Elvira, "Mistress of the Dark," give ghostly party pointers on how to have a successful Halloween party. In addition, each caller received a life-size stand-up Elvira, identical to those displayed in the stores. IdealDial of Denver designed and operated the line.

TBS Superstation used 900 in its "Win a Hog!" sweepstakes run in conjunction with a television special, *Harley-Davidson: The American Motorcycle.* The special featured one promotional ad letting viewers know that, through a 900 number or a postcard, they could enter a sweepstakes to win a motorcycle. When callers dialed the promotion's 900 number, they were asked a few short questions and were then entered into a drawing to win a Harley. Participating callers tolerated the short marketing research questions because the prize was so attractive. The draw was strong enough for people to sit through. This kind of balance between response and enticement is critical to a promotion's success. Each call to the 900 line cost 99 cents. The special aired twice. The first airing drew 2,262,000 households as viewers. In total, 10.7 percent of the households viewing dialed the 900 number. Omaha-based West Interactive Corporation, the service bureau for the number, processed more than 400,000 calls during a five-day period. 500,000 postcard entries to the sweepstakes were received, for a combined response rate of 24 percent.

Multimedia Promotions

Burger King pulled together a multifaceted interactive telephone and print media promotion. Burger King's approach to reaching a new target audience (young adults-sports fans) helped them market their food products as well as establish loyal Burger King football fans.

The marketing campaign started with full-page spreads in *USA Today.* Burger King's advertising promoted the 900 number, football codes and prizes. The campaign was then supported by additional advertising in *Sports Illustrated* and on network television sports. Several promotion opportunities were combined.

- For example, Burger King encouraged people to come to restaurants to pick up game cards.

- Once they were at the restaurants, Burger King promoted the 900 number on their restaurant takeout bags, tray lines, drive-through windows, and football code books (give away with each purchase).

- Halfway through the promotion, Burger King launched their College Football Cup Promotion. This promotion attracted people to the restaurants where they were educated to call the 900 Fan's Poll.

Burger King's promotion established rapport with college students because $1.3 million was donated to the Burger King's College Football Scholarship fund. Every week results were posted in *USA Today* and *Sports Illustrated*. Sometimes results were announced during the college games. Burger King identified itself as the official College Football promoter while their 900 number enabled them to poll fans cost-effectively and of course sell more Whoppers. Burger King was a customer of record with West Interactive, and AT&T provided transport.

On not quite the same scale but with similar objectives, *Scary Larry* was developed for *GamePro*, a monthly magazine for young computer game players. The players compete against each other in a monthly contest using either a rotary or touch tone phone to avoid Scary Larry and move through a maze while competing against the clock. The five fastest players are listed in the magazine along with their winning times. They receive *GamePro* T-shirts and the fastest of those five is dubbed "King of the Coffin." Interactive games are often used to enhance brand awareness, and Scary Larry has helped *GamePro* to top of mind awareness and recognition. When a new issue of the magazine hits the homes of the callers, call volume goes up.

Telephony and Internet Services

No chapter on the Interactive Telephone would be complete without discussing the use of the phone and the Internet. It's not just selling 900 to the Internet home page developer so surfers can gain access to home pages without having to use a credit card. That works out when the surfer calls the 900 number and is issued a Pin number which is used to gain access to the page. Then the cost for the call shows up on the phone bill.

For example—Fish Phone: the amusing name doesn't take away from the efficacy of this award-winning program. The application enables fishermen in remote parts of Iceland to contact a central database by telephone and provide information about their trips in and out of port. The information is then made available on the Internet. This unique application used by fishermen in Iceland forms the basis for a quota fishing management system for small boats. Using the simple and accessible infrastructure of the telephone, the Fish Phone makes real time information gathering from all parts of Iceland possible and inexpensive. Here the computer, the telephone and the Internet are combined. Information is collected from fishermen about their departure and arrivals. This information, through the Internet, is then made available to the authorities and other fishermen. To get information, callers punch in the number for an individual boat; then the Telsis telephony computer talks to the PC, which in turn issues a query to the MS-SQL server, accessing the records for the particular boat. Fishing authorities use the Internet to access and process the data for statistical purposes.

The sampleNet Card is a promotional calling card that awards consumers with a predetermined amount of long-distance telephone service or Internet access. It allows sponsors to extend interactive promotions beyond the relatively small group of consumers who access the Internet.

The Net presents a challenge and a tremendous opportunity. It can be used to attract more business for a company or an ongoing application. Voice personals are a good example. Companies like MicroVoice, Tele-Publishing and Advanced Telecom Services who were doing voice personals in newspapers added the Internet. The advantage for the user is that all the searching that would normally be accomplished by entering in touchtone commands takes place online without charge. When their search is complete, the matching ad and mailbox number are displayed for the user, and he or she can call, for a charge, and hear the corresponding greetings and leave a message. One of the advantages is that unlike print, updating on the Internet is ongoing. Fresh content is an incentive for the caller to check the page. Further, the web sites take advantage of hypertext capabilities to package content from the newspapers in ways that cannot be accomplished in print.

In Conclusion

The effective use of media including print ads, direct mail, direct response and television spells the difference between success and failure for any interactive telephone application or campaign. Anyone who thinks that telephone applications are relics of a past age is mistaken. The potential is still there. Remember the consumer has a love-affair with the telephone. What *is* happening is the convergence of the new electronic media. Interactive telephone and online/Internet services, telecommunications, television and computing are converging into cohesive and hopefully innovative products.

The phone will be an integral part of Cybermarketing. It's as simple as that. How to integrate secure billing solutions with breathtaking applications is the question to answer. It's not unreasonable to project that there will be a merging of all the technologies with most of the information you receive in the future being over the telephone—be that fax, modem or whatever.

CHAPTER

14

Interactive Television

Broadcasting to Millions— One at a Time

V. Tyrone Lam

V. Tyrone Lam is Director of Marketing for NTN Communications, Inc., based in Carlsbad, California. He is responsible for marketing and advertising sales for NTN's ITV network, which is located in more than three thousand restaurants and taverns in North America and distributed on home ITV and airline networks. Previous to NTN, Ty was with EON Corporation (formally known as TV Answer), where he managed sports and games development. Lam currently serves as Chairman of the Interactive Television Council of the Interactive Services Association.

Interactive television (ITV) is the promise of the computer age. By combining a networked computer with the family television, the potential of ITV will be limited only by the developer's and user's imaginations.

This new version of television—which has been traditionally broadcast—is a continuation of the evolution that cable has recently delivered to the viewer. People have a greater choice of what they want to see and will have an even greater choice of when they want to see it and how they may want to *act* on it once they see it.

The ITV family of the future can select the television programs they want to see, when they want to see them. This is commonly known as video-on-demand, or VOD. Viewers will also be able to select interactive programming: for example, predicting the outcome of a sporting event and playing along with a game show will pit viewers against each other coast-to-coast. On-demand news, sports, weather, and traffic will be available and personalized to the viewer's tastes. Finding your new favorite restaurant or the nearest movie theater to see the latest release are just a few remote clicks away.

There is a blur between interactive television and personal computers connected to online services or the World Wide Web. The primary differences, which we will discuss later, concern the types of activities performed and the environment in which they occur. Either way, the current success of the personal computer connected to a global network of services bodes well for the future of interactive television.

As more features are added and customization becomes possible, control of the medium is being placed with the keeper of the remote control rather than the content provider. The user will have more options and will be empowered to create a viewing atmosphere based on personal tastes. In turn, the increase in bandwidth has given programmers and marketers the opportunities to create more personalized content in order to reach their marketing goals more efficiently.

ITV's Stuttered Start and the PC's Opportunity

Only three years ago, the press labeled interactive television as the biggest media revolution since the television itself. It was touted as the convergence of the personal computer, the telephone, and the television that would create the ultimate communication tool. In the last two years, however, the online services such as American Online and easy-to-use Internet web browsers signaled the death of ITV to the industry.

ITV resources have been reallocated to PC online and Internet services; telephone companies are refocusing on wireless cable due to delays in ITV network buildout and uncertainties in set-top boxes; and cable MSOs are planning entries into PC modem-based services as opposed to ITV applications. The same press that couldn't write enough about couch potatoes ordering a pizza through TV has pronounced victory for the PC.

If you look at ITV- and PC-based delivery services as two separate, completely evolved products, I can see how this misunderstanding could take place. View it as an evolutionary process, however, and you will not only see the growing popularity of PC-based services expanding, but a breeding ground for the ITV content of the future.

The magnitude of building a broadband, switched consumer network and the difficulty in designing an affordable set-top box based on a moving target of requirements has pushed back the public's expectation of delivery. This could be a blessing in disguise. Before ITV's break-even point drops over the horizon due to the enormous cost associated with doing something that has never been done before, we can learn more about what content the people want and how to effectively use it as a marketing tool.

Let's look at the basics. It's safe to say that the initial market for ITV services already owns a PC and subscribes to an online service (or will soon). So, the majority of the ITV target market is enabled to participate in interactive services—and better yet, at their own expense. What better way to learn and hone our ITV production skills? Although we cannot directly answer the forbearing VOD question, we can test the demand for non-video dependent applications such as games, information services, banking, news, and so forth. At the very least, if no one wants to pay a few cents for your service online, why will they pay at least that much on their TV?

ITV vs. PC-based Interactivity

Will the same content be delivered to the TV and the PC? It may be, but the dynamics of how each is used today will probably not change so quickly. We spend time alone, staring at a PC screen 12 inches away— usually in an office or den. The time spent is usually task oriented and proactive in nature. We go to the PC to *get something*—information, a

EXHIBIT 14.1   GTE Mainstreet's Main Navigation Screen

game, a conversation—and this mostly happens alone. We also have the ability to search topics in depth.

The television, on the other hand, is more of a community entertainment medium. We turn it on to be entertained, 12 feet, rather than 12 inches, away. We are more inclined to surf between channels rather than to sit down with a specific agenda. Cable has permitted us to have more control over what type of entertainment we see, and through near video-on-demand, when we want to see it.

The control we have on a personal computer and the casual entertainment we experience from our television will become more blurred as the years pass. But today, the PC serves as a relatively inexpensive way to learn more about what type of content the consumer wants on any interactive medium. The interactive *screen* will evolve from a combination of the PC and the television, but the dynamics of the household and how we interact in each room should serve as a guide to how we will use it.

Not Killer Apps—*Killer Attributes*

Hundreds of millions of dollars have been spent trying to find the killer ITV application—the one (or more) function that will make the customer see the value in paying for this service. We have tended to think of content in categories, similar to how the online services do today, and want to know which category will provide the best opportunity for revenue.

The following is a basic set of application groups for ITV:

- Video-on-Demand: Selecting a movie or television show to air at a specific time. Near-VOD, selecting from an assortment of various time starts, has become more prevalent in testing based on the high costs of VOD and customer satisfaction with NVOD.

- Information-on-Demand: Getting the latest news, sports scores, schedules, traffic, interest rates—you name it—all in a format that is personalized for your needs.

- Games: Viewers can compete with other ITV viewers in a wide assortment of games including popular game shows, making predictions of live action in sporting events, traditional board and card games, and standard video games of today.

- Shopping: Searching through a "virtual mall" to find and view the product or service in the style you have in mind. Purchasing the product directly through the television with a credit card.

- Education: Distance learning, where the instructor has constant feedback from the class while they sit in their living rooms. Children receive personal feedback based on their responses to educational programming questions.

- Communication/Polling: Talking back to your TV has been going on since the first broadcast. Now viewers will be able to give their opinion and have it register in seconds. The on-screen announcers will be able to use the feedback to keep the programming in-tune with the audience.

- Banking/Bill Paying: The functionality of your bank's ATM machine—except for the cash and deposits. Viewers will also be able to check account balances and make payments to those accounts from their bank account.

At first glance, these applications seem to comprehensively support the needs of the electronic household. The interactive television will

EXHIBIT 14.2   Time-Warner Full-Service Network's Pizza Hut Page

enable us to accomplish these activities from our home. However, several companies have tested these applications, and with a few exceptions the tests have stuttered or failed.

Let's look at the opportunities these applications present to the household. This may help us to determine if an application will be successful, as the feature will have to provide a specific benefit before becoming successful—even if it accomplishes the task for which it was designed. We need to look at the attributes the system brings to the home as opposed to just the features of the applications. Instead of a long applications list, consumers want the technology to give them empowerment, control, saving of time/money, and be intuitive and sometimes fun to use.

This is substantiated by the features that have been successful in interactive television tests thus far. Applications such as an electronic programming guide, advanced remote control featuring easy-to-use timing features such as VCR recording, and program reminders, have been heavily used and successful. Each of these applications provides a tangible benefit. Imagine bringing up a list of movies for the upcoming week sorted according to your favorite topics and then have the TV turn on automatically when the show begins. This empowers the individual and saves them time from having to search through the television guide manually. These attributes go to the core of the promise of interactive technology and must be met in order to provide a value proposition to the consumer.

The Value of Advertising with ITV

The advertising and marketing communities are still trying to determine the details of selling in an interactive marketplace. The PC-online arena is finding it difficult to move from "hotlinked" banners that take the user directly to an advertiser's web site and electronic catalogs that enable electronic purchases.

Interactive television will benefit from these efforts, but will also provide more of a marketing opportunity based on a current mainstay in television viewing—commercial interruptions. We are accustomed to marketing messages, based on the demographics of the majority of the viewers, coming up at the most opportune time for the marketer.

The requirements of connecting the advertiser with the consumer through an interactive television network are enormous. A business relationship and an electronic link must be in place between the ITV supplier and the advertiser. This is no small task, but will be accomplished in the future due to the fantastic opportunity it brings.

Previous ITV advertising tests have given the viewer the opportunity to respond to an ad by clicking on a button on the screen. The user usually has a choice of asking for more information or possibly ordering the product directly from the TV.

We, of course, need to take this idea further in order for interactive advertising to become successful. Advertisers will be willing to pay a premium for the opportunity to market directly to their audience and take advantage of impulse buying situations. The following model demonstrates the correlation between features and the cost per thousand (the current standard pricing measurement for advertising).

The advertising community has begun to make entries into the World Wide Web and will do so with ITV when it becomes more prevalent. The type of advertisement we see in ten years may not look anything like today's. It will allow viewers to save time by learning about products or services they need and save money by finding the best value

EXHIBIT 14.3   Relative CPM Values

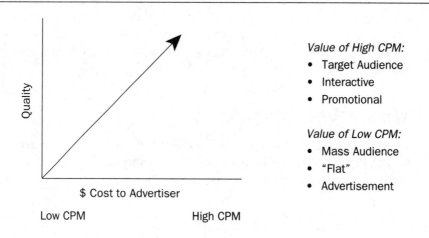

Value of High CPM:
- Target Audience
- Interactive
- Promotional

Value of Low CPM:
- Mass Audience
- "Flat"
- Advertisement

based on their requirements. Consumers will be rewarded for participating in market research—either directly or indirectly—and we should see a more educated consumer as a result.

It's rare to find something that clearly benefits both marketers *and* consumers, but ITV can do just that. There will be a match between advertisers and potential end-users based on current, relevant data as well as *by invitation* of the consumer.

The End of "Junk Mail"?

Using interactive technology to give the customer what they want, when they want it is delivering on the promise of this new medium. The following application can deliver on that promise and is given as example to help create new ideas to creatively bring the consumer and the marketer together.

One of the biggest dilemmas of direct marketers today is how to get costly product information in front of their potential customers. When you go home to your mailbox this evening, odds are you will find several pieces of direct mail (O.K., junk mail) which make the short trip to your waste basket with barely a glance.

Filtered marketing lists are helping to target those mailings to consumers who are more likely to be interested in the product, but the few that hit the mark sure don't make up for the thousands that don't. It's easy to tell if your name has been sold to other marketers by the volume of offers you receive in a product group. If you subscribed to any hobby magazines, you know what I mean!

Imagine if every household would only receive mail about products they were interested in at that time. The decision of whether the customer was interested in a direct mail piece would occur before they received it—and could change at anytime. Better yet, only the consumer would know what product literature was requested, so their privacy remains intact.

Marketers can broadcast their message to every interactive television household. ITV programming will enable each household member to create a personal profile which will filter *out* any marketing message that does not interest them. "Junk mail" is never received, the customer learns what they want to learn, the marketers get their personal message in the hands of a qualified buyer—everyone gains.

Although I designed this concept several years ago while working at a wireless—thus broadcast—ITV company, I am surprised it has not become a featured product today from the major online merchandisers. It fulfills the promise of interactive marketing.

Marketing and Privacy

A conversation about interactive advertising rarely gets too far without the topic of privacy coming up. And rightly so. Even as people continue to entrust their most private personal and financial secrets to ever-expanding wired and wireless networks, we need to be sensitive to the balance between consumer privacy and marketing profiles.

Users of interactive devices today understand the basic workings of the technology they are using and the flow of their data over networks. Consumers will understand if the decisions they are making on their television are affecting the marketing messages they see on their screen. The more interactive the experience, the greater the opportunity for a third party to learn about the user.

As marketers, we must continue to use captured data to make interactive media a beneficial experience for the consumer. Control of marketing information needs to be visibly in the hands of the rightful owners—the people they describe.

The Future of ITV

Interactive television has had a frustrated beginning, especially in light of the unforeseen success of the Internet and PC online services. In 1997 however, the major television manufacturers plan to take advantage of this success. Companies such as Sony, Phillips, Mitsubishi, and RCA plan on shipping televisions or TV set-top boxes which enable TV viewers to access the World Wide Web. Although the success of these efforts is being debated, the impact of these major consumer electronics companies using a standard communications system to enter the PC business will undoubtedly change the marketing landscape.

This initial push of interactive features to the American public will do more than just create a new market for television manufacturers, it will help educate the consumer about the real benefit of this new medium. As representatives of companies that deal with interactivity on a daily basis, we may forget that the general public at best may have heard of interactive television, but few really understand why they should own it. This could be the first major test of marketing interactive television.

Technology creates more choices which leads to more time spent making a decision based on a greater number of options. This is not what ITV should be, but probably will be at first. The current example of 100+ cable channels and the volume of content on the Web will probably hold true for interactive applications as well. People will have their favorites and stick with them.

As we become more comfortable with interactive television in our home, the user, programmer and marketer will learn how best to use the medium to save time and make a better user experience. How the information is customized and presented is what will benefit everyone—not the quantity. ITV will have evolved when we can focus on context rather than content. Tools such as profiling, filtering, personal preferences will provide valuable benefits.

As providers and leaders in interactive technology, we must understand that the real promise of interactive television is not quantity of selection or finding the "killer app"—it's making today's entertainment and educational experiences on the television better, faster, cheaper, easier, and more personal. Stay tuned . . . .

CHAPTER

15

Anatomy of a Web Advertisement

A Case Study of Zima.com

Charles Marrelli

Charles Marrelli, a senior copywriter at Modem Media, was one of the key strategists in the conceptualization and development of the Zima.com World Wide Web site. The father of the serialized character, ì Duncan, î Marrelli is a member of the Modem Media creative team.

One of the first advertisers to venture into cyberspace was the alcohol beverage, Zima Clearmalt. The reasons for reaching out so strongly to the online consumer were obvious. Zima was targeting consumers 21-34, opinion leaders, relatively upscale, and skewing heavily male. Sound like the Internet audience? Absolutely.

It all started with an e-mail address cryptically printed on the inside label of the bottle, "youcan@zima.com." From that channel, the brand received thousands of e-mail messages from curious consumers around the country. Shortly after that, the advertiser set up shop on the burgeoning World Wide Web (http://www.zima.com), where it became the first national consumer packaged good to have a dedicated Web server. The following article breaks down the original web site into its component parts in an effort to illustrate the strategy and the mechanics behind building a massive advertising presence in cyberspace.

The Home Page: Priority One

Probably the most important aspect of any web site is the first thing that users see upon entering. It's analogous to the cover being the most important feature of an entire magazine. Let's examine the reasons. With online surfers visiting anywhere between ten and one thousand sites in a given Web experience, a site's graphic statement becomes a tremendous factor in the decision to stay or leave. Within seconds, the consumer should get an idea of what the site is all about and where to go within the site. If the opportunity is missed, the surfer may never return, given the wide array of choices at his/her disposal.

Another truism of Web usage behaviors is that many consumers only see the front page regardless of how compelling the internal content may be. These folks are more interested in the breadth of content on the Web versus the depth. An advertiser's best wish in this scenario is that the consumer says, "Zima.com . . . cool!" and bookmarks the site for future reference.

In the case of Zima, the design team created a banner graphic that leveraged imagery directly from the television commercials. It's a good example of integrated marketing communications, where high familiarity with the television spots was used to the brand's advantage in cyberspace.

Ideally, the graphic element(s) on a home page should be as small as possible (in kilobytes) without compromising the visual strategy. A

EXHIBIT 15.1 Zima Banner Graphic

handy rule of thumb is to keep individual graphic elements less than 50 K and not to exceed 150 K for the entire front page. The majority of consumers surf the Web at a 14.4 baud rate. This is certainly adequate. However, tremendously large graphics can be time consuming and troublesome for these individuals. Many will stop the process and abandon the page once they begin to feel impatient. At the risk of sounding Zen, graphics are only useful if they can be viewed.

Product Information—Re:Zima

One of the most obvious uses of the World Wide Web or any online service is the attainment of information. Despite my previous section, imagery and fluff only get you so far with the wired audience. Whether surfing for the population of Bolivia, the minority opinion in *Brown v. Board of Education,* or the number of home runs Wade Boggs had in 1987, the online consumer is constantly on a quest for information.

A popular convention on the Internet is the FAQ (Frequently Asked Questions), where an authority compiles a listing of the most common questions, along with their answers, on a given topic.

For Zima, a key requirement of the marketing team was to publish accurate product information. Zima Clearmalt was introduced nationwide in 1994 and completely defined an entire category of alcoholic beverages. By default and by design, there were a number of questions in the marketplace (". . . what is this stuff, anyway?).

The Zima.com Q&A, known as "Re:Zima" (Exhibit 15.2) was developed to address the most common consumer questions. Consumers received answers to questions like "How many calories are in Zima?"

EXHIBIT 15.2 Zima Q&A

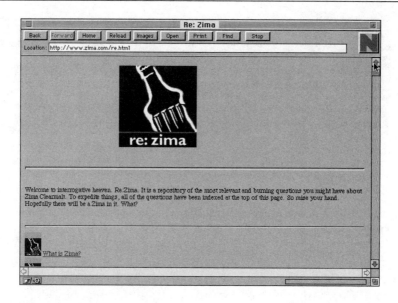

and "What are the ingredients in Zima?" Through traditional advertising, there was no cost-effective way for consumers to delve into so much information. The Web enabled consumers to satisfy their curiosity about an ambiguous product.

The copy strategy behind Re:Zima was to take the brand team's stock answers to questions and "jazz 'em up," making the responses more palatable and entertaining for the online audience.

The E-mail Feedback Loop: Write to Us

The most basic, yet crucial aspect of online advertising is the e-mail component. The wired consumer is intelligent, inquisitive, and more often than not, has something interesting to say.

Any online site, commercial or not, should give its audience the opportunity to interact. To a large extent, the comments are innocuous (". . . . love your product. Keep up the good work!"). In other cases, the comments may reveal a problem that the brand management needs to know ("I've had a difficult time finding Zima on the shelves in my area."). In any event, it becomes incumbent upon the advertiser to reply in some way to all e-mail correspondence.

EXHIBIT 15.3 The E-mail Feedback Loop

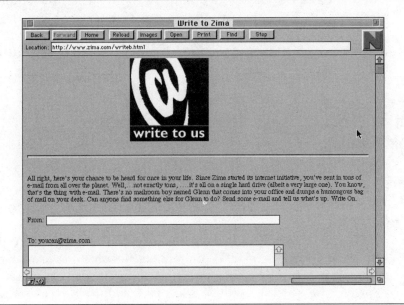

With Zima, the sheer volume of incoming e-mail necessitates a program that automatically sends a message back to the consumer. Such a program is commonly referred to as a mailbot, or an infobot, which acknowledges the message and thanks the consumer for the feedback. Next, every message is individually scanned by the brand's customer service department. If a second level of response is necessary (". . . sorry you've had trouble finding Zima," for example), a more personal correspondence is sent out, sometimes directly from the brand management. It's this one-to-one dialogue that underscores the essence of truly interactive marketing.

For the purpose of consumer research, all e-mail is bundled monthly and delivered to key members of the brand team. By scanning the collective consumer feedback, the team can qualitatively assess the performance of the brand, the effectiveness of the web site, and the psychographics of the consumer.

A final component to the e-mail feedback loop is a proactive Zima e-mail strategy that broadcasts messages to the "Tribe Z" affinity club on roughly a monthly basis. Once a consumer has voluntarily placed himself/herself on the list, he/she can expect things like "Zima Holiday Facts," an informative and slightly irreverent report on the history of certain holidays. Holiday mailings arrive the day before the holiday, St. Patrick's Day, for example. Along with the entertaining message, late-breaking product news and site enhancements are also listed. Through this channel, Zima maintains consistent contact with the online audience, whether they have visited the site recently or not.

Online Product Usage Scenarios: Interactive Gold Sipping

Online environments allow software marketers the opportunity to make samples of their product available online. But, how does a beverage marketer do the same? After all, Zima is not a digital product. Or is it?

When the brand introduced a new product, Zima Gold, to the marketplace in the spring of 1995, there was a clear need to drive consumers to sample it. Hence, the Zima Gold virtual sipping demonstration.

Here, we see the creative use of copy and visuals to simulate a consumer trying Zima Gold for the first time. Each time the viewer clicks on the Zima Gold bottle, less beverage appears in the bottle. The copy walks the viewer through the thought processes of a first time Zima Gold drinker. Such an execution, although possible in traditional print or broadcast media, would be very expensive (print) and not nearly as interactive (print or broadcast) as the interactive version.

EXHBIT 15.4 A, B, C Zima Gold Virtual Demonstrations

Navigation Structure: The Fridge

Any web site needs some way to get at the information on the server—a method for internally surfing the site. This is known as a navigation structure. Some sites have a text-based clickable table of contents. Other sites employ various kinds of graphical buttons. Still other sites use more complex, visually rich image maps. An image map is a single graphic which has multiple hotspots programmed into it. These hotspots can hyperlink internally to the site or elsewhere on the Web.

For Zima, the decided navigation structure was a combination of buttons and an image map. The various buttons were clearly evident on the top of the home page The image map utilized in Zima.com was branded "The Fridge." It points to ten discrete areas (other pages) within Zima.com.

The reason for utilizing a virtual refrigerator as a navigation structure should be obvious. A refrigerator is an excellent real world metaphor for a virtual beverage to be located. Where can one get real Zima? In a refrigerator, of course. Where does one access Zima digital content? Naturally, in "The Fridge."

EXHIBIT 15.5 The Zima Fridge

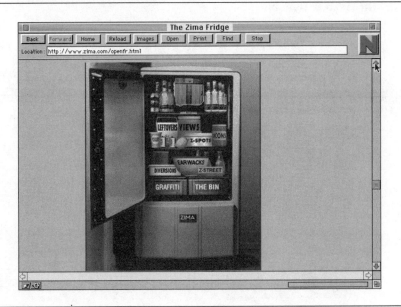

The "Duncan" Installments: An Exercise in Frequently Updated Content

A Web page is analogous to a diner. It may have its burgers, fries, and milkshakes on a daily basis. Indeed, it is even open 24 hours. However, in order to keep the "regulars" coming back for more, it must frequently change the menu. A site that is unchanging is ofttimes left for dead by the Web audience. In order to provide a degree of freshness to the Zima site, a character named *Duncan* was developed to deliver a biweekly journal that kept the site fresh for the online audience.

Duncan was created as the typical Zima drinker. The strategy was to give the character a number of different occasions for drinking or purchasing the product. Duncan was also built to convey a sense of "coolness" and "regular guy" appeal for the Zima product.

Duncan is never seen by the online audience. His journal writings appear every two weeks without fail on the Zima.com site. Duncan journal installments range from things like mountain biking to paying taxes to dating his virtual girlfriend, Alexandria.

Multimedia elements are woven into the copy in order to exploit the potential of the Web as a medium. In addition to the copy, each

EXHIBIT 15.6 Duncan

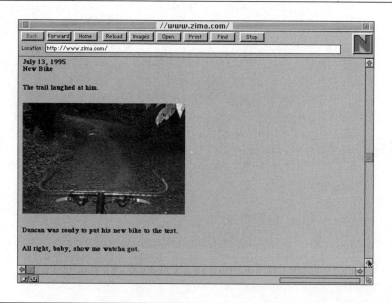

Duncan installment features an image, an icon, a sound, and a pointer to an external site on the Web. Of course, each installment also features a reference to Zima.

For example, when Duncan bought a new bicycle, the image was a bike trail, the icon was a bicycle helmet, the sound was the character sighing as he began his journey, and the pointer went to a bicycle manufacturer on the Web. Every time the installment changes, the multimedia elements are also changed to fit into the story. By providing fresh content at Zima.com through Duncan, the site is always timely and relevant for Web surfers who frequent it often.

Consumer Research: Web Questionnaires

The online environment is well suited for the collection of consumer demographics. In keeping with the tradition and culture of the Internet, survey respondents should always be self-selected. To exemplify the relative ease of collecting consumer data on the Internet, let's examine two other direct marketing channels of research: direct mail and 800/900 automated telephone systems.

In the direct mail environment, it is incumbent upon the consumer to fill out the survey, insert it in an envelope, and mail the survey back to the advertiser. This is not impossible; it is simply a great amount of work. It is not surprising that a *successful* direct mail campaign generates a one or two percent response rate. Additionally, the advertiser usually foots the bill for each response. Thus, a direct mail program can become a victim of its own success via the relatively high cost of postal service.

In the Telephone Voice Response (TVR) arena, data collection has another set of complications. Like direct mail, the advertiser is often handed the bill for each interaction. With a phone survey, the advertiser is paying for minutes, so the longer the interaction, the more costly the phone call. Additionally, the medium itself is cumbersome at best for administering surveys. A multiple choice question that might be answered in five seconds on a printed or online survey can take over a minute on the phone, because *each choice* must be read until the respondent answers the question.

Form-driven online surveys offer significant advantages over traditional methods. A recent e-mail survey given to "Tribe Z" members generated a phenomenal forty-five percent response rate. The online demographic is much more willing to respond to surveys due to:

EXHIBIT 15.7 Web Survey

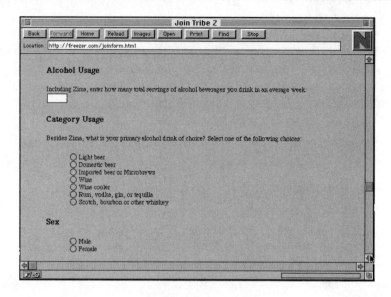

1. The relative ease of response—consumers merely select "reply"
2. There is nearly instantaneous feedback from the advertiser by using an automated mailbot.

In the Web environment, survey research is incredibly simple. Consumers need only to click on the appropriate radio button to register a selection. Thus, the process becomes incredibly expedient and easy for the consumer to participate in. A word of warning. Even on the Web, long and obtuse surveys become tiresome unless there is some compelling incentive for the consumer to fill out the questionnaire.

Affinity Clubs: Tribe Z and The Freezer

Online advertisers are enabled with an environment that makes it incredibly easy to create affinity clubs for self-selected consumers. There is a tremendous allure for the online user to be included in special or secret areas of the Web that only he or she can access. Web advertisers can utilize secured servers to create exclusive environments for high affinity groups.

Early in the Zima online initiative, "Tribe Z," an online affinity group was originated to develop a better communication channel between the Zima brand and self-selected Zima drinkers. Members of Tribe Z filled out an online survey and gained access to an exclusive area of Zima.com, known as "The Freezer." All Tribe Z members were enabled with their own passwords to access this area.

The purpose of The Freezer was twofold. It gave high affinity consumers a sense of exclusivity in their own *private* online environment. For the advertiser, it provided an extra level of data collection. Since each consumer was given a unique password, unobtrusively tracking the consumer within the environment was possible.

From the content perspective, The Freezer is an experiment in *participatory design.* The Freezer's visual metaphor is an unfurnished loft. Every few weeks, the members of Tribe Z are enabled with a set of decisions upon what elements go into the loft environment. The purpose is for consumers to derive a sense of ownership and involvement in the site based upon the decisions they collectively make.

The long term strategy for The Freezer is to allow consumers to eventually "move-in" and place their own home pages within The Freezer. In this sense, the brand becomes a haven for the Tribe Z

EXHIBIT 15.8 An Affinity Club

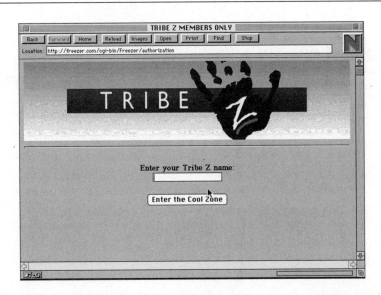

EXHIBIT 15.9 The Tribe Z Table Vote

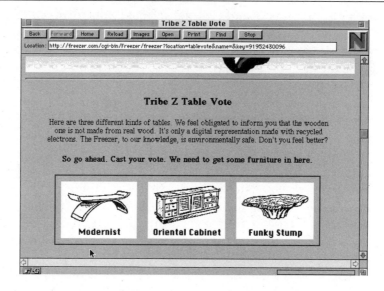

member to personally inhabit. The Tribe Z member then becomes a cohort with the brand, a contributor of content, in the online advertising campaign.

Pointers to Other Web Sites: Z-Spots

One of the most fascinating things about Zima.com is that you get to *leave* it. Huh? Now why would an advertiser ever want a consumer to leave? Stay, stay, stay, right? Well, not exactly.

The entire World Wide Web is built largely upon the notion of *hyperlinking,* whereby a Web surfer jumps from one site to the next like digital hopscotch. One minute the consumer may be on a server in Dallas, with a single "click" he/she may be on a server in Brussels, another click may take the consumer to a server right around the block. It is the notion of an interlinked community that makes the World Wide Web such a dynamic and thriving environment. Hyperlinking is what the Web is all about. At the risk of being trite, no site is an island.

Strategically, a major component of the Zima site was to point to other web sites that offered interesting and relevant content for the

EXHIBIT 15.10 Z-Spots

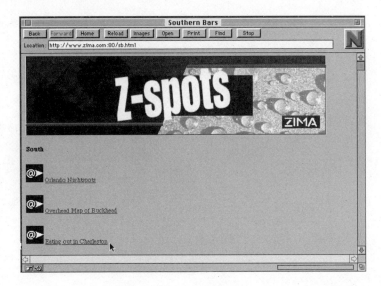

Zima target market. Labeled "Z-Spots," the purpose of the page was to give consumers an index to other compelling sites on the Web.

The showpiece of "Z-Spots" is the Zima Bar and Restaurant Guide, which serves as a "directory of directories" for consumers looking for local nightspots across the country. The guide segments into four separate geographic regions: Northeast, South, Midwest, and West. From this listing, consumers can find places of interest all over the country.

Z-Spots is an excellent example of an advertiser as a gatekeeper of content. Instead of driving consumers *away* from the site, it actually draws consumers *to* the site, since the guide is actually a useful tool for finding other sites around the Web. The advertiser becomes an "arbiter of coolness" for the online audience.

Downloadable Multimedia Files: Views, Earwacks, Icons, and Diversions

In this article, much has been said about "the online consumer." So, exactly what is it that this individual *consumes*? Certainly, information.

EXHIBIT 15.11 Zima Views

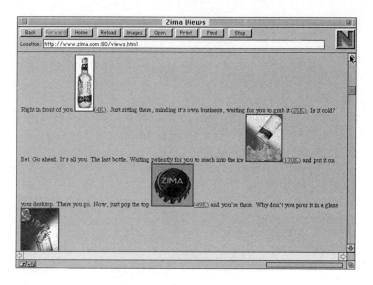

That has already been discussed in large part. Another thing which this individual wants is *digital stuff,* for lack of a better expression. Images, sounds, icons, games. In other words, the online advertiser, particularly an advertiser like Zima, has to offer the digital equivalent to T-shirts, caps, buttons in cyberspace. This *stuff* might be more commonly referred to as "downloadable multimedia files."

Within Zima.com, there are four areas that primarily offer these files, all accessible through "The Fridge." They are labeled "Views" (digital imagery), "Earwacks" (small sound files), "Icons" (desktop icons for Mac and Windows), and "Diversions" (shareware video games).

Let's investigate the Views section. Within Views, consumers have the opportunity to preview and potentially download a number of different Zima images. Once the consumer clicks on an image, it is downloaded to the user's hard drive through the ftp site. The size of each file is given in parenthesis next to the image. This way, the individual knows what to expect in terms of download time for a particular image.

A residual benefit to offering these items online is that they can become a part of the consumer's daily computing experience. Many consumers within the Zima demographic like to use images on their desktop as backgrounds or they like to customize their icons. By making such "refrigerator magnets" available, Zima is given the chance to be on thousands of computer monitors every day, whether or not the consumer is online.

Advertising for Advertising

A subject that has yet to be discussed is promoting an advertiser's web site. It's perfectly fine to invest the time and resources to build an online presence, but if nobody sees it, the entire exercise has been futile. For a web site, user traffic is the equivalent to television ratings. It validates that Web surfers are indeed visiting the site, and thus being exposed to the marketing communication.

There are typically four ways to publicize a web site. They are:

1. Paid pointers
2. Reciprocal/voluntary pointers
3. Web directory registration
4. Traditional media channels.

For the purpose of this article, I'll give a detailed description of each tactic.

Zima was an early pioneer in sponsoring other Web publishers in exchange for a premium banner links. A premium banner link is ideally a large graphic at the top or the bottom of a Web page that links back to the advertiser's site. The basic criteria that Zima employed to evaluate media purchase was:

1. Content relevance to the Zima demographic
2. Verifiable traffic that the sponsorable site generated
3. Zima's banner size and positioning within the sponsorable site.

Content Relevance

Like traditional media, Zima sought to advertise within sites that interested people in the target market. Sites like Hotwired (http://www.Hotwired.com), Word (http://www.word.com) and Virtual Radio (http://www.microserve.net:80/vradio/) fit the bill by delivering Zima a demographic and psychographic profile of its users that was consistent with the brand's targeting objectives.

Verifiable Traffic

Quite simply, a web site has to demonstrate a large amount of traffic. One of the most compelling features of Web publishing is that traffic volume and server accesses are quantifiable. Sites like Hotwired actually require readers to presubscribe to the service, thus guaranteeing an addressable readership for the purpose of selling ad space.

Banner Size and Positioning

Another important factor in paying for pointers is actual size and positioning within the sponsored site. In Web advertising, size and positioning are everything. Obviously, the more real estate a banner occupies, the more likely the chance that it will be accessed. With regard to positioning, ad space is more valuable relative to its closeness to the home page. A banner placed on the main home page will receive more impressions than the same banner placed a couple levels deep. Placement within a page is also a significant variable. For example, a banner placed on the top of a page typically generates more clicks than a banner on the bottom of the page.

Unpaid and reciprocal pointers are also very important. For example, citation of Zima as "Cool Site of the Day" generated the single largest amount of one-day traffic the site has ever seen. In many instances, Zima receives pointers from other sites merely because they like the Zima site. This can be a highly cost effective way of generating traffic to the site. Reciprocal pointers ("I'll scratch your back . . .") can be incredibly beneficial as well, particularly from highly trafficked sites.

Directory listings can make a tremendous impact collectively. Many web surfers employ directories like yahoo (http://www.yahoo.com) to search for content on the ever-expanding Web. In most cases, registration with these directories is free. By registering Zima with all the major directories and search engines, Zima was able to maximize its reach and guarantee that it would be "discovered" by Web surfers that had employed these various research tools. Another strong grassroots tactic for publicizing a web site like Zima was to post the site's address to all the relevant usenet newsgroups.

A final method for publicizing a web site is to utilize traditional vehicles like television ads, magazine ads, outdoor placements, and T-shirts. Any marketer that has made an investment in online advertising should make the additional effort to publicize the site in *every* other piece of marketing communication. Although the message may go unnoticed with non-wired consumers, it will be picked up and appreciated by consumers that do have Internet access.

Alcohol Issues: 21 Means 21

The final issue that must be discussed with regard to an alcoholic beverage advertiser like Zima is responsible marketing.

To be certain, online demographics tend to match up tremendously with the brand's target market. However, the truth is that there are some members of the online audience that are below the legal age limit to consume the product. Although Zima can never police its site to be 100% sure of a 21 plus audience, certain tactics can be employed to combat the occasional attendance of minors at the site.

EXHIBIT 15.12 Controlling Club Membership

A message directly accessible by clicking on the main banner advises consumers that Zima is for "Adult Humanz Only," and that "21 Means 21." By placing the message directly on the banner, Zima is making a statement to younger members of the audience that the site (and more importantly, the beverage) is not for them.

On the same accord, Tribe Z membership is limited to individuals 21 and over. Age disclosure is a necessary component of the Tribe Z survey and any individuals citing their age as younger than 21 are forbidden membership in the affinity club. To be certain, the brand only wants to communicate with consumers who can legally purchase the product.

The Future of Zima.com

The Zima brand has made a clear investment in cyberspace and Web advertising. The site will continue to be maintained, with major interface overhauls occurring on an annual basis. Zima's future uses of the World Wide Web include increasing participation from the ranks of Tribe Z, an ongoing investment in the latest Web multimedia technologies, and a more intelligent e-mail system that automatically reads consumer mail and attaches the appropriate feedback. Since Zima arrived to the party early, so to speak, the brand can enjoy the advantages of experience. However, with a medium like the Web being constantly in development, the only way to maintain an advantage is to continue to stay on the edge of the technology curve.

SECTION III

Research and Measurement Strategies

There is a great deal of excitement about interactive media. In mid-1996 WebTrack identified about 4,000 companies in the United States that spend more than $0.5 million on traditional advertising. Of this group approximately 19 percent had web sites, and with the explosive growth of sites in general this percentage will grow by a percent or two each month. There is a significant amount of money being invested in new media.

And advertising on the Internet is on the rise. In 1996 it is expected that between $200 million and $300 million will be spent on web advertising, with that number expected to more than double in 1997 and then rise even more dramatically over the next few years. In the face of these numbers it is obvious that current spending on advertising is capturing only a tiny portion of corporate America's total advertising budget.

Why is this the case? The simple answer is that there are major differences between traditional and interactive media. Interactive media are, for the most part, still evolving. The audiences are different in size, composition, and use. And there are different metrics in place for measurement. For example, let's look at an advertiser who places an ad in a print publication and on a web site. The advertiser knows a lot about the target audience they are reaching in the print publication. Yet they do not know how many readers actually saw the page where their ad was displayed, nor do they know how many readers actually stopped to read their ad. On the Web the advertiser knows exactly how many people saw their ad banner and how many people actually clicked on their banner to view their ad. But they don't know much about who has seen their advertising.

The beauty of the Web is that every interaction can be tracked. "Clickstream" tracking allows advertisers to see where their viewers came from and how many times the viewer interacted with their ad. Advertisers can even infer how long the viewer spent looking at their message. There are also auditable tracking mechanisms in place with both the BPA and the ABC now involved in certifying cyberspace.

There are many challenges new media must face to begin to attract a sizable portion of advertising budgets. This section provides thoughts and insights into what is already in place today and takes a look at where we need to move in the future.

"Measuring the Effectiveness of Interactive Media: Internet Media Evaluation and Buying Strategy" provides an overview of how advertising placements and measurement have evolved in the time since the first paid advertising appeared on the Web in September 1994. In that not-too-distant past there were a limited number of sites available for the consumer to visit; consequently, advertising was a novelty and results were stellar. Today web sites proliferate, ad banners are more ubiquitous, and click-through rates have fallen. John C. Nardone discusses how to approach Web-based media planning and highlights considerations that have not been part of the traditional equation. For example, search engines and directories have been able to deliver higher response rates by targeting ads based upon customers' psychographic interests. Others are targeting based on the browser type (this has major implications in terms of the creative presentation), computer operating system, time of day, or Internet service provider.

Nardone's look at measurement provides a primer in how to gauge web media performance. But he challenges advertisers to be sure to look beneath the surface. Hits and click-through rates only tell part of the story because they look at the traffic delivered to the advertiser's site. What is even more important is what that traffic did after it arrived. To be effective advertisers must examine both sides of the equation.

In "Hits, Views, Clicks, and Visits: Web Advertisers Face Data Jungle" Jamie Murphy and Ed Forrest provide more depth on this critical issue. At best, measurement is still an inexact science and the fundamental question remains: just who's doing all this hitting, visiting, and clicking? Some of this is being done by "spiders" and "crawlers" from the various search engines. The use of "frames" and "page caching" have also had an impact. To the uninitiated this may sound like meaningless jargon; but Murphy and Forrest clear up the mysteries and provide a thorough explanation of why these are important concepts to understand to successfully exploit cyber-space. They also point out that not every visitor need be anonymous. Marketers and advertisers can set up registration areas that will allow them to capture user demographics and interests through simple surveys.

There are many web management systems available today and Murphy and Forrest provide a survey of this field. As advertisers increase their monetary commitments, they need to be able to evaluate the reported information they receive. This raises the question of how advertisers will pay for their ad placements. Procter & Gamble recently challenged the interactive community by their declaration that they will only pay for "clicks" or traffic delivered to their site. This is an interesting position for one of the largest traditional mass media advertisers to take. Interactive site owners are very uncomfortable with this standard for payment and argue that so much depends on the advertiser's creative. Even if the creative is "dead on," other factors can influence performance such as time of day, computer type, domain name, and derived profile information.

Mickey Bennett looks at measurement from a different perspective—that of consumer research. Market research has traditionally developed ongoing consumer panels, and he believes that this methodology can deliver the marketing insights required to successfully compete. "A Blueprint for Syndicated Online Research: Consumer Panel Research Methods Applied to the Online Economy" argues that there need to be overall standards for measurement on the Internet. The Coalition for Advertising Supported Information and Entertainment (CASIE) was founded to develop common recommendations for research of online and interactive media. CASIE recommends that a universal standard be developed to calculate a user's "clickstream" or path.

As interactive advertising grows in volume, the role of the advertising agency will be challenged to change. Advertising in cyberspace has creative requirements that will tax the old-school-agency way of thinking. Major agencies are now showcasing their interactive capabilities, but there are also smaller upstarts who are aggressively going after business and positioning themselves as purely interactive shops. Compensation is also an issue here. It is probable that the agency compensation model will expand to include pay-for-performance and less of their total revenues will be derived from the traditional commission structure.

For advertising to flourish, user demographic and activity information needs to be much more robust. There is a clear need for third-party auditing. The advertising agencies want a much better understanding of media habits such as "site visit time, length of visit, repeat visitation, responses, interactivity and GRP rating, and share of voice equivalent for that individual's demographic group."

There are sophisticated tracking and measurement standards in place for traditional media such as network television. Recent studies show that traditional network television is losing its vise grip on the consumer as the number of media choices proliferate. Online and World Wide Web studies have found that the time consumers are spending in cyberspace has displaced television viewing in particular. "The Convergence of Database Marketing and Interactive Media Networks: New Sources, New Uses, New

Benefits" brings the focus back on the consumer. Rob Jackson and Paul Wang are excited by the communication possibilities brought by information networks including CD-ROM, online services, and the Internet in reaching the customer effectively. It is all about creating, keeping, and managing customers. It is their firm belief that the key to managing customers is a marketing database for it "allows a marketer to cost effectively understand customer behavior and maximize customer value." Electronic media can effectively utilize databases for the information hungry consumer to create a powerful resource. Database marketing has the opportunity to play a powerful role in the future of electronic communications.

CHAPTER 16

Measuring the Effectiveness of Interactive Media

Internet Media Evaluation and Buying Strategy

John C. Nardone

John C. Nardone is the Account Director for Consumer Products at Modem Media. In that role, he manages the overall strategic direction for all consumer-oriented business. He has been responsible for the development of IRIS, the first pricing model that can be used to evaluate media properties on the Internet. Prior to joining Modem Media, Nardone was a product marketing strategist at such leading consumer product companies as Procter & Gamble and PepsiCo.

Things change. And in this period of rapid growth and expansion of the Internet, things change *fast*. For this reason, I have focused on some broad brush theory behind interactive media planning, which I hope will remain more stable than aspects of implementation.

The first-ever paid advertising appeared in *HotWired* (Sept., 1994). At that time, there were no standards for measurement or valuation. There were no industry structures to support the buying and selling of ad space. There were no information sources, and no history. And there were no choices, since *HotWired* was the only game in town. But, as I said, things change.

Today, there is an active and growing market for Internet-based advertising which is likely to surpass $100 million spent in 1996. There are emerging standards for measurement, led by companies such as Internet Profiles Corporation and NetCount. There are numerous firms, such as SoftBank Interactive and Double Click, that specialize in representing interactive media properties to the advertising community. There are emerging information tools, such as Market Match from Focal Link, and traffic resource from I-Traffic. And there are plenty of choices.

Since the launch of *HotWired*, virtually every major U.S. media company has made an effort to play in the interactive media space. Time-Warner dove in head first with its ambitious Pathfinder site. Condé Nast moved more cautiously with Epicurious and Condé Nast Traveler Online. The cable ventures have all made significant efforts, from ESPN Sportzone, to CNN Online to Discovery Online. Newspapers from *USA Today* to the *New York Times, Wall Street Journal* and the Times Mirror publications are putting up quality content. And Internet-only publishers such as 1-Village have emerged with quality editorial products like Parent Soup, while integrated Web/TV projects like C/Net and MSNBC further complicate the landscape. In all, over 700 individual publications now accept advertising on the Web.

So planning an interactive media presence is not an easy task. Hopefully, the following information will provide the beginnings of a theoretical framework for addressing the challenges, as well as some useful how-to's. It must be noted, however, that the information reflects Modem Media's current view of the world. And that world is still anything but stable. So take everything with a grain of salt, and remember: things change.

The Evolution of Media on the Web

Beginning in late 1994, the rush to the Web began with technology focused toward forward-thinking companies building their own web sites. It seemed that for a company to "own" a corporate site was a point of prestige. It was a sign that the company was looking toward the future; that it was "hip"; and in some ways the web site provided a source of corporate pride. There was competition in the marketing community as the press wrote reviews and evaluated those with the most impressive site. So in many ways the corporate web site was viewed as another lobby to the company headquarters. And because there was little on the Web that could be considered "slick" or graphically interesting, consumers flocked to view what companies such as IBM, Microsoft and AT&T posted.

But as true editorial content from the publishers of the world began to emerge on Web, it quickly became apparent that consumers would not simply volunteer to go to corporate sites for entertainment value, or for the privilege of being advertised to. So, with *HotWired* as the first model, advertisers began to place banner ads in the emerging editorial sites. These ads offered some promise to the consumer, overtly or implied, and a convenient hypertext link to the advertiser's web site. This method effectively "herded" consumers where marketers wanted them to go, with click-through rates routinely in the 15 percent to 25 percent range and higher.

Of course, at that point, banner ads were still a novel thing. But, as more and more content emerged on the Web, and advertising became more prevalent, those click-through rates quickly fell to the 2–3 percent range. All of a sudden, it began to get expensive to herd large numbers of consumers. At the same time, web development services were also getting more expensive, just as companies were getting more ambitious about building the web sites. So companies that had begun by spending relatively small amounts of money to fund test efforts began to face the challenge of investing "real money." By the end of 1995, the typical corporate web program was a minimum of a one million dollar investment, leaving little in the budget for substantial traffic-driving media.

Yet, misled by the very early reports of high visitor counts, many corporate executives were surprised to find they had built large, impressive web sites that no one visited. They mistakenly thought they were in the cyber real estate business, but soon found that the "field of dreams" strategy was ineffectual. Just because you build it does not mean they will come. In fact, despite the new medium, advertising was still needed to alert consumers of the corporate presence.

Basic Theory

The overall objective of any media plan on the Web can be defined as follows: bring consumers to your interactive message, or bring your message to interactive consumers. The first part reflects the "herding" model of driving consumers to a web site. The second reflects a wider view of the Web as a flexible communications vehicle. But before beginning to think about a given project's web media strategy, we have to back up to the beginning of the marketing process and understand the overall objectives and priorities of the program.

- Are we trying to build awareness?

- Change consumer perceptions?

- Drive traffic to a web site?

- Is it a "direct response" program, in which we are asking consumers to take immediate action?

- Or is a "branding" assignment, in which we want to build a certain image or association with the product?

The Web is a very flexible communications vehicle that can be utilized in different ways to meet any one of or combination of these objectives. But these objectives cannot be addressed by any one advertising discipline in a vacuum. On the Web, functions including advertising, distribution, customer care, and research can all be tied up in the same initiative. So it is essential to begin the media planning process in conjunction with the creative development process, because the form the creative takes influences the form the media take and vice versa.

For example, in traditional advertising, we must decide if the appropriate medium for a client is TV or "out of home" or radio or print. But once we have decided that we want to advertise on the Web, we must still face a similar decision regarding the ad format or creative unit. It may not always be necessary to build a web site in order to convey a message to consumers on the Web. This might be accomplished directly through banner ads. It might be accomplished through sponsored content in an editorial environment. It might take the form of an "intermercial," a dynamic banner space that uses new technologies to create involvement without transferring to another web site.

So the creative unit and format along with its delivery from a media standpoint are integrally linked. This is decidedly a different situation than is usually encountered when working in "traditional media," where a TV or radio commercial can vary only in its length, and a print ad or outdoor billboard in its size or shape. In these media, the ad unit is fundamentally separate from the content that it resides in. This may not be the case on the Web, where it is possible to create very tight linkage between an ad and the editorial environment that surrounds it.

Sites vs. Sessions

As noted, early web advertising efforts were very "site-centric" in approach. The advertiser owned a piece of web real estate, and tried to herd consumers to it. But we now recognize that there are dynamics to consumers' online behavior that we must consider and exploit when making our creative and media decisions.

Our research has shown that there are two main types of web behaviors: needs based and interest based. In a needs-based web session, the consumer has a specific information need and has a pretty good idea of how to fulfill it. He may go directly to the URL of a known company to get the information or use a search or directory function to find it. But in either case, he is focused on a specific goal.

In another instance, the same consumer may be online to pursue an interest. He might start with a search or directory, but is likely to follow links from one site to the next, pursuing items that catch his attention. This is the classic "surfing" behavior, which is much less goal oriented.

Thus, when we think about an ad campaign, we must try to imagine how our target consumer is likely to use the Web, in regards to our product or service. Are they likely to be task focused or interest focused? At what point during their Web session will they be most receptive to our message? Do they want to reach them at "destination sites" or at the start of their web sessions? Do we need to employ different creative strategies and ad forms to correspond to different points in the session?

So as a guiding principle, we believe good web media plans start with the anticipation and recognition of the consumer's chosen web session. This approach recognizes the consumer and his individual session as the center point of the strategy. It is a user-centric approach, as opposed to an advertiser site-centric approach, which leads us to try different creative approaches that make the advertising part of the session, not a departure from it.

Targeting

Traditional media is most typically targeted at consumers based on demographic information. For example, we can buy TV or radio based on a broad range of age and gender breaks. But few web properties have demographic information on their users. So we typically target based on "psychographics" rather than demographics. In practice, this really boils down to targeting by interest and related editorial environment. However, since the Web has so many publications to choose from, we can focus on very specific and narrow targets: sports enthusiasts, online investors, do-it-yourselfers, etc.

We can also use the technology of the Web to take our targeting efforts to another level. We can target our ads to specific search words on the search engines and directories, so that if a consumer searches on the word "stocks," we can show him an ad for online brokerage services. If he is "drilling down" through a directory to "life insurance," we can sponsor that page with an ad for John Hancock insurance products. This is the most common targeting now taking place on the Web. But new and very sophisticated methods are emerging.

There are several sites they are beginning to target by users' technical characteristics, such as computer operating system, browser type, Internet service provider, etc. They can target by time of day or use intelligent agents to dynamically match ads to the users that would be most interested in them. And they can control the "reach and frequency" of ad delivery, in order to ensure that the same few consumers don't view the same ad over and over.

When designing our media plans we always explore the opportunities to employ these new targeting technologies. Through them, we have the potential to greatly increase the effectiveness of our creative and can help our money go farther by showing ads only to the most likely prospects.

Choosing Sites

After you have examined your own marketing goals, examined your target audience's expected behavior, determined your creative units and established your targeting criteria, you must still choose your ad locations. By now you have narrowed down your considerations list, based on obvious editorial and targeting options. But most likely you still have to choose between numerous, and sometimes similar, sites in order to refine your list. Consider the following:

- Is a site the acknowledged "Best in class"?

- Based on time spent per page, which site has the most involved readers?

- Which sites, on average, have the highest click rates for advertising?

- Which sites are most flexible in terms of creating unique, custom ad programs?

- Does the site have "building visitor counts," showing healthy growth over time?

- Does the site have a wide user base, or a small base that returns over and over?

- Are any of the sites sister properties to those on the traditional media plan, offering synergies?

- Do any of the sites have unique technical or targeting capabilities that we can utilize?

- Can any of the sites offer unique added value, such as e-mail lists, custom content, etc.?

- Can the sites deliver comprehensive and timely post-buy reports?

- Are the sites' media delivery audited by a recognized third-party organization?

It may be necessary to investigate these questions with each site's representative, but this time will be well spent. You will develop a deeper understanding of the properties that will allow more complete evaluation and ranking against your marketing goals.

Measurement Criteria

There are three main measurement criteria we use to evaluate web media performance:

- **Cost per impression**—the cost of exposure to an advertising message. This is typically expressed as a cost per thousand; for example $20 per thousand ad views.

- **Cost per click**—total media cost, divided by the total number of times an ad is clicked on. Related to this is the "click rate," which is the percentage of ad views that result in clicks.

- **Effective yield**—It is often valuable to have consumers click on ads and transfer to a web site, *but only if they do something when they get there.*

Effective yield refers to the cost per click divided by the number of pages of content consumed by the consumer, once they reach the desired web site. This measure gets to the delivered value of a web visit, and begins to differentiate the quality of audience delivered by different media properties. For instance, if one property delivers consumers to the advertiser's web presence at a cost of $1.00 per click, but they tend to consume four pages on average, then the second property delivers a more efficient "effective yield."

In general, media web sites report on impressions delivered and click-throughs. It is the responsibility of the marketer to analyze his own server logs to develop the effective yield measures. Coordination of this "server side tracking" can get technical and requires planning and cooperation with the host provider and the website production team. However, if done correctly, it yields valuable performance and diagnostic information.

Test and Re-apply

Because web media has such a robust feedback mechanism built into it, through site reporting and server log analysis, we have the opportunity to refine both media and creative choices "in real time." If something is not working, we can change it—quickly—while there is still time to make an impact on the program. So even the best laid media plans are subject to constant re-evaluation and change. This is both the blessing and the curse of the medium: it gives you the information you need to make decisions, but then you are obliged to constant, ongoing analysis and replanning in order to exploit it. It can be as tedious and labor intensive as it is valuable. But it is the only medium in which it is possible.

Depending on the goal of the program, impression delivery, click-throughs and effective yield may provide all the information you need to evaluate your success. However, in most cases this information can only tell you that your ad messages were delivered in a cost-effective way (or not). They cannot tell you if they achieved the desired effect on the consumer. So in order to determine if a program created awareness, built favorable attribute associations or increased intent to purchase, you must conduct primary research. This is most often accomplished by setting down a baseline of these measures in a pre-wave survey before the program runs, and then following with a post-wave survey after the program is complete. This approach is tried and true in traditional advertising and is the best gauge of a program's ultimate success or failure.

Summary

Web-based media planning is built on the same principles as traditional media planning: understand the marketing objectives, understand the consumer and his behavior, determine the targeting criteria that will reach that consumer, and choose the most appropriate editorial environments to complement the audience and the creative. In traditional media, we must make decisions about the appropriateness of different media channels to reach the consumer, while on the Web we must make similar decisions about ad forms. And in both media, we must determine our measurement and success criteria and provide the post reports against those measures.

The differences between operating in the traditional and web environments center on two things: the types and amount of information available and the time frames we work within. Traditional media has sophisticated systems, models, and information resources that have developed over time to assist the media professional in his decisions. These systems, if available at all, are still in infancy on the Web. Yet the information that is available comes in real time, requiring constant attention, evaluation and reaction. So we must work with imperfect and incomplete information that requires rapid turnaround—not an ideal combination. Nonetheless, interactive resources and systems are improving, and will continue to develop over time. We can look forward to a day that we will have complete and reliable information and feedback, and the systems to analyze and react to it. When this time arrives, the Web will fulfill its promise as the most powerful and accountable medium available.

CHAPTER

17

Hits, Views, Clicks, and Visits

Web Advertisers Face Data Jungle

Jamie Murphy
Edward Forrest

Jamie Murphy is a doctoral candidate in communications at Florida State University.

Edward Forrest is Professor of Marketing at Griffith University, Brisbane, Australia.

Brian Massey, a doctoral candidate in Communications at Florida State University, contributed to this article.

Advertisers rushing to buy a banner on the World Wide Web find themselves wading through a jungle of data and statistics that set the price for apples by counting oranges.

Useless data don't seem to be slowing the rush of advertisers to the Internet. Forrester Research of Cambridge, Mass., projects that web-based ad revenues will grow from $200 million this year to more than $2 billion by 2000.

As they funnel all that money into this medium, all advertisers really want to know is how many people visit a web site in a given period of time and how many of those visitors see a banner and then click on it to view the advertiser's web page.

But determining such figures is at best an inexact science. Many web-site operators will glibly rattle off the number of "hits" recorded on their sites, but the actual number of people who visit a site are typically only a fraction of those hits. What's more, only a few visitors click on an advertiser's banner—and even when they do, there is no guarantee that they will actually arrive at the advertiser's site.

So, while the hit remains the current standard by which ad rates are set, content providers and advertisers alike are eager to create new and more meaningful measurement models.

"In this crazy state of the market, ad prices are set by the hype surrounding your site or Initial Public Offering, rather than by hard numbers," said Terry Myerson, president of Interse, a leading provider of Internet tracking software.

Katharine Paine, chief operating officer of the Web consulting firm The Delahaye Group, said:

> Most top-level management doesn't know enough about the Web,— or didn't six months ago—to know the difference between "hits" and "visitors." But that's an important distinction for a company to make before it pulls thousands of dollars from its wallet to buy its very own Web site banner.

A hit is not a visitor is not a click. And whichever of those three you measure, none answers an equally fundamental question: Just who's doing all this hitting, visiting and clicking?

Chip Bayers, writing in the April issue of *Wired* magazine, playfully suggested that at some point in the future only 1 in 10 hits would come from a human being. The rest, he predicted, will be logged by "spiders" and "crawlers," search-engine robots blind to banners and with nary a dime to their names.

The seeds of that future are already sown. Search engines like AltaVista, Lycos and WebCrawler send out spiders, or broods of spiders, to catalog and index the Web. The developers of HotBot, the latest mega-search engine, claim it will index the roughly 50 million pages on the Web every week. (Related May 21 article: "HotBot Advances Web Search Technology")

And a growing number of "para sites," which glom off the work of existing search engines, generate hits for a search engine yet return to the human searcher a display that is stripped of the search engines' ad banners. (Related April 9 article: "'Para-sites' Raid Search-Engine Data")

Either way, a computer-generated hit does not have a pair of eyes, nor does it make consumer purchasing decisions.

Hits, visits, registration, impressions, and clicks are all web-speak for measuring the popularity of a site to set ad rates.

A hit is the most basic traffic measurement; it simply means that a web server transmitted a requested file. A hit can be a page—a text file coded in hypertext markup language, or HTML—or any element on that page, including a graphic, video, audio, a Java applet, an ad or a script, among other things.

So, for example, when a visitor accesses a page with five graphics and a script, that server's log file typically will record it as seven hits—one page, five graphics and one script. (Even the drop cap—the big red "A"—at the beginning of this article registered as a hit when you came to this page, because it is not coded in HTML like most text on the page but is a graphic file.)

Sites that use frames combine two or more pages on one screen and consequently multiply the number of hits on an opening screen, perhaps accounting for upwards of 30 or more hits from what is really a single view.

Counting hits "is a beginner's mistake," said Kevin O'Connor, chief executive of DoubleClick, a web marketing company. "Typically, once a person realizes the confusion they immediately drop the term. I would like to see the term banished from web speak."

The web community would do well to remember a baseball basic: the difference between a hit and a pitch. Web servers are pitching files, not hitting them.

To complicate matters, there's a difference between hits and "qualified hits." For example, the server may be too busy to deliver the file or the visitor may click on the web browser's "stop" button and abort the file transfer. Yet in either case, the server will register a hit.

Two web-traffic counters, NetCount and Nielsen I/Pro, compensate for this problem by measuring both requested and delivered files.

Another form of hit is the HTML, or page hit. This measures how many text pages have been requested, ignoring all other types of files.

HTML hits would provide a fairly straightforward measurement if it were not for "caching"—that is, storing web pages on either the visitor's computer or on the server of a service like America Online.

Caching decreases download time and keeps Net traffic at a minimum. When a web browser is told to get a page, it first checks to see if that page is cached. If it is, then that's what the user gets—and the web server from which the page originated isn't credited with a hit.

Even harder to gauge are visits to a web site. Like simple hits or HTML hits, visits are measured largely by rough guesses.

In I/Pro's scheme, a visit represents consecutive file requests all made by one visitor at one web site. If that visitor stops requesting files for (generally) 30 minutes, then starts asking for files again, a new visit is tallied for that site.

However, most web sites include links to other, external sites. So someone could start at Site A, then link to Site B and spend a half hour there. If that user returns to Site A via the browser's "back" button function, Site A will register it as a new visit. And if an online connection was left open during a work break, a new visit would be recorded when that user becomes active again—that is, clicks anywhere—on the already open site.

An ideal way to measure a web's site's popularity would be to count how many unique visitors it attracts in a given period of time. But that kind of count is foiled by page caching. A page that has been cached by a private network, like a university or America Online, may be viewed by one or thousands of people, so a publisher has no idea how many people are viewing a page.

Registration is one way to clear the measurement hurdles of page caching. Sites that require registration typically allow free access but require visitors to complete a short questionnaire to receive a user name and password.

But registration presents problems of its own. First, a visitor might be unwilling to answer the questions and so simply leave the site. And a registered user might well forget his or her user name or password or confuse them with the dozens of other user names and passwords that people must remember when navigating today's digital society. In many cases, rather than go through customer service to straighten out the problem, a visitor will simply re-register and get a new user name and password.

In addition, user names and passwords may be shared by many users—family members or classroom students, for example—so registration may be a more accurate measurement of computers than of human users.

Despite these drawbacks, registration offers web-site managers an attractive advantage: user demographics drawn from the registration questionnaire, which can help advertisers determine whom the site is attracting.

The effectiveness of traditional advertising in newspapers or on television is often gauged by impressions (a.k.a. exposures or ad views) and I/Pro's Erin Gaffaney argues that this measurement can also be applied to the web.

Impressions represent the number of times an ad banner is seen. Typically, impressions are calculated from a web server's log files, yet the resulting number can be misleading because of caching or the problem of qualified hits vs. simple hits.

Impressions usually are sold on a cost per thousand, or CPM basis. Such rates vary from $10 to $100, depending on the site, the hype surrounding the site and the demographic profile of the site's average user.

For DoubleClick's O'Connor, however, "CPM is only useful when comparing two sites that deliver your target audience."

Delahaye's Paine agrees: "CPM can be very misleading on the Net," she said, "since you really don't know what 'thousands' you are really reaching."

But Will Margiloff of Jumbo!, one of the largest web sites, with more than 100,000 cataloged pages, is a "big believer in cost per impression." Advertisers "want to put fannies in the seats," he said.

The best measurement of all might well be clicks—that is, counting the number of people who actually click on an advertising banner. AdCount takes the click concept a step further to measure "click-throughs"—that is, how many times the user successfully arrives at the advertiser's web page after clicking.

When counting clicks, if 100 users are exposed to an ad banner but only two click on it, the usage rate is tallied at 2 percent. But click rates are harder to measure than impressions, and most web traffic measurement companies are only now getting into position to offer the sophisticated software this kind of counting requires.

But ultimately, ad banners might well turn out to be the wrong ad model for many web sites.

"Advertisers want to bring people to their site, and the publishers want to keep them in their site," said Interse's Myerson. "Obviously, there is conflict here."

From that conflict, he said, new models for web advertising could emerge. He envisions different models for three categories of web sites: navigational, news, and content.

"For the navigational sites, like Yahoo/Infoseek, the current ad model is fine," Myerson said. "For the content sites, like HotWired and ESPN, they have the opportunity to produce branded content or sponsorships, where the advertiser is integrated into the content."

The news sites, however, are "pinched the most as they try and maintain the separation between editorial and advertising," Myerson said.

The recent demise of *Web Review*'s Net Daily News supports Myerson's theory. In a closing letter to his readers, *Web Review*'s publisher, Dale Dougherty, stated, "The advertiser-supported model isn't really covering costs for targeted publications, and *Web Review*—which requires a dedicated staff of editorial, design, production and technical resources—is expensive to produce."

Who's Doing All This Measuring?

A number of companies now are trying to bring some calm to the seeming madness of measuring traffic on World Wide Web sites—and on the banners advertisers pay to place on those sites—though each has its own view of how and what to measure.

Devising more accurate and efficient methods of a web site's popularity among Internet users is a battle that's just now beginning.

"Staying ahead of the rapid pace of Internet evolution, including Java, VRML and digital certificates," said Terry Myerson, president of Interse, "is by far our biggest challenge today."

Interse's "Market Forces 2" is a leading web-server software package that provides measurements of site and ad-banner traffic. Similar independent third-party measurement services are offered by NPD's "PC-Meter," Neilsen I/Pro, and NetCount.

DoubleClick and Focalink's "Smart Banner" and "Market Match" offer just-in-time advertising delivery, or ad-placement services, in addition to measuring the effectiveness of ad banners. NetGravity's "AdServer" is a software package for web-site managers that measures ad-banner traffic and also customizes the banners and ensures that messages are rotated for the characteristics of site visitors.

Newshare's "Clickshare" measures web traffic, but also includes a user registration and micro-transaction payment scheme.

As for the nuts-and-bolts of measuring the traffic, I/Pro uses sophisticated algorithms to infer web-browsing behavior, while NetCount uses a full count of all web-server log files. Yet there are two roads to the actual counting—the Net surfer vs. the web server. PC-Meter tracks usage on a surfer's personal computer; I/Count and NetCount track traffic on a web site's server.

"Current measurement techniques are basically site-centric—drawing conclusions from the number of visits that occur on a particular web site," said Pamela Smith, PC-Meter's Marketing Director.

PC-Meter installs its software on a user's computer, and it currently is monitoring the moves of a panel of 3,000 potential web-ad consumers. This panel is projected to reach 10,000 in order to increase predictive accuracy. PC-Meter's software tracks all the files it finds open on a computer—regardless of whether it's dialed into the Internet—as well as the time the user spends with each file.

However, PC-Meter's small panel doesn't include education or business users, and focuses instead on home users. Also, PC-Meter's software can work only with IBM-compatible PCs.

I/Count and NetCount install their measurement software on the web site's server to track each user's trip through the site. It records such information as the user's domain address, pages viewed, and whether the user hits the browser's "stop" button to abort any file download. Unlike PC-Meter's software, these measurement software packages can't accurately measure site visits.

Newshare's "Clickshare" and Nielsen I/Pro's "I/Code" offer a one-stop user registration process. Once a user is registered with Clickshare, for example, he or she can surf from Clickshare site to Clickshare site without having to re-register at each stop. Clickshare registrants can also use their account with the company to pay what they owe on any web purchase.

Netcount's "HeadCount" registration system is due out soon.

Clickshare, designed for publishing sites, tracks registered users to measure web traffic across multiple, unrelated servers. Currently, the

Christian Science Monitor, American Reporter, and *Studio Briefing* use the Clickshare system.

I/Code registrants can choose from more than 20 sites, ranging from Audio Net to Visa. Like their Clickshare counterparts, users registered with I/Code have only one ID and password to remember. I/Code encourages registration through contests and sweepstakes.

And there are plenty of users who are willing to sign up to click around. "Currently, a quarter million web site users have registered for I/Code at a rate of approximately 50,000 a week," said I/Pro's public relations manager, Erin Gaffaney.

For web-site managers Eric Meyer of Newslink and Charlie Hofacker of Hall of Malls, however, sophisticated measurement software and tracking services may be fine, but there's still nothing quite like a bit of old-fashioned—and far less expensive—counting.

"I can easily use standard statistical analysis packages or one of the many Unix-based freeware programs to give me the information I need," said Hofacker.

"It comes down to a matter of trust between the advertiser and the web site," he said. "Measuring services or software are an additional expense that many web sites might not be able to afford."

Banners: Bullying, Boosting and Blocking

Increasing click rates is becoming an abiding goal of advertisers and web-site owners, especially since Procter & Gamble recently rewrote the rules for buying advertising banners.

Not content with the cost-per-thousand, or CPM, model, P&G is playing hardball with web sites, forcing them to accept a different payment design. For example, it pays search engines through a scheme that factors in the number of clicks on its banners. The broadcast industry has long used a similar strategy, typically during early morning hours on low-traffic cable TV stations, where advertisers pay per call to a 1-800 telephone number.

Yahoo! was the first search engine to acquiesce to P&G's terms. Still, Yahoo and other sites have argued that click rates depend on a well-designed banner.

"How do we distinguish between a great site and a lousy ad?" I/Pro's Erin Gaffaney asked. "Do we blame the ad or blame the site?"

Few sites so far have bowed to the P&G model.

A recent Nielsen I/Pro study found that click rates varied from 2.4 percent to 17.9 percent, depending on the advertiser's banner. DoubleClick has shown that a few simple banner changes can increase the click rate by 200 percent. DoubleClick's Test It! program allows an advertiser to compare two similar banners and in 48 hours see which has a higher click rate.

C/Net claims that an animated Java-enhanced icon increased the click rate nearly four times over that of a static design for the same ad.

Click rates also depend on the type of web site hosting the ad banners. The Nielsen I/Pro study found that the click rate varied by as much as seven times between different sites.

A study by Jumbo!, released to *CyberTimes,* suggested that click rates fluctuated from 2.2 percent to nearly 6 percent, depending on the web site hosting an ad banner. This translates to a cost per click of 31 cents to 35 cents, far below other rates.

Will Margiloff of Jumbo! argues that the true cost of web advertising lies somewhere between the old and new models. "CPM is fine, but it should work in conjunction with cost per click," he said, "because both are needed to understand the true value and effectiveness of an ad buy."

If hits, visits, clicks, impressions and registration weren't enough to toss into this salad of web ad rates and measures, consider "smart" or "targeted" banners. These are aimed at increasing click rates and impressions by taking advantage of software that recognizes such user characteristics as time of day, computer type, or domain name—.edu or .com—to deliver an ad banner tailored to a specific user profile.

DoubleClick provides this service on a real-time basis between the user and the web site. User information is first sent to DoubleClick, which then transmits the ad banner to the site's page as it's displayed on the user's computer. NetGravity offers a similar software package that resides on the web site's server. Search-engine sites like Yahoo! work smart banners based on keywords. A keyword search for "Florida," for example, would likely return to the user ad banners specifically related to that state.

And those who mourn the web's commercialization can take heart in a new category of software known as ad blockers.

PrivNet's "Internet Fast Forward" is a sort of anti-ad radar that detects and blocks out all ad banners appearing on a requested web site. Basically, this means a free lunch on advertising-supported sites.

Ad blocking isn't a big concern yet, said DoubleClick's Kevin O'Connor, who sees less than 5 percent of users rigging themselves with such anti-ad radar. But he added: "If it were to ever become a big problem, we would simply defeat it. The consumer choices are 'take ads or pay the site.' There is no such thing as a free lunch."

CHAPTER
18

A Blueprint for Successful Syndicated Online Research

Consumer Panel Research Methods Applied to the Online Economy

Mickey Bennett

Mickey Bennett is Vice President, Consumer Information Systems, for ACNielsen, which uses personal scanning technology to report purchasing of nondurable consumer goods. He has directed the development of consumer analytic systems, which are used to gain strategic insights from consumer transactional data.

© 1995, 1996 Mickey Bennett

Analyzing consumer activity captured over time from the same consumers yields some of the most insightful behavioral information a marketer could want. As a marketer, I want more than a report card of market share and total sales. I would love to know:

- Where do the buyers of my brand shop?

- How frequently do they shop?

- Who are my heavy buyers?

- What else are my buyers buying in my category?

- Where do buyers of my new brand come from?

- When I lose buyers, what brands do they buy?

- Am I getting good trial purchasing? From Whom?

- Who is the trier of my brand who didn't come back?

- Who is the trier who is coming back a lot?

- How can I get more of them into my brands franchise?

Anyone responsible for growing a business has asked questions like these to help set marketing strategy and tactics. Imagine the competitive value of identifying a new segment of consumer interest before your competition, or having better knowledge of consumer behavior in your market. Marketers of all consumer goods and services are better armed for competition when they understand consumption patterns and trends of consumers in their respective markets or categories.

Since the late 1950s, consumer packaged goods marketers have had the benefit of consumer panel information to help them set competitive strategy. This type of consumer activity measurement is reported from the same set of households over time and is broadly classified as a longitudinal methodology. Tracking the same set of households over time yields insights from a view of the total consumption activity for each household. Proper sampling and recruiting techniques allow a relatively small sample to statistically represent a larger population. Every online marketer should be demanding the consumer behavior insights which only consumer panels can deliver.

Capturing this type of longitudinal consumer information is a complex research challenge. Consumer panel research demands the researcher strike and maintain a delicate balance of capturing a robust activity database and keeping the data collection process as passive as possible. The data gain marketing value when a representative set of consumers consistently and accurately report on their consumption.

Consider the question of tracking PC online consumer activity. Why do I say a consumer panel is the best methodology to capture consumer online activity? Today's technology, which has enabled PC online activity, should obviously be able to capture consumer online activity to allow marketers the insights noted above without the need for expensive and sophisticated consumer panel data capture. After all, the online services know who their users are and what their users' activity is while they are in the online service! Why can't marketers gain access to the consumer activity information which online service providers will easily be able to capture?

It is a fair question, but the fact is online marketers will not be able to acquire actionable marketing information from the services themselves. It is true that third-party researchers doing independent site audits will help business-to-business advertisers and agencies as well as marketers of space on less popular or niche sites. But the competitive situation and revenue pressures of the online services will prevent them from allowing their information to be used to deliver the consumer insights needed by online marketers to compete. The sophisticated insights packaged goods marketers enjoy can only be delivered by longitudinal consumer panel research.

In this chapter, I will compare the measurement of consumer activity from an on-going consumer panel versus measurement from an online service provider. I have 13 years experience with in-home scanner consumer panels as large as forty thousand households. I also have experience with third-party consumer information captured when retailers sell their sales data to third-party research firms for processing. In this chapter, I will analyze the dynamics of these two methodologies. Each methodology has its unique issues of quality, utility and cost. As advertisers and marketers in a consumer online economy, I believe you will see that only the consumer panel methodology delivers the marketing insights required to succesfully compete in the emerging PC based online economy.

It is difficult to exist today in a media business without any measurement of the audience. Looking at the importance of advertising to the cable and magazine industries, it is clear that accurate consumer activity measurement is a critical component of an economy fueled by advertising. As we consider the case for consumer panel measurement of the PC online economy, we will also examine the development of the advertising industry and its capacity to support the PC online medium because of its revenue importance to the online economy; advertisers, agencies, Value Added Networks, online content providers and of course researchers.

The PC: Today's Interactive Medium

As the recent media hyperbole surrounding the "Information Highway" subsides, we are seeing real, albeit immature, Personal Computer Based Interactive technology available today as well as television-based interactive technology being field-tested. Interactive television tests are underway with several big name backers. These tests have shown one consistent finding for all involved; Interactive Television (ITV) is expensive to implement without vast industry expenditures to upgrade current signal delivery infrastructure. Everyone also agrees that standards for signal delivery and in-home signal processing will be very slow to arrive, given the attractive market size, potential payouts to winners and the long-term revenue stream afforded to the owners of the appliance technology which will eventually earn a place in most people's homes. Given the technological challenges and industry realignments required to develop and fund this gargantuan effort to bring television-based shopping, entertainment and communication to the majority of U.S. homes, it is unlikely that this nascent industry will achieve significant economic mass in the next five years.

Only recently featured in the public media, the Internet has been gaining notoriety at an astounding rate, driving awareness deeply across the population. The Internet's rate of growth is itself newsworthy, as is the daily number of new Internet home pages and e-mail addresses mentioned in newspaper and magazine articles, print advertisements and direct mail announcements. The Internet has become such a de facto standard for interuser connectivity, that even the established commercial online networks (Prodigy, America Online, CompuServe)[1] have rushed new software releases to market which feature access to the Internet via their commercial service. Established software publishers (such as Microsoft, IBM, Adobe and Netscape)[2] as well as new aggressive firms (Spry with Internet-In-A-Box, or private networks like Business MCI, Mecklermedia, Commerce 2000, Ziffnet and others) are being attracted to the Internet environment bringing new capabilities, competition, cost efficiencies and innovation to those engaging in commerce in the emerging online economy.

Given the cost issues associated with a materially significant implementation of Interactive Television, the PC, not the television, will be the interactive medium used by the most people for the foreseeable future. Forrester Research (Cambridge, MA) took the position in December of 1994, that "The PC will be the only viable interactive device in the next 2–5 years." [3] I am personally convinced it will be around in the next twenty years as well, although it will be more PDA[4] like in form factor and cheap wireless broadband will be commonplace. The PC has proven to be a sustainable medium as evidenced by the rapidly growing popularity of online services and the increased penetration of PC's with modems across commercially important consumer segments of the United States.

Consumer PC Ownership Reaches Critical Mass

The penetration of PC's into American homes has increased by 30 percent in the last two years. In 1996 about 36 percent of all households also have PC's.[5] Two-thirds of those PC's have modems. Forty percent of the total PC population in homes are connected to an online service. The competitive economic forces at work have driven down prices and consumers are showing that this market is very elastic.

As seen below, the absolute numbers are not only impressive, but the rate of growth is increasing although it is expected to grow at a slower rate through the next three years. Falling PC prices, intense competition for PC's in the home market, new generations of pre-installed, ready to switch on, CD-ROM, multimedia, online service ready PC's are all keeping the consumer market hot. Loads of new CD-ROM software and constantly improving online service offerings are also supporting the PC becoming a ubiquitous household appliance. *The Wall Street Journal* recently reported that in 1994 more households purchased PC's than color televisions.

Today's Consumer of Online Services

A recent study by AST Computers of two-thousand United States computer buyers confirmed the likelihood that the PC is truly a new consumer medium. The study revealed that nearly 34 percent of these

EXHIBIT 18.1 Projected U. S. Household Penetration of PCs, Modems, and Online Service Access

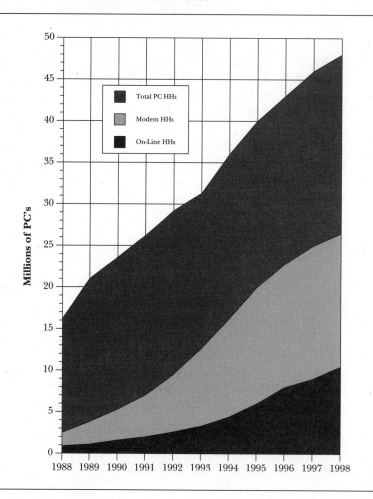

Source: Forbes ASAP, p. 72, April 10, 1995 [6]

PC owners were connected to an online service. The total user base reported spending an average of 13 hours per week on the PC. The average person only spends 9 hours per week watching prime time television! America Online (AOL) alone is accessed by about 1/25 of the audience of a single television network on a given day, but ABC and NBC were both working hard to "brand" areas on the AOL service until NBC jumped to the Microsoft Network to produce programming content.[7] My interpretation of this network interest is that that we will have a very broad, heterogeneous universe of users with a mix of online behavior. This emerging consumer behavior dynamic can only be understood through the thorough tracking and analysis of consumer activity by the various user segments. Consumer panel research is the best methodology for capturing a full range of analytic measures of consumer activity.

Dependable information about actual users is very vague at this point, since research services are only beginning to explore and learn about this market themselves. It is generally recognized that the profile of those using online services is a very desirable advertising target: male, upscale, affluent and well educated.[8] Current estimates of 1995 Consumer Online Service access is about 4 to 4.4 million consumers. These consumers bought $200 million worth of goods and services through online vendors in 1994. By 1998, 19.5 million consumers are expected to purchase about $4.8 billion in goods and services.[9] While these estimates predict an optimistic five-fold increase in business per household, the fact is that commerce is rapidly adapting to the PC online environment. As industry quickly fills the gaps in required technology, such as enabling online banking and shopping by providing secure transactions and enabling better, faster graphics by providing increased bandwidth, competitive pressures will make access cheaper and improve services and innovation. The best advertising method of all, "word of mouth" from friends and co-workers, becomes more commonplace everyday, so we can be sure the PC based use of interactive online services will continue to grow at its rapid pace. Consumer panel research will provide the means to understand the trends and changing dynamic of the consumer marketplace as the online economy evolves.

Online Advertising Activity Parallels Postwar TV Growth

In the Spring Special Edition of *Advertising Age,* the focus was a retrospective into the last 50 years of television advertising. Scott Donaton, the respected *Ad Age* columnist, brilliantly related today's interactive challenge for advertising agencies to a nearly identical challenge when television was the upstart technology, much as interactive, online media are perceived today. Back then, radio and print media were so entrenched, that advertisers were reluctant to "test the waters." At that time (late 1940s), Leo Burnett urged the industry to experiment: " The courage of Agencies to change long-established habits and procedures and to get wet all over . . . is, in my opinion, the index to the strength of the advertising agency business of the future."[10] That message seems remarkable when considered with a more recent message from Ed Artzt, then Chairman of Procter & Gamble, delivered last May to the American Association of Advertising Agencies (4A's) annual convention at the Greenbrier Resort. Artzt said: "Our most important ad medium, television is about to change big-time. . . ." He asked the 4A's to get together to "understand how consumer viewing habits will change as a result of these new technologies." Jay Chiat (Chiat/Day Agency) described the agency reaction as, "Hey, my agency doesn't know anything about interactive media, we'd better do something about it."[11]

They did do something about it. In the nine months since Artzt's call to action, ad agencies have added Interactive or New Media Units which are aggressively fighting for recognition as "Interactive Agency of Record" for their clients. On April 2, 1995, the country's eighteenth largest advertiser, AT&T, announced that Modem Media, of Norwalk, Conn. would be their Interactive Agency of Record. Modem Media also lists Coors, Zima, and CBS as clients. Other advertisers are also reviewing agencies' interactive capabilities. To ensure it had the right online advertising skill sets on hand, America Online purchased Ted Leonsis's interactive media agency, Redgate, last year.

ONLINE ADVERTISING—A DESCRIPTION

The creative requirements of online advertising will also tax the old school agency way of thinking. Obviously the interactive model of message delivery changes from the broadcast environment, since people will have to be shopping for information on a product, in the process of buying the product, or interested in the editorial or entertainment value of an advertiser's online message to reach your message. The ad agencies that are already working in the interactive area will deliver value to their clients by drawing the customer's interest to the message effectively, and delivering a positive experience to the consumer, whether the experience is making a purchase, getting information or being entertained.

Scott Kurnit (an interactive marketing leader with tenure at both MCI and Prodigy) describes a scenario where advertisers can place "Activerts" on any online service for a fee. The consumer can press on the button (example: Colgate has a new article on their site which describes "Five ways to get a toddler to brush his teeth without a fight.") to transparently get to the Colgate area, where, just like a magazine, the consumer can browse, place a bookmark, print an article (unlike a magazine), or scan the content to learn about toddlers and tooth care.

Consider the tone of this approach. The advertiser delivers a real interactive message which the consumer values. The online service gets paid as a deliverer of the interested consumer, plus some base fee similar to a slotting allowance for the activert on their system. The agency can be compensated its percentage for the slotting fee, the responses, and with the ratings produced by the proposed enterprise, the demographics of the buy and the demographics of the responders will all be reported in GRP terms, which can be rolled up in a total delivery number as the agency does today.

FOLLOW THE MONEY: AN ONLINE ECONOMY NEEDS A COMMON CURRENCY

The audience of this new PC-based media is a new audience, which has yet to be identified and measured to support advertising sales. The measures must be expressed in terms that traditional advertising media planners and buyers can understand and use. Media buyers require audience measurement including demographics of individuals exposed to the advertising and a measure of the exposure frequency to develop Gross Rating Point equivalent measures.[12]

To ensure the industry gains acceptable metrics to use as a common currency, a new group, CASIE (The Coalition for Advertising Supported Information and Entertainment) was formed in early 1995 to establish online and interactive research standards. As David Marans, SVP, Director of Media Research at J. Walter Thompson said of CASIE, "The goal is to have some kind of common currency." The coalition represents the American Associate of Advertising Agencies, the Association of National Advertisers and the Advertising Research Foundation. This organization has already developed preliminary recommendations for research of online and interactive media. The group is trying to balance current industry measurements with the capabilities of the new media.

CASIE recommends that a universal standard be developed to calculate a user's "clickstream" or path through the online service. They would also like to see "second-by-second" measurements of usage as opposed to several second interval of today's TV measurement systems. They also recommended that passive people meters be tested for online and interactive TV services. The most relevant recommendation was for a "sample to be formed for interactive and online measurement and monetary incentives offered to participants, as with Nielsen's People meter sample."[13]

Delivering required advertising metrics such as GRP's and demographic information to advertisers, agencies, online service providers, Value Added Networks (VAN's) will enable a growth in advertising placements on these online media by quantifying the audience delivered at a given cost. Dollars available for this media will grow as online services penetration reaches the majority of the US population, because budgets for advertisers could then be drawn from larger national advertising budgets. Until recently, most online advertising was considered a learning experience and was funded from ad-hoc adver-

EXHIBIT 18.2 Tracking Online Advertising "Clickstream" Links

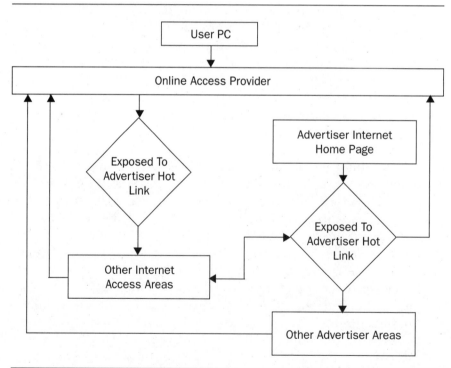

tiser budgets. With high quality metrics available to report on the reach and frequency of the advertising delivery, the advertisers and agencies will know what they are buying and it can be included as part of a typical media buy.

Are the Big Agencies Ready for Interactive?

As Exhibit 18.3 indicates, even back in August of 1994, major agencies have made their interactive capabilities a very visible part of their strategic offerings. If this table were updated today, not only would we see more agencies, like Ogilvy and Mather Interactive, but we would also see the inclusion of some aggressive upstarts in this area, such as Modem Media, CKS,[14] and others who meld technological understanding with the new marketing communications demands.

EXHIBIT 18.3 Advertising Agencies With Dedicated Interactive Groups

Agency	Advertising Agency Interactive Media Group Activity					
	Internet	Commercial Online	PC Software & CD-ROM	Kiosks	Interactive TV	Electronic Retailing
Ayer	•	•	•	•	•	
Bates USA					•	
Bozell		•	•		•	
Leo Burnett		•	•		•	
Chiat/Day	•	•			•	•
Earle Palmer Brown						
Fallon McElligot	•	•				
Foote, Cone & Belding		•	•	•	•	
Grey Advertising	•		•	•	•	
Martin Agency			•			
Ross Roy Communications	•	•	•		•	
Wells, Rich Greene/ BDDP		•				

Source: Mike Garvey, *Advertisng Age;* August 15, 1994

Interactive Advertising Industry Economics

The consumer panel will report detailed activity on popular business-to-consumer advertising sites (Internet or VAN). For the business-to-business, specialized and niche industrials, the custom audit service of the Network Cooperation Model would usually be the best methodology for measuring business-to-business advertising effectiveness.

It is important to recognize the culture and power at work today concerning how advertising is bought and sold. All advertising purchased by media planners, and funded from the general advertising budget of the advertiser, must be measured in terms of GRP's. The most valuable GRP's are those targeted and delivered to the right buyer demographic group. Most advertising which cannot be quantified as part of the general advertising activities will fall under other specialty budgets which are not always administered by the agency, hence removing any interest on the part of the agency to recommend this specialty type of advertising. Typically, the media buys are placed by agencies and paid for by advertisers. The majority of these buys will be national, so that the funding will come from a general advertising budget. Many advertising efforts to date have come from ad-hoc advertising budgets, which are much smaller than the general funds. The larger, nationally represented access providers will capture the lion's share of the advertising dollars available, much as today's broadcast networks capture the lions share of total television advertising dollars. These national access providers will be likely to use an in-house sales team to sell ad placements. Local and regional providers will probably see their advertising revenue develop more slowly.

Compensation based on pay-for-performance methods will not be readily embraced by ad agencies. Pay for performance neglects the fact that good ad work cannot salvage an inferior product, a bad offer or a poor service. Today, agencies need to be compensated for more than just the creative fees. Agencies will want to place buys and perform planning functions within this media just as they do today for traditional media, but a commision or other compensation plan will have to evolve. The ratings metrics, which could be drawn from a consumer panel, will mirror the statistics used today by agencies to measure delivery effectiveness; and it would be a key part of that agency compensation infrastructure. Additional sources online related revenue for agencies will be advertising client Internet areas via traditional media such as television, radio, direct mail, or print ads.

Will Businesses Pay for Online Advertising?

Internet usage has increased an average of 8 percent per month, roughly doubling in size every year. As Clinton Wilder notes in his recent article[15] on business and the Internet, "If you haven't already added a '.com' electronic mail address to your business card, you will soon." He cites recent improvements in Internet access, such as the World Wide Web (WWW) and graphical browsers like Mosaic as driving the explosive growth of businesses using the Internet and WWW for communication and commerce. Mary Cronin, author of *Doing Business on the Internet,*[16] feels that "Critical mass has arrived." With secure financial transactions coming online this year for some networks, Cronin expects this to advance Internet commerce viability even more in 1995.

Businesses detailed in the *Information Week* Special Report included: JP Morgan, Hyatt Hotels, Schlumberger and GE Plastics. These companies all cited valid and quantifiable reasons to justify Internet and WWW access. Wilder points to Ford's interactive CD-ROM disks, Fidelity Investments (Boston) with online ads on Prodigy, and Hyatt's Internet Web page of vacation and resort information as examples of good business sense. He summarizes ". . . for big ticket items, it makes good business sense to give buyers as much interactive information as possible."

Gateway and Oracle both signed on as advertisers on Ziff-Davis web sites. Hot Buttons and point and click icons will appear on the home pages of ZD Net to "lure"[17] users to ads and additional product or usage information about the sponsors' products and services. The cost per advertiser for a full rotation across ZD magazine home pages will total $25,000 per quarter. David Schnaider, V.P. General Manager of ZD Interactive said that rotating the ads will ensure a broader exposure for the advertisers' messages. This network in total has one million pages viewed per month, with 250,000 "accesses" and users spend an average of 5–7 minutes per site.

Almost singlehandedly making a case for online consumer panel tracking, General Motors announced it would buy 2–3 million dollars in online advertising, provided the "commercial online services (VANs) and Internet web sites must be accountable for their users by hiring a third party service to certify their subscriber bases." In the same article from *Inside Media,* Wayne Friedman reported that GM planned to "buy a number of hyperlinks" and messages on a mix of online areas.[18]

VAN and Online Service Provider Advertising Revenue

Another reason to support online consumer panel research is to measure the audience and consumer activity such as shopping and game use across different services. They can also report on the relative audience delivery of larger "hyperlink" areas. Online service providers act as "directories" capable of delivering users to areas (via hyperlinks), such as commercially sponsored areas in the service or commercially sponsored areas on the Internet where advertiser messages and advertiser/consumer interaction can occur. These services will always present a "Home Page" or a Welcome Page which presents what's new or lists available directories, such as shopping or advertiser directories. Each of these areas will attract a different audience based on their mix of content or services.

This directory capability is like a "Link" from one cyberspace area to another. The user just sees the information requested. Advertisers will buy schedules of links much as with Cable interconnects or Local TV Stations, or TV networks sell today to advertisers. Jeffrey Dearth, presi-

EXHIBIT 18.4 Online Advertising Delivery Model

Consumer	User PC Session			
Access Method	Online Access Provider			
Content Mix	Editorial	Entertainment	Reference	Retail
Exposure Methods	Activerts	Hypertext Links	Static Ads/Notices	
Exposure Types	Active Exposures		Passive	
	Advertiser Controlled Areas			
Advertiser Areas	Internet Home Page	Private BBS	Sponsored Areas/Forums	

dent of *New Republic* magazine points out the "explosion of web pages" will make links between pages the key, calling them "the new currency on the Web." Advertisers will buy "schedules" of these links. He further proposed that as the Web grows and moves toward more vertical markets, there will be web sites relating to "particular special interests" linking together forming the equivalent of special interest "cable" channels.[19] In the figure above, the *Active* exposures include activerts and hypertext links. These active methods of advertising take a consumer to the message, or advertiser controlled area, such as an advertiser's home page.

The service providers will make money from advertisers for the posting of the directory notice or ad, and more from the "pay-for-performance" aspects of delivering consumers to advertisers areas (through these electronically linked addresses). Of course, they also receive the revenue stream for providing the dial-in connectivity to their service or a gateway to the Internet. However, these revenues will not increase and in fact have actually dropped by over 30 percent from several service providers as competitive pressures to rapidly acquire online subscribers continue to mount. This pressure to hold the line on subscriber connectivity costs and the pressure to upgrade infrastructure and services to compete will increase the importance of advertising revenues for these service providers. The advertising-related compensation will clearly drive these service's revenues as advertisers respond to the increased penetration of online services. Other infrastructure services to enable this advertising growth include ratings measurement availability (one service provided by the proposed enterprise) and standardized advertising placements[20] and rate cards from online services.

Research Methodologies for Advertisers, Agencies, VAN's, and Online Service Providers

Data will be captured in two forms: audit and longitudinal consumer panel. The first methodology, site-specific audits, would be proprietary studies sponsored by an advertiser or its agency. These would be best suited for business-to-business sites or smaller niche consumer sites which may not be reported in syndicated studies. The audit data will be provided via a purchase of site activity tapes from the specific online service. These tapes could be enhanced with site visitor demographic information provided by the online service to aid "audience" analysis. The permissible uses of the data will be dependent on the cooperation of the specific online service for all data. Wayne Friedman in *Inside Media* reported[21] the online services do not want "third party concerns revealing imperfections in their service" and "they want to resell their own user information data because they perceive it to be of tremendous value." Taking a lesson from the consumer packaged goods industry, where retailers resell their own store data tapes to market research companies such as IRI and Nielsen, the online services selling their data will ensure that the data is very costly to purchase and that the services will be very restrictive in the allowable uses of the data they provide.

The second methodology, using a longitudinal consumer panel, yields a much more robust and actionable database of media and marketing information. The consumer activity will be captured via a consumer panel research methodology using very passive proprietary data capture techniques. Unlike the site-specific audits mentioned above, where the data are owned by the online service, the panel data collected is owned by the enterprise and is fully syndicatable. The most fundamental measure, and the most valued in the next few years, will be GRP types of ratings: measures of audience reach and frequency of exposure to an advertising message. Later, shopping and other "pay-per-use" features (such as online games) can be measured to help the players in the online economy value their services and set competitive strategy.

The consumer panel methodology will also allow reporting on total online activity by consumers which will deliver advertisers, advertising agencies, content providers and online services a common measure of consumer advertising impact of PC activity and trends. This type of syndicated information has never before been available for use by online services themselves. Online services will find the cross-service, independently gathered consumer panel information, very useful for strategic decisions such as where to place online advertising, evaluation of service performance relative to other services. This information will also lend input to the services strategy: to acquire new visitors or enhance repeat visits by current visitors.

Using the consumer panel methodology, a syndicated panel operator skilled in this type of research could also provide high-end, value-added strategic analytics. These strategic analyses were developed over many years of consumer packaged goods data capture. Dr. Al Kean of

Management Science Associates created and refined many of these approaches using longitudinal consumer panel information. Having started their careers at MSA, Tod Johnson and Andy Tarshis join other eminent analysts of these panel data, including Greg Starzynski of the NPD Group, Bernie Ryan of MSA and Todd Hale, Greg Ellis, Rich Maturo, Meredith Spector and Robert Tomei from A.C. Nielsen. Traditional longitudinal consumer panel data enables analysis of a specific site or VAN for Visitor Demographics, Site or VAN Trial & Repeat, Cross-Site Visitation, VAN Loyalty (Share of Online Requirements), Activity Group based analytics (such as profiles of frequent visitors) and many others.

Several years ago, while working with Andy Tarshis on "Single-Source" consumer panels, Rich Maturo and I produced some very exciting analyses where consumer panel purchasing was tied to the households actual television viewing. We gained unique experience analyzing commercial viewing and consumer purchase activity from a panel of 6,000 households in New York, Chicago, and Los Angeles. This experience is directly applicable to tracking consumer online advertising exposure and online purchase activity.

For an example of these analytics, picture a report covering online shopping area visitors. The report would list demographic groups, and for each group the report would list the online shopping areas. Shoppers visiting multiple "virtual malls" in the report period would be tracked and an interaction index could be generated revealing cross shopping patterns.

Another useful analysis would be a conversion measure which would be the ratio of buying visitors at a site to the total site visitors for the same time period. Using a consumer panel methodology, buyer demographics could be reported, as well as repeat visitation frequency and information on items purchased.

Another report could detail sites visited by heavy online game players, and detail the interactions of those heavy players with other sites. This would highlight the best areas on which to place advertising to reach heavy online game players. The same analysis could be done for sites on gardening information, sports information, fashion, automobiles, travel and other sites. Since we are considering a longitudinal consumer panel, we can track consumer exposure and flow not only on the Internet and web sites, but also on Value Added Networks.

PC MEDIA MARKET SEGMENTS

Besides the customer segments listed in Exhibit 18.5, other major purchasers of these data will be Financial Analysts; Telco/Cable/Television strategic planners, banks, and credit card issuers and advertising sales brokers (like today's local television station sales rep firm) who will sell advertising space for regional Internet access providers who won't have an internal advertising sales force like the larger network providers will.

ONLINE SERVICES FACE INCREASED COMPETITION

This potentially huge advertising market has attracted the attention of some very well-funded competitors who have already started, or are starting, new Value Added Networks (VAN's) and other online access services.

EXHIBIT 18.5 The Market for Online Research by Type of Data

Market Segment	Consumer Online Usage		Consumer Off-Line PC Usage		Consumer/Business Custom Audits	
	Basic Syndicated Analytics	Value Added Analytics	Basic Syndicated Analytics	Value Added Analytics	AD-Hoc Custom Audits	On-Going Custom Audits
Ad Agency Media Buyers	✓		✓			
Advertiser Strategic Planners	✓	✓	✓	✓	✓	✓
Software Publishing Planners		✓	✓	✓		
Value Added Networks–Consumer	✓	✓		✓		
VAN Content Providers–Consumer	✓	✓	✓			
Internet Site Producers–Consumer	✓	✓			✓	✓
Internet Site Producers–Business					✓	✓
Private Network Producers–Business					✓	✓

Microsoft and IBM have each established their own online networks and will bill users monthly for access through their networks.[22] Leveraging their broadly installed user base for their operating systems, both firms will have the phone numbers for their respective networks included as defaults in their new operating system releases. Microsoft included "one-button" access to the Internet in its new release of Windows 95. IBM announced similar access in its new release of OS/2 Warp.

AT&T has just released its online service. Pacific Bell (California) is aggressively signing up its installed telephone customers to Pacific Bell's access network. Netcom, and other Internet access providers are also marketing their firms, although more through niche media. These smaller Internet providers are typically regional, drawing business and advertising opportunities from their respective regions. These larger access providers will have the ability to deliver and sell national "advertising" in an online format, and that will enable agencies to allocate funds from a larger general advertising fund, moving away from current ad-hoc budgets.

Times-Mirror Co., Tribune Co., *The Washington Post*, Knight-Ridder and the Newhouse Family's *Advance Publications* have all purchased a $20 million equity stake (about 15 percent) of NETSCAPE, which is the most popular (estimates at 90 percent) web browser in use today. The Bozell business to business unit handling Netscape advertising says ". . . the home page of the upgraded Netscape navigator will have ads from AT&T, EDS, General Motors, MasterCard, Adobe, and Netcom.[23] These advertisers paid a $40,000 fee to appear on the Netscape home page.

The newspapers mentioned above were motivated to pursue their own online service access because of the unattractive financial terms offered them by the other established online services. As content providers and advertisers negotiate the best placement and "distribution" channels for their content, longitudinal viewer research will be critical to support this industry's marketing information needs as the technology and industry competition continues its evolution.

The Competitive Environment for Online Research

One of the first Interactive research services, Pathfinder, was announced from ASI/Arbitron/Next Century Media, and it validated the advertising industry's interest in this information. General Motors announced an agreement with this research entity for $200,000 worth of information. Others, including Bell South, were announced as expected to sign deals soon. The consortium (CASIE), formed under the auspices of the Association of National Advertisers , American Association of Advertising Agencies and the Advertising Research Foundation, has validated their approach using what is being referred to as "clickstreams." The panel approach uses this same "approved" clickstream methodology, expanding it to track unique consumer activity across services. Within weeks, ASI dropped out of the earlier alignment and joined a new entity with Nielsen Media and Yankelovich called ANYwhere research. While this new group was announced in *The Wall Street Journal* in early June, there were no products or services announced, only that the entity would look into research on the Internet.

Several companies have reportedly talked with online services to discuss subscriber demographic and activity information which the services should be capturing. These services expect to purchase data directly from the online services to act as "third party validators," reporting user visitation frequency and length of stay. These competitors will be limited to reporting only through cooperating services probably for an increasing percentage of revenue, and will be forced to use inaccurate household level demographic overlays for user information since detailed personal information is not likely to be readily available from service users given current privacy concerns. At the least the information will be of limited marketing value at an individual user level. The information captured from each service, and the quality of that information is also likely to vary for each online service.

These third-party audit-type research services would deliver more commodity-like information when compared to the information available from a consumer panel. A consumer panel would be the industry's sole resource for interaction and trial and repeat types of information across services and sites. The consumer panel operator would be in a competitive position which would not be dependent on service provider data cooperation or payments to those services. In the long term, costs for data will be a marked advantage of the consumer panels, since there will be an incentive for the services to sell their usage information at an increasing cost to the "third party validators." I would draw comparisons between packaged goods research suppliers like Nielsen and IRI who purchase data tapes from retailers for a price and they are dependent on broad industry participation by the retailers for their data "raw materials." A panel service, which collects data directly from the consumer, is usually a syndicated service with the freedom to compare effectiveness and audience across services and competing sites. This panel service would not require without requiring online service cooperation, restrictive covenants regarding the permissible uses of the data or onerous payments for data access.

The audit approach will provide more accurate accounting of less popular or niche consumer online sites and a means to measure business-to-business site visitation. Each methodology of capturing consumer behavior has its advantages, and there is a place for both in the market. In any case, we can be sure that a consumer panel service will provide unquestionably superior insights into online user behavior, trends and attitudes.

Alternative Consumer PC Media Research Methodologies

TRADITIONAL "RECALL-BASED" AD-HOC CONSUMER RESEARCH

Methodology description. This broadly described set of traditional non-longitudinal research methods for conducting direct consumer research is the most typical type of research currently being conducted on today's consumer PC media usage. Telephone, mail, and even some Online Survey methods are all being employed by a variety of firms to serve their respective interests.

These sample sizes have ranged from several hundred to several thousand, although none have been conducted on a longitudinal sample. Arbitron had announced a periodic survey to be conducted named PATHFINDER. This survey was recall-based and asked a broad range of questions on online media usage. It earned the firm publicity in *Ad Age, Inside Media, The Wall Street Journal,* and other publications. Next Century Media of Woodstock New York and ASI of Glendale, California, also cooperated with some of the Pathfinder project.

Odyssey Research conducted a frequently cited study which clustered users into technology receptive groups, and providing demographics for the groups. This was a one-time study not likely to be repeated. Specialty consultant firms such as Frank Magid Associates, Arlen Communications, and a handful of others, including management consulting firms like Andersen Consulting and Coopers and

Lybrand[24] have conducted studies which are frequently intended to provide public relations exposure for the firms within their area of recognized expertise, such as retailing, catalogs, direct marketing or technology management.

Dr. Sunil Gupta[25] is conducting a business panel survey to attempt to assess business uses on the World Wide Web, and it will probably be the most definitive work in this area. Dr. Gupta had completed a similar survey of consumer use last year and the results will be forthcoming shortly.

Methodology Strengths and Weaknesses. All of the ad-hoc approaches mentioned above are designed to provide early indications of the attitudes and opinions of users, self-reported users and recalled usage of online services. The shortcomings of any recall-based methodology are readily known. Plus the ad-hoc approach cannot deliver actionable marketing insights into usage patterns and the user graphics important for setting accurate ratings information.

One clear advantage of these traditional random sample research methodologies is that a sample can be asked questions which may be inappropriate for an on-going consumer tracking panel, such as personal questions on religious affiliation or political opinions. They may also allow fast reads of specific questions via phone studies. A disadvantage of this technique is respondent representation within a small "random" sample.

Important Trends. These traditional researchers mentioned above will find it increasingly difficult to attract quality random samples given increased unlisted numbers, privacy concerns, the recurring threat of increased government legislation and the increase of unscrupulous firms selling under the guise of research. Consenting participants in longitudinal panels typically exhibit a response rate of 75 percent or more to monthly attitude and opinion surveys.

Specialized ad-hoc research will always be an important research tool, and firms will continue to provide this type of research to the PC media industry through a mix of field methods and with varying degrees of quality.

Valuable Custom Ad -Hoc Survey capabilities is another service that can be sold in the form of custom monthly surveys which are distributed electronically to the PC consumer panel. These survey data, including attitude and opinion information can be linked to actual PC usage for unique marketing insights. For example, a survey of user's print media reading habits might be compared to online magazine access areas for the purposes of cross media promotion. Heavy game users online may exhibit very specific attitudes about certain other recreational interests off-line, which could lead to special Internet links being promoted on those game areas home pages.

Online Network Cooperation Model

NETWORK COOPERATION METHODOLOGY DESCRIPTION

This area is the most popular area of research being focused on by Arbitron, Nielsen, possibly Audits and Surveys[26] and other research suppliers. Under this model, a third-party "auditor" such as Nielsen or Arbitron, could be contracted by the online service provider such as America Online or by an advertiser, such as Colgate to perform an audit of the number of "hits" or online users exposed to that area. The networks are logging household data by account ID and they are thus able to provide information on which users went where and for how long on their service.

The key point for the online services is that the processing of this information is required to help sell and value the consumer traffic and exposures in those areas. The services cannot do this themselves because of credibility reasons. However, to adopt a census approach, such as reporting on all users' activity for each minute of every day would not be very cost effective. Some summarization of the data will be likely.

Comparing these data to Supermarket data tapes Nielsen and IRI currently get from their retail panel,[27] the amount of data will typically have a time value for the service and they will summarize the records. Supermarkets report on unit sales by UPC each week, and what the price was. To store every transaction and every product for an average of 15,000 trips per week, and an average of about $125 per week of UPCs would be very expensive for each retail store to capture, log and transmit. With several million users logging in to an ever broadening mix of areas and services, the costs to maintain transactional data for each user will force some level of summarization to balance costs with the minimum information required to sell advertising.

Methodology Strengths and Weaknesses. The major strength of this methodology is that a "census" approach is expected. All users of the service will have all actions tracked and logged at all times. This is not a realistic expectation because of two reasons: (1) the cost of storing and accessing these detailed data transactions for all users, and

EXHIBIT 18.6 Service Provider Cooperation Data Collection Model

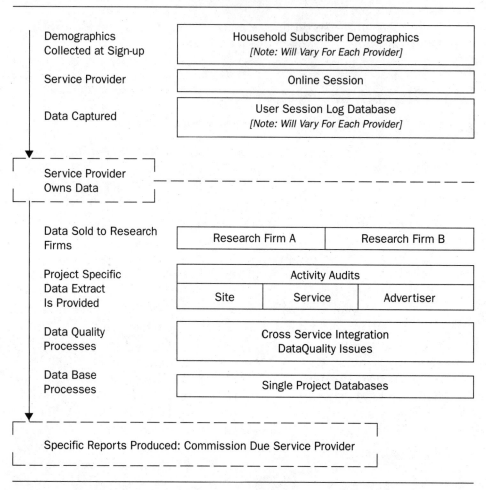

Demographics Collected at Sign-up	Household Subscriber Demographics *[Note: Will Vary For Each Provider]*
Service Provider	Online Session
Data Captured	User Session Log Database *[Note: Will Vary For Each Provider]*

Service Provider Owns Data

Data Sold to Research Firms	Research Firm A	Research Firm B
Project Specific Data Extract Is Provided	Activity Audits Site / Service / Advertiser
Data Quality Processes	Cross Service Integration DataQuality Issues
Data Base Processes	Single Project Databases

Specific Reports Produced: Commission Due Service Provider

(2) The difficulty and expense of capturing and maintaining user demographic, attitude and opinion and purchasing transactions. As supermarkets have learned, these services will also learn which records are relevant for them to store and resell to third party auditors. There will be a clear marginal expense at some point which will not justify logging all data for all customers. These services will be in the business of selling advertising access. Technology offers the hope of total information, but the fiscal realities do not.

Third-Party Auditors' Costs. The major cost a third-party auditor will bear is the cost for data access. Since these data are acquired and "owned" by the online service provider, there will always be the need to "pay the piper." Supermarket chains learned within a few years that reselling their already captured sales (front-end scanning) information would yield a new profit center. Nielsen and IRI both bid up the value of these tapes, and without any replacement goods, they are still forced to pay onerous fees to the retailers for the retailers' tapes of store-scanned sales. Neither vendor could deliver on its contracts without the weekly retailer tapes. A similar model applies to third-party auditors seeking "tapes" of online user activity. Costs will only rise as the online services realize their monopolistic pricing and attempt to maximize value for their firm through increased cooperator costs for data tapes. Therefore, each sale will already be burdened with a commission fee due to the online service provider which could be 10 to 25 percent of the project cost to the client,[28] usually the advertiser.

Additionally, the data will be delivered in disparate media and formats. The actual detail and accuracy of the data collected will vary for each separate service. Most services will also place restrictions and covenants on the legal use of the data sold to the third party vendor. For instance, the data may not be released for publication without prior clauses and will almost definitely not be approved for release or comparison to other online services. The differences in data collected mentioned above will likely contribute to a confusion under this multi-supplier scenario as well.

Measuring Unique Site Visitors—An Issue of Data Quality. Advertisers are interested in the effective exposures of their message to the targeted audience in the method and frequency which will deliver the desired result and lead to a purchase decision of the advertiser's product or service. Most methods used today to capture information on-site visitors have several shortcomings. They only measure "hits," which is generally a gross count of the number of times a site is accessed. This does not allow the capture of repeat visitation, key indicator of most sites' long-term success or delivery on the promised benefit.

A new service from Internet Profiles Corp., named I/Count[29] assigns a unique ID code to the IP address coming into a site. This helps with repeat read, but many users have multiple Internet accounts, like one at work and another from America Online, each will have a different IP address. The next question important to a marketer is "Who are these people accessing my site?" Internet Profiles president will introduce I/Code in the third quarter which will be a standard software registration form that will give users an incentive to provide demographic data voluntarily. Because of privacy concerns mentioned earlier, and the obvious annoyance factor associated with entering personal information to just about every home page, users will get tired of logging onto those sites and many sites will sacrifice key data for less valuable information on its site attendees.

Online Service Competitor Cooperation. It is extremely unlikely that any online service will allow release of its ratings data to any other service. It is even more unlikely that the larger VAN services would actually provide data consistently over time for ratings purposes. These proposed service reported data, being supplied by the service themselves, would also be suspect to most savvy advertisers and agencies.

As an early example of industry cooperation, Prodigy conducted an independent audit by the print industry auditor, Audit Bureau of Circulation. Other online providers did not follow suit and thus Prodigy gave its competitors an unfair advantage, forcing Prodigy to cancel its audience measurement attempt.

In this period of increasing competition with new services competing for the hotly growing pool of potential subscribers, it is extraordinarily unlikely that online service providers would release or make public in a cooperative mode, what they will consider to be proprietary marketing information. This reinforces the need for the independently operated, statistically supported consumer based panel methodology for measuring ad performance and "audience" for this and other PC based media.

CONSUMER PANEL RESEARCH MODEL

Consumer Panel Methodology Description. Consumers have agreed to join and cooperate on panels since the 1950s in the United States. They will typically be selected via acceptable market research standards in order to represent an appropriately geographic and demographic population. The most recent U.S. Census projections are typical targets. Since these individuals volunteer to participate, lifestage and demographic information is more readily captured at a convenient time only once per year at their choice of time to complete. The information captured is generally more accurate and complete than ad-hoc phone or mail surveys. This person based information is then analyzed together with logged activity information captured from the person's PC

EXHIBIT 18.7 Consumer Panel Data Collection Model

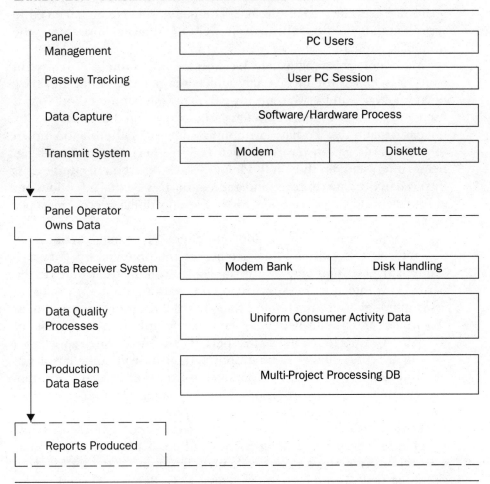

Panel Management	PC Users	
Passive Tracking	User PC Session	
Data Capture	Software/Hardware Process	
Transmit System	Modem	Diskette
Panel Operator Owns Data		
Data Receiver System	Modem Bank	Disk Handling
Data Quality Processes	Uniform Consumer Activity Data	
Production Data Base	Multi-Project Processing DB	
Reports Produced		

Media habits, such as site visit time, length of visit, repeat visitation, responses, interactivity, and GRP Rating, and share of voice equivalent for that individual's demographic group. Specialized reference resources are also created to understand the types of programs, services and activity users are accessing through their PC media. Highly customized proprietary analysis and basic syndicated analytics would be deliverables.

Consumer PC Panel. The sample will be controlled to balance PC ownership across major census age, income, education and other demographics such as to present a projectable sample to the total U.S., in terms of PC ownership and usage. The panel will also be balanced to represent modem ownership as well as CD-ROM ownership, among the home PC population.

Methodology Strengths and Weaknesses. Consumer participate in Consumer Panels for surprisingly similar reasons each time they have been surveyed and for whatever type of data collection methodology is used, even diaries or questionnaires. The reason cited most frequently for participation is "To have my opinions heard." Other factors noted to drive participation have included feeling special by participating, being interested in the methodology (such as when technology is involved in the data capture) and getting the gifts. Actual gift values per year are typically in the range of forty to seventy dollars per panelist per year.

Since panelists volunteer, and with effectively managed continuity programs, they continue to participate for multiple years.[30] They also willingly release their activity information to you for their time on the panel. This information is owned by the venture, and constitutes an asset, although there is a limited value for old inventory, referred to as "back data" and usually being more than six months old. The privacy of the participating individuals is respected, but since they represent a sample of representative demographics, their individual behavior will be projected to represent the estimated universe of PC-using consumers. The data will always be reported on at a reasonable level of aggregation for analytical or market targeting purposes.

Shopping Online. Even without the secure transaction capability, shopping services are making money online. There are eighty merchants in CompuServe's electronic mall. Shopping 2000, the internet shopping mall from Contentware carries J.C. Penney, Spiegel, and a dozen other high-profile marketers. The two major CD-ROM catalog "malls" are Magellan's "The Merchant" with 39 catalogers and Redgate's 2Market with 28 catalogers. These catalogers pay between $20,000-$40,000 per release to include their products in the CD-ROM.

ProductView is an advertiser supported service which seeks to be paid by advertisers for only the "hits" it delivers, including the names and addresses it hopes to capture from information seeking online shoppers.

Financial services, leisure and travel, and automotive marketers have been very active online and with interactive disks or CD-ROM interactive advertising efforts.

Security is cited as a real concern among businesses and consumers when asked about actually selling on an online service. Wilder reports that dozens of security software suppliers are working to solve the security problem.[31] Two noteworthy partnerships in this area are Microsoft-VISA International and CommerceNet-RSA Data Security. Although expected soon, adequate security for financial transactions does not currently exist. When it does, expect consumer online shopping to increase. Online ordering capability would enable households with one phone line to order and interact with customer service while active in the shopping area. Today, an online shopper (usually) must exit the online area and then phone an 800 number and order as via a catalog.

A consumer panel should include tracking of the various PC-based shopping applications and the online shopping applications. As connectivity bandwith becomes both cheaper and widely available, this area will explode. Catalog marketers continue to face sharply rising paper costs and continual postal rate increases. Bandwidth and security will enable Online Shopping to be the next "killer app" of PC Media.

Marketing Issues Best Answered Through Consumer Panel Information

Since these panelists will be reporting unique activity within the household and by each active member of the household, our mix of marketing information services will be quite robust. The unique mix of marketing information available will address issues for online marketers, advertisers and service providers as well as software publishers and distributors.

Issues addressed will include: Which services provided the highest access period in prime time? What was the demographic profile of the frequent visitor to an advertiser's Internet home page? How many repeat visitors are there per month? How many accessed each of the advertisers who had "links"[32] from my site? Am I charging enough for my effective spots as a network service? Am I paying a reasonable fee and am I reaching the right target audience if I am an advertiser? Who is advertising where? How frequently? How successful is it for them? Which services and which times are the best for me to reach my audience? Who's shopping, and how many come back to buy? What software publisher's software is losing ground, and which need a re-stage? What software retail channel (online, catalog, DM, retail) is doing better with what types of software? Who is buying and what are they paying? Who are my heavy users and what else do they do with their PC time? Do I have copromotion opportunities? As an online service, are there PC applications for which I should be selling or renting access time? How else can I reach other people like my heavy users, to attract new site visitors?

Key Trends Supporting Consumer Panel Research

Misuse of personal information gathered under the guise of research (Selling-Under-Guise) is a problem already impacting the research industry. Powerful headlines pressure government to focus on privacy, such as through Vice President Gore's Privacy Working Group. They were presented guidelines for online service privacy by the Interactive Service Association[33] which allowed the services to sell subscriber names by notifying the subscriber at sign up time and there will be an easy "opt-out" method to allow users to say no to disclosure of their names. Most relevant to this proposal is the following reported stipulation "Only names, addresses and *broad usage patterns may be exchanged or rented; no list may include data on individual session activities.*" In that same article Editor John Featherman of *The Privacy Newsletter,* called the ISA's self-regulation a farce noting that the profit-minded will ignore no-penalty guidelines.

A few very public abusers of privacy, some of whom may try and capture lists under the guise of research will cause laws to be passed limiting the value of the demographic and activity based reporting of the Service Network Cooperation model, and will support the voluntary consumer panel method. Even when collected, the marketing value and useability of the information collected will limit its research value.

Privacy issues online are hot topics, and it is likely the government may pass privacy laws which would restrict release of information passively captured from the online services without the permission of users.

More likely, users will be very wary of releasing their demographic information online when asked online. As Iang Jeon, Director of electronic marketing at Fidelity Investments noted "Just because of technology, we can't lose sight of the customer. We wouldn't ask a customer walking into an investment center to fill out a questionnaire. People will accept commercialization of the Web, but you have to do it the right way."

The panel allows information to be collected once per year, and the panel operators credibility must be established with the panelist for those first contacts. This could be addressed by judicious use of selected direct mail contact, the use of unique ID numbers when online, and ongoing panel participation compensation/incentive plans.

People will always respond to certain human wants and needs. Based on historical levels of cooperation, we can always expect people to participate in research, provided it is real and they feel they are being heard and making a contribution to how we live. The consumer panel is the only viable methodology for online marketers to measure switching behavior between networks, and to report on comparative shares and marketplace strengths. It will be the best way to measure online advertising, online sales of consumer goods and services and the sources of online links. Online marketers will then have the powerful consumer insights that have been used for years by sophisticated packaged goods marketers.

References

1. These large Value Added Networks (Commercial Online Services: CompuServe, AOL, Prodigy) as well as new Internet Connection Services recently announced by Pacific Bell (focused on California market) and MCI (national focus) provide a "directory" type of service to users and advertisers since these services represent a Users Point-of-Entry into the online environment. They can sell space to promote other product or service commercial areas in other parts of the Internet. This function of funneling or directing users to certain areas will make these Value added networks valuable "Virtual Real Estate", much as Supermarkets control product placement on their shelves, and thus directly aid a given products sales by placing it on an end-aisle display.

2. Adobe announced a pending commercial release of a version of Adobe's ACROBAT graphical design and layout software. This release, which has been in beta test for four months, is expected to be released this April. It was co-developed with Netscape, and will be distributed via the Internet. The new ACROBAT graphical software will allow easy creation of Internet Home Pages without forcing a user to learn HTML (Hypertext Markup Language). This will facilitate Internet use for business and consumers. *InformationWeek,* March 24, 1995.

3. Jeffrey Dearth, President of *New Republic* magazine; *Electronic Marketplace Sourcebook,* January 1995, Thompson Publishing Group, p. 4.

4. Personal Digital Assistant—PDA's are essentially PC's designed for maximum portability with very small form factors, typically with touch screens, stylus pointing devices and wireless communications capability.

5. *Forbes ASAP,* April 10,1995, p.72; Additional reference is given to information from Veronis, Suhler & Associates, Jupiter Communications, Electronic Industries and Wilkofski, Gruen Associates.

6. Ibid

7. Tom Noglows & Tom Steinert-Threlkeld, *Interactive Week,* May 22, 1995, p. 15.

8. Katy M. Bachman, American Demographics, Marketing Tools publication, March/April 1995, p. 59.

9. Forrester Research, as quoted in *Forbes ASAP,* April 10, 1995, p. 69.

10. Scott Donaton, *Advertising Age,* Spring 1995 Special Edition, p. 54.

11. Richard Rappaport, *Forbes ASAP,* April 10, 1995, p. 66.

12. Nielsen Media provides these surrogate GRP ratings and demographic services for several types of alternative media such as Airport News Channels and other place based media. Having these ratings available enables buying and selling of advertising on these media within existing agency/client relationships.

13. Wayne Friedman and Jane Weaver, "Calculating Cyberspace: Tracking 'Clickstreams'", *Inside Media,* February 15–28, 1995, pps. 1, 44.

14. Founded in 1987, clients include United Airlines, Motorola, *TV Guide On-Screen,* Pacific Bell and Apple Computers.

15. Clinton Wilder; "The Internet Pioneers", *Information Week,* January 9, 1995, pps. 38–48.

16. *Doing Business on the Internet,* Mary Cronin, published by Van Nostrand Reinhold, 1994.

17. Martin O'Loughlin, "Home-Page Positioning"; *Inside Media,* p. 13.

18. Wayne Friedman, "GM Dangling Cyberspace Dollars"; *Inside Media,* p. 8.

19. Jeffrey Dearth, President of *New Republic* magazine; *Electronic Marketplace Sourcebook,* January 1995, Thompson Publishing Group, p. 4.

20. An Advertisers Internet site, created using HTML, follows the de facto standard available now. These sites can be found using a Mosaic type "Browser." The site can also be transparently accessed from network areas where "featured" or regular service listings in the major value added services are included.

21. Wayne Friedman, "GM Dangling Cyberspace Dollars", *Inside Media,* May 24, 1995, p. 8.

22. Christine Hudgins-Bonafield; "How will the Internet Grow?", *Network Computing,* March 1, 1995, p. 84.

23. John Motavalli, *Inside Media,* March 29, 1995, pp. 4 and 45.

24. Emerging Retail Formats Conference, May 26–27, NYC, Sponsored by International Business Communications.

25. Research Project on the Commercial Uses of the World Wide Web, University of Michigan Business School, Ann Arbor. Conducted 4/95–6/95.

26. Audits and Surveys presented an audit-based approach for analysis of online service usage at the ARF conference in March 1994, although their PR since has been minimal.

27. Nielsen and IRI acquire data from approx. 3500 supermarkets nationally each. They are beginning to capture "census" or all data, each transaction, all stores, but it is expensive to maintain because the data are voluminous.

28. While this fee is clearly negotiable, the percentages mentioned are typical cooperation fees seen with retailer data sales for test projects in the consumer packaged goods industry.

29. Clinton Wilder, "Know Your Net Surfers," *Information Week,* April 17, 1995, p. 30.

30. To avoid panelist bias, whether perceived or real, some panels are rotated (panelists are regularly removed from the panel and new panelists are added. This approach does have operations expenses which may or may not be justified in designing the panel methodology.

31. Wilder, p. 39.

32. Hotlinks between internet sites activated by clicking on a logo or an ad space in one area which automatically takes you to the next "linked" space.

33. Jeffrey O'Brien, "Just A Slight Omission", *DIRECT* magazine, May 1995, pps. 1, 43.

The Convergence of Database Marketing and Interactive Media Networks

New Sources, New Uses, New Benefits

Rob Jackson
Paul Wang

Rob Jackson is Vice President, Corporate and Marketing Communications of CMS/Customer Management Services. He is former Vice President of Marketing and Information Services at Donnelley Marketing, Inc., and is Past President of the Chicago Direct Marketing Association. A frequent speaker, he also writes on database marketing and database enhancement for *DM News* and other industry publications.

Paul Wang is Associate Professor in the Graduate Direct Marketing Program at the Medill School of Journalism, Northwestern University. He also is Technical Editor of the *Journal of Direct Marketing*.

Jackson and Wang are co-authors of *Strategic Database Marketing* (NTC Business Books).

We are witnessing a marketing evolution and revolution. It is an evolution for the consumer and revolution for media and communications. As the two come together in the interactive communications world, database marketing applications move to the center stage in the battle for share of mind, time and the attention of consumers.

The Power of Information Networks

You cannot help but be aware of interactive media in general, and interactive information networks, in particular. In an average month, there are over 3,000 news stories about the Internet, information networks and marketers venturing out into cyberspace. PC owners are accessing online services by the millions. By conservative estimates there are more than 5 million individuals accessing interactive media via their computer. Our best example is a nurse we talked to. She purchased a computer and accessed America Online because she was tired of dating services and print ads she used to attempt to find "Mr. Right." On AOL, in the chat areas, she met many new friends, including her current boyfriend. Being wired was, for her, a social experience—proof positive, that it is not just computer jocks, but nurses, teachers, children and housewives who are using the new media. Many come and look around, but the question is . . . how many stay and for what motivations? The $64,000 question is, What will it take to get and keep Everywoman and Everyman wired and tuned-in on a ongoing basis? And, once they are on and stay on, what level of commerce can and will be conducted online?

The vision and today's reality are still far apart. Many visionaries see the electronic world becoming the center of commerce in the future as retail is today. Some do not agree. Microsoft is determined to position itself as the conduit for all electronic commerce of the future via the Microsoft Network and links to the Internet. The answer lies in understanding very complex dynamics of communications, media, distribution, acceptance of technology and change itself.

Dramatic Changes in Consumers and Media

We must first look at the changes in the consumer and the media that have helped create the dynamic growth in interactive communications. From this change and our observations, we can start to develop models of how to market effectively to the consumer in the electronic world.

Mostly by accident, the traditional mass media has helped create the demand for the interactive world. Nowhere has change been more pronounced than in the communications media. This convergence of media and consumer behavior is best illustrated by today's best mass media successes. For example, one of the top-rated television shows, "Home Improvement", is watched by about 18 million households per episode. But many marketers communicate more effectively via targeted (non-mass) media to 25 or 30 or more million households. For example, Donnelley's Carol Wright Co-op mailings reach 30 million households each month. The envelope-opening rate per thousand household exceeds viewership of the top-rated show. With longer exposure time and more information per advertisement, direct mail in this case can provide better sales punch than mass communication.

Traditional network television is losing its vise grip on the consumer as alternatives become available. Media represents content. Consumers watch because the media has content that they are interested in. Changes in technology have brought changes in control. It was not so many years ago that if you wanted to watch the news, you had to be sure to be home by 5:30, and if you missed it, you were out of luck until 10:00. Then came the VCR which enabled you to tape your favorite program for viewing at your leisure. Content did not change, just the ability of the consumer to exert control on how and when he/she interacts with it. Enter the world of cable and 50 to 100 or more channels, providing the consumer with a significant increase of programming that appeals to almost any special interest and is available at almost any time.

There is, however, only so much news and weather and each must repeat the same thing over and over. The interested viewer comes in and out based upon need, interest, and time. This communications process, however, is only one way. It allows for no interaction between viewer and content provider.

Now, multiply this by the 50 or more stations available to the average wired household. Thus, the media has driven two changes in the consumer. First, it has created a consumer who is overloaded with options and little control which leads to frustration. Second, in the process, we have created an information-aware, almost information junkie consumer who is now conditioned to many options for information and entertainment in the media. There is specialty programming to interest almost any consumer, but no easily available road map to chart, access and control content. The consumer has little control over the content, timing and programming that he/she must choose from and no hope to interact with the content or content providers in a meaningful way. It is no wonder that when presented with the ability to choose content, timing and access that the consumer gravitates toward interactive media applications.

Just as the dynamics of media communications have changed, so has the consumer. With exception of some commodity products, most consumers base their purchases on information. We all search for information before we make purchases. Many products require more information search than others. Consumers expect today's communications to be information based, to help expedite the information search process. If a piece of communication does not provide useful information, consumers will go to other sources to gain the information they require to make an informed decision.

The purchase of an automobile is an example. Until recently, consumers relied on the manufacturer as their primary source of information. This was delivered in 60 second spots, print ads and visits to the showroom. Many consumers no longer accept the credibility of those communications without verification—and they have many sources to turn to other than the manufacturer. From *Consumer Reports,* auto magazines, online services and networking to services that provide cost-plus pricing to negotiate the best deal, massive amounts of information are available from third parties. This same process is true for any considered purchase from PC software to a hair dryer and the books and magazines we buy and read. The bottom line is that the consumer has raised the bar on the information required in order to make purchases.

Fundamental Change in Acceptance of Technology

In addition to the convergence of media and consumer change and information delivery level, we are seeing a fundamental change in the average consumer's lifestyle delivered by acceptance of technology. This change has been driven first by the technologically enabled, then the early adoptors and gradually by the consuming public. Cellular phones are a great example. Ten years ago, most cellular phones were limited to CEOs or super sales reps. Today, most are not sold to businesspeople, but to family members. Proliferation of cellular phones has become so great that many areas are being forced to add additional area codes to handle the volume of numbers and activity. Fax machines are another example. As little as five years ago, fax machines were primarily found in offices. Now the fastest growing segment is for home use. Similarly, PC sales have now overtaken TV's in dollars sold each year. It is estimated that by the end of 1995, there will be more than 50 million multimedia PC's in use. We as a society, are gradually becoming more technically enabled and less phobic of new technology.

The Proof is with the Children

The most telling example, though, is our children. Four-year-olds are taking computer classes in pre-school and eleven-year-olds take class notes on laptops and e-mail them to classmates. High school students turn in their papers via e-mail, and most college students are active on the Internet. It matters only a little whether we as today's older generation embrace technology and electronic media; it is already the present for our children. They have embraced technology and online communications. The move to full electronic commerce and online content usage will be as common and easy as flipping on the TV remote is today.

Characteristics of Information Networks

To learn how to master electronic media, we first must understand how it serves the needs of the consumers who are using it and the dynamics that make it a powerful medium. The information networks have three important characteristics. They are:

- Information networks are a highly effective communications medium.

- Information networks are a significant distribution channel for a wide range of products and services.

- Information networks are sophisticated marketing databases.

Information networks such as Prodigy, America Online, CompuServe, and The Microsoft Network effect communications in three important ways. First, they communicate information and entertainment content similar to existing mass media communications channels. You can view news, weather, sports and entertainment of all types: both original content designed and produced for electronic media and content duplicated from existing mass media. Several networks are experimenting with audio and video transmission. Limitations today are down load time for the information to reach the consumer's PC based upon data delivery restrictions. It is inevitable that data compression technology will eliminate this problem and full video/audio will become as common on the information networks as text and graphics are today.

The biggest difference between information networks and traditional media is its fully interactive capabilities. Individuals can customize the information they want from the massive volumes of information available. They can also interact to ask questions, gain in-depth information or target just plain entertainment value. Interaction can be with other consumers, content providers or personalities such as politicians, entertainers, authors and individuals with other specialty expertise— none of which is possible with traditional media channels.

Exhibit 19.1 is a model relating interactive capabilities with capability to deliver compelling content to consumers. The delivery of content is described technically by the term *bandwidth,* which represents the size of the pipeline required to deliver data to the consumer's PC or television. The richer the content (i.e., video and audio data), the wider the bandwidth required. Today the bandwidth available for delivery of interactive data to PCs is limited. In order to provide richer content via PCs, compression technology must advance to deliver richer content, or the pipeline capability must increase to accomplish the same result.

Today, online services have great content and strong interactive communications capability with the data. However, given the narrow bandwidth restrictions, there is limited distribution of rich content defined by video and audio transmission that are received in traditional broadcast media. CD-ROMS, on the other hand, have strong video/ audio content, but are limited in their interactive capability relative to the amount of data that is captured on the CD-ROM. Interactive broadcast that will come of age in the later 1990's, will have rich capabilities for audio and video transmission, but less interactivity and content than the interactive networks.

The second important aspect of communications is targeted directional communications. The information networks can watch patterns develop in consumer online behavior and direct the consumer, online, to similar content or related areas of communications value. This has

EXHIBIT 19.1 Comparison of Information Density and Delivery Capability

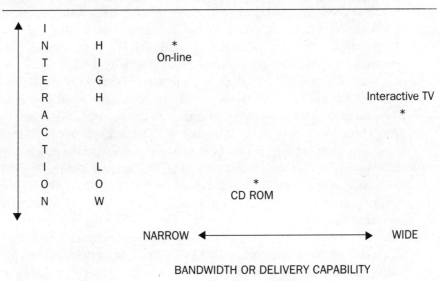

important implications for advertisers and marketers. Not only can marketers develop a communications and content center on an information network, but they can also build targeting models that will identify online subscribers with propensity for their products/services/information and direct them to their locations on the services.

The third important area of communications is one-on-one message delivery. Via e-mail or network generated communications or advertising communications, marketers can talk to individual consumers in a cost-effective manner. Since each subscriber that entering an information network is tracked by a unique ID code while online , custom and targeted messages can be delivered to any subscriber who directs them to content-, interaction- or marketer-sponsored areas. This delivers on the ability to truly implement one-on-one marketing activities.

The information networks are also significant distribution channels. Traditional media have limited ability to directly effect the distribution of products and services. In fact, they are limited to direct response offers and TV shopping activity such as the Home Shopping Network. To purchase a product or service, the consumer must go to another intervening distribution channel, such as Retail, to actually purchase the product or service. Electronic networks offer the opportunity to bypass this process. With detailed information on any marketed product or service, including video and audio, the consumer can gain all the information required to make an informed purchase. Consumers can even purchase their groceries and specify delivery time in some areas of the country. The day is coming when you will be able to enter your online department store, stroll down the aisles, stop and browse merchandise, pick it up and examine it in detail, and choose to put it in your electronic shopping cart—or not. The experience will duplicate the traditional retail experience down to the noise in the store. . .except that you will never leave your chair and PC in your home. Information networks and electronic media delivery offer dramatic potential for major change in how we view and implement distribution of products and services.

Information networks are also sophisticated marketing databases. Each online consumer is tracked by his/her behavior on the network. Thus, each network knows what content the subscriber accesses, how long he/she stays there and what products/services he/she is interested in or purchase. Marketers who sponsor areas or sell merchandise/services online, also know who stops in their area as well as who purchases or inquires. The database allows for significant interaction with a marketer's customers in an online environment. This facilitates information search, targeted marketing and relationship marketing, providing customers with a fast way to get help if they have a problem with the product or service they have purchased.

Six Requirements for Developing Successful Applications

There are six characteristics required to develop successful communications and marketing applications on information networks.

- The content must be compelling and take advantage of multimedia presentation capabilities.

- The content must be dynamic in nature.

- The content must be information-rich. It must provide the necessary information and "deliverables" to satisfy the consumer's purchase requirements.

- The content must have high entertainment value. With a high level of competing programming and advertising, a successful application must stand out from the competition.

- The content must be personalized to the needs of the user and his/her interests. It must look like the application was developed just for them, not for thousands or millions of viewers.

- The content must be interactive in nature and delivery.

With these six requirements in mind and a detailed understanding of how to maximize the marketing value of the three key characteristics of information networks, marketers can proceed to develop online applications.

Database Marketing Is the Key

Do not start electronic media marketing communications without understanding the power and function of database marketing. Maximizing the value of online marketing applications requires a detailed knowledge of the subscriber and that subscriber's propensity towards the purchase of a product or service. Product propensity can be determined by past purchase behavior or by modeling common characteristics between and among consumers and individuals who have exhibited the particular purchase propensity in the past. A marketing database makes the bridge from subscriber to customer.

A marketing database is a collection of data about customers and prospects that effects what and how you sell them. At its simplest, it can be a list. At its most complex, it links together all the information needed to manage a complex business. The process of database marketing communications can be represented by a model that has three phases (Exhibit 19.2).

Identification involves accessing the database to target appropriate customers or prospects. The next step is to develop the appropriate communications effort based upon the requirements of the business and the targeting program. Once the communications program has been completed, the results (consumer response) are recaptured in the database for analysis that will modify the process of selection of customers or prospects for the next communications effort.

EXHIBIT 19.2 Database Communications Model

IDENTIFICATION ——> COMMUNICATION ——> CAPTURE

As explained in detail in our book, *Strategic Database Marketing,* most database applications can be classified into one of three points of entry:

- Capturing and managing historical data—Marketing databases are used primarily to track data captured from tactical marketing programs. Data in the database is usually limited in scope. Applications from the database are limited to tactical programs.

- Marketing intelligence—Marketing intelligence databases build on the data captured in a historical application. The major difference is that customer data is enhanced with other overlay data, and sophisticated modeling techniques are used to provide analysis for detailed decision making capabilities.

- Integrated business resource—This type of database serves as an information resource for the entire business. This is accomplished by integrating all key business information sources or functions in the organization. Examples might include finance, customer service, distribution, inventory, manufacturing, research and marketing.

No matter which database marketing model is correct for a business and its data-driven marketing applications, each requires a combination of three key building blocks. With the three key building blocks, a marketer can build databases as sophisticated or simple as the needs dictate. These building blocks are also the key to the link between database marketing applications and information networks. For a detailed discussion of the three building blocks and how they vary in combination by the three points of entry into database marketing, see *Strategic Database Marketing.*

The three key building blocks are:

- Data—A marketing database is only as powerful as the data it houses. To accomplish effective database marketing applications, the marketer must develop a source data strategy to maximize the collection of the right data for their applications.

- Technology represents the ability to manage customer data and access that data for decision making capabilities. The marketer must learn to harness technology to provide a platform to access the information you collect about customers and prospects.

- Research techniques—Segmentation and modeling techniques complete the final building block. Via research, marketers unlock the power of the data they capture and store.

Each marketing database application will require a different combination of data, research and technology for successful application. First, you must determine the appropriate applications for database marketing for your business. Then, you can determine the data, research and technology required to explain, house and access your customers.

Once you have developed a database application, you can develop ongoing communications programs that maximize the value of your customers or develop new customers. Traditionally this has been accomplished via the communications media of direct mail or telemarketing. Both are highly targeted, one-on-one mediums that can deliver unique messages to a customer or targeted prospect. It is this aspect of database marketing that allows for a perfect match with electronic media applications on information networks.

Linking Database Marketing and Information Networks

A marketing database provides the perfect resource to maximize information network applications. In fact, you can draw many parallel comparisons between the key aspects of data driven marketing and information networks. As with information networks, except in a more limited context, marketing databases allow for control and management of communications with customers. In a database, communications are based upon the relationship that the consumer has with the company. Normally, this is based upon the purchase of a product or service or an inquiry about the same.

The communications effort is delivered via direct mail or telemarketing or some other targeted medium. A marketing database allows for distribution of products and services via mail or other channels instead of or supplementing traditional products distribution. A marketing database can also support other distribution channel efforts. Similar to information networks, a marketing database is the repository for customer information. This includes information collected as a part of the interaction with the customer, or added to enhance the existing information collected about the customer.

Current communications programs are passive based efforts. The standard model of communications is shown in Exhibit 19.3. The seller communicates to the buyer via a medium such as television, print, radio, newspaper or magazines or direct mail and the buyer (consumer) must purchase via an intervening distribution channel such as a retail store. In the electronic network environment, the medium and distribution portions collapse into the medium itself. The network is the communications medium and controls the distribution process for the product or service.

The first level (Exhibit 19.6) represents the current state of the bridge between information networks and a marketing database application. In this model, there is no direct bridge or link between the information network and its subscriber database and a marketer's database. Neither can communicate directly to the other, and neither share data or customers with the other. The best that a marketer can do is to ask customers for their e-mail address if they have one or develop an online presence and capture subscriber names and match those to the existing marketing database. The link is used to provide persuasion on the seller's behalf to create interest by a current or potential buyer.

Three Models Bridging Databases and Networks

Three models of the convergence of marketing database and information network for customer communications applications represent three levels of sophistication of the communications and targeting process and the bridge between the information network and the marketing database.

The second level (Exhibit 19.7) represents data sharing and interaction between the information network database and the marketing database. However, this is accomplished in an off-line environment.

In this model, an information network and a marketing database compare files at a third-party location. Each can then determine the overlap between the two. The marketer can then target communications directly to its customers who subscribe to the online service, either by online communication or by direct mail. The information network

EXHIBIT 19.3 Passive Communications Model

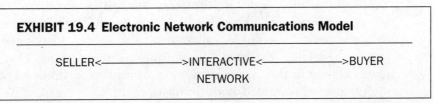

SELLER<———>MEDIUM<———>DISTRIBUTION<———>BUYER

EXHIBIT 19.4 Electronic Network Communications Model

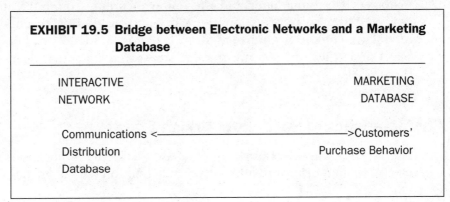

SELLER<———————>INTERACTIVE<———————>BUYER
NETWORK

EXHIBIT 19.5 Bridge between Electronic Networks and a Marketing Database

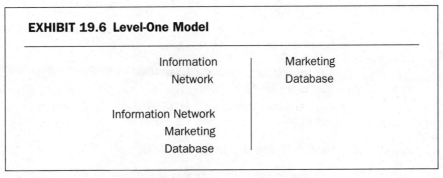

INTERACTIVE   MARKETING
NETWORK   DATABASE

Communications <———————————————>Customers'
Distribution   Purchase Behavior
Database

EXHIBIT 19.6 Level-One Model

Information   Marketing
Network   Database

Information Network
Marketing
Database

EXHIBIT 19.7 Level-Two Model

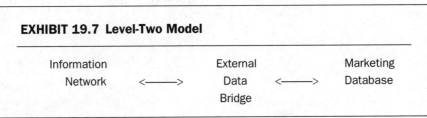

Information   External   Marketing
Network   <———>   Data   <———>   Database
                         Bridge

can deliver targeted directional messages to the marketer's customers via e-mail and opening screen messages sponsored by the network or jointly with the marketer. Thus level two communications represent targeted dialog between the buyer and seller via the information network.

The third level (Exhibit 19.8) represents a integrated bridge between the information network and the marketing database. Here, the two are electronically linked, matching customers and prospects for individual or joint marketing communications programs. This offers the marketer and the information network the opportunity to provide fully integrated, targeted communications linking the past behavior managed by the marketer and the power of online communications delivered by the information network. The process represents full interactive communications based upon dialog and feedback between buyer and seller with the information network as an active partner in the process.

Characteristics of Successful Bridge Efforts

Successful applications bridging database marketing applications and electronic networks must all have several common characteristics:

- They must start with an existing customer base that allows for targeting and tracking opportunities between the marketer's database and the information network.

- They must create an environment that makes commerce and communications more effective for the consumer. They must present an interesting and value-driven alternative to the consumer.

- They must facilitate the coming together of buyers and sellers.

- The communications between buyer and seller must be easily accessible and easily reachable.

- There must be clear benefits that clearly drive the consumer to the electronic network commerce opportunity as compared to current options.

- They must facilitate the sale by making it easy to buy.

EXHIBIT 19.8 Level-Three Model

| Information | | Marketing |
| Network | <———> | Database |

Marketing programs developed for this new world of media, distribution and tracking are still basically the same as traditional database marketing applications. They are designed to make and keep customers. If you target your offer correctly, you will make the sale. If you reinforce the sale and keep customers happy, they will buy again over time.

Database-driven programs are customer driven . . . not sales driven. Information networks are and will be powerful facilitators of commerce- and customer-based marketing. We have identified 15 specific applications that can be developed by bridging a marketing database effort with an information network. Each can be implemented by accessing one of the three levels of interaction between a marketer's database and an information network (Exhibit 19.9).

Starting Your Own Database-Driven Information Network Marketing Effort

Once you have determined the appropriate database-driven information network applications for your business, you must next figure out where to start. We suggest that you start by reviewing, again, the characteristics that we feel are required for a successful effort. First, you must develop and manage a marketing database. It will form the basis for tracking customers and their relationship to your business both inside and outside the electronic media world. Then, based upon the applications of electronic customer marketing that you feel are appropriate, you need to test, test and re-test again. Once you have gained experience with selling/prospecting and communicating with customers and potential customers in the online world, you can effectively develop financial and communications models that will facilitate a successful effort.

The model in Exhibit 19.10 represents an example of a test to rollout grid for entry into database-driven information network marketing.

EXHIBIT 19.9 15 Marketing Opportunities Linking Marketing Database and Information Networks

1. Communications efforts targeted to customers—The most important aspect to database marketing is targeting and reaching customers. By identifying the overlap between a marketer's database and an information network, this can maximize the strength of commerce in this new environment.

2. Prospecting for new customers—By effectively developing information and selling presence in the information network environment, prospecting can be extended to electronic media

3. Delivering communications based upon prior purchase behavior—By capturing and managing prior purchase behavior in your marketing database, a marketer can communicate in the on-line world based upon the consumers prior purchase behavior.

4. Reinforce customer purchase behavior—By communicating with the customer after the sale, the on-line e-mail communications environment allows for cost effective and efficient means to keep customers happy

5. Cross-sell/up-sell and complementary sell—By capturing and tracking a customer's prior purchase behavior, the marketer can sell other products and services to the same customer.

6. Communicate with prospects/customers based upon purchase potential—Communications can be implemented based upon customer potential models. This controls the costs involved with selling a customer and maximizes sales potential

7. Targeted delivery of sales promotion—Delivery of sales promotion based upon customer purchase behavior with no waste due to one-on-one targeting.

8. Increase the effectiveness of multichannel products and services distribution—Tracking provides detailed information on customers and products and equalizes the power of traditional distribution channels over products and goods delivery to consumers.

9. Understand customer/product dynamics via customer interaction By communicating with customers and tracking purchases, the marketer gains invite into the marketing process.

10. Eliminate communications waste and deliver highly targeted communications—By reaching customers with targeted messages based upon information needs and purchase behavior, sales are maximized. Targeted communications represent traditional savings over mass communications efforts in the electronic media environment.

11. Conduct market research—Electronic information networks represent captive audiences for product, customer, media, distribution and communications reach.

12. Provide immediate and personalized customer service—E-mail offers the ability to keep in contact with customers to maximize their experience with the product and service. It identifies problems that will keep the customer from making future purchases.

13. Create integrated communications programs—Information network based programs can provide consistent messages with other customer directed communications and marketing activities. The nature of the medium allows for reinforcement of brand equity and delivery of greater levels of information and reinforcement leading to the sale.

14. Manage customer communications and sales potential—By tracking customers in a marketing database, the marketer can practice customer communications management. In this process, customers that wish to be contacted primarily via electronic networks can be pulled from other communications efforts. In the future, entire customer segments may be managed via different communications alternatives.

15. Reach new customer segments not available with traditional media—Certain customer segments, such as younger consumers, will be more reachable via electronic media than traditional media.

EXHIBIT 19.10 Bridge Testing Model

| | FUNCTION | | | | | |
	ID Customers	ID Prospects	Info. Delivery	Lead Gen.	Sale	Customer Service
MODE						
Test						
Stage 1	X	X				
Stage 2				X		
Stage 3			X			
Stage 4					X	X
Roll-Out	X	X	X	X	X	X

The model represents several stages of testing. First, the marketer tests the ability to identify customers and prospects who are in the marketing database and can be reached by marketing on an information network. At this stage, information can be analyzed to identify characteristics of each group and the overlap. The next step is to use a network to develop leads, communicate with customers and facilitate the information search by consumers. Finally, customers can be moved from other distribution channels to online sales and customer service if appropriate. If successful at any testing level, depending upon the nature of the applications you have chosen, the effort can be rolled out to one or more information network environments.

Ultimately, the success of the effort will based on an economic value to customer-based communications for either facilitating the sales process or by selling and delivering via the electronic network. By linking the information network effort to a marketing database, you can match current and new customer behavior patterns and develop payback analysis for your applications. To some degree, getting involved will require a leap of faith. In truth, you may not be able to figure out the payback until you "get there" with your applications, and it may take some time to determine where and when the payback occurs.

Summary

Information networks represent an exciting new world of communications possibilities. However, it is important to remember that all marketing communications are about customers: Creating, keeping and managing customers. If you manage customers effectively, you will create sales. And the key to managing customers is a marketing database. It allows a marketer to cost effectively understand customer behavior and maximize customer value. With this knowledge, the database becomes the bridge to the world of electronic media via information networks. A marketing database facilitates all the key aspects of information network marketing—communications, distribution and data capture. By bridging these, the marketer creates a powerful resource.

The convergence of database marketing and information networks is both an evolution and revolution. It is also an opportunity that is unparalleled in communications and targeting history. The emergence of consumer interest and information networks has created the opportunity for database marketing to play a powerful role in the future of electronic communications.

INDEX

TITLES OF INTEREST IN MARKETING, DIRECT MARKETING, AND SALES PROMOTION

SUCCESSFUL DIRECT MARKETING METHODS, by Bob Stone
PROFITABLE DIRECT MARKETING, by Jim Kobs
INTEGRATED DIRECT MARKETING, by Ernan Roman
BEYOND 2000: THE FUTURE OF DIRECT MARKETING, by Jerry I. Reitman
POWER DIRECT MARKETING, by "Rocket" Ray Jutkins
CREATIVE STRATEGY IN DIRECT MARKETING, by Susan K. Jones
SECRETS OF SUCCESSFUL DIRECT MAIL, by Richard V. Benson
STRATEGIC DATABASE MARKETING, by Rob Jackson and Paul Wang
HOW TO PROFIT THROUGH CATALOG MARKETING, by Katie Muldoon
DIRECT RESPONSE TELEVISION, by Frank Brady and J. Angel Vasquez
DIRECT MARKETING THROUGH BROADCAST MEDIA, by Alvin Eicoff
SUCCESSFUL TELEMARKETING, by Bob Stone and John Wyman
BUSINESS TO BUSINESS DIRECT MARKETING, by Robert Bly
COMMONSENSE DIRECT MARKETING, by Drayton Bird
DIRECT MARKETING CHECKLISTS, by John Stockwell and Henry Shaw
INTEGRATED MARKETING COMMUNICATIONS, by Don E. Schultz, Stanley I. Tannenbaum,
    and Robert F. Lauterborn
GREEN MARKETING, by Jacquelyn Ottman
MARKETING CORPORATE IMAGE: THE COMPANY AS YOUR NUMBER ONE PRODUCT
    by James R. Gregory with Jack G. Wiechmann
HOW TO CREATE SUCCESSFUL CATALOGS, by Maxwell Sroge
101 TIPS FOR MORE PROFITABLE CATALOGS, by Maxwell Sroge
SALES PROMOTION ESSENTIALS
    by Don E. Schultz, William A. Robinson and Lisa A. Petrison
PROMOTIONAL MARKETING, by William A. Robinson and Christine Hauri
BEST SALES PROMOTIONS, by William A. Robinson
INSIDE THE LEADING MAIL ORDER HOUSES, by Maxwell Sroge
NEW PRODUCT DEVELOPMENT, by George Gruenwald
NEW PRODUCT DEVELOPMENT CHECKLISTS, by George Gruenwald
CLASSIC FAILURES IN PRODUCT MARKETING, by Donald W. Hendon
HOW TO TURN CUSTOMER SERVICE INTO CUSTOMER SALES, by Bernard Katz
ADVERTISING & MARKETING CHECKLISTS, by Ron Kaatz
BRAND MARKETING, by William M. Weilbacher
MARKETING WITHOUT MONEY, by Nicholas E. Bade
THE 1-DAY MARKETING PLAN, by Roman A. Hiebing, Jr. and Scott W. Cooper
HOW TO WRITE A SUCCESSFUL MARKETING PLAN
    by Roman G. Hiebing, Jr. and Scott W. Cooper
DEVELOPING, IMPLEMENTING, AND MANAGING EFFECTIVE MARKETING PLANS
    by Hal Goetsch
HOW TO EVALUATE AND IMPROVE YOUR MARKETING DEPARTMENT
    by Keith Sparling and Gerard Earls
SELLING TO A SEGMENTED MARKET, by Chester A. Swenson
MARKET-ORIENTED PRICING, by Michael Morris and Gene Morris
STATE-OF-THE-ART MARKETING RESEARCH, by A.B. Blankenship and George E. Breen
AMA HANDBOOK FOR CUSTOMER SATISFACTION, by Alan Dutka
WAS THERE A PEPSI GENERATION BEFORE PEPSI DISCOVERED IT?
    by Stanley C. Hollander and Richard Germain
BUSINESS TO BUSINESS COMMUNICATIONS HANDBOOK, by Fred Messner
MANAGING SALES LEADS: HOW TO TURN EVERY PROSPECT INTO A CUSTOMER
    by Robert Donath, Richard Crocker, Carol Dixon and James Obermeyer
AMA MARKETING TOOLBOX (SERIES), by David Parmerlee
AMA COMPLETE GUIDE TO SMALL BUSINESS MARKETING, by Kenneth J. Cook
AMA COMPLETE GUIDE TO STRATEGIC PLANNING FOR SMALL BUSINESS, by Kenneth J. Cook
AMA COMPLETE GUIDE TO SMALL BUSINESS ADVERTISING, by Joe Vitale
HOW TO GET THE MOST OUT OF TRADE SHOWS, by Steve Miller
HOW TO GET THE MOST OUT OF SALES MEETINGS, by James Dance
STRATEGIC MARKET PLANNING, by Robert J. Hamper and L. Sue Baugh

For further information or a current catalog, write:
NTC Business Books
a division of *NTC Publishing Group*
4255 West Touhy Avenue
Lincolnwood, Illinois 60646–1975 U.S.A.